WOMEN AND ENTREPRENEURSHIP

WOMEN AND ENTREPRENEURSHIP

Issues and Challenges

Editors

Dr. Asha Patil
Dr. Anuradha Mathu

Publications

KALPAZ PUBLICATIONS

Delhi - 110052

Women and Entrepreneurship: Issues and Challenges

ISBN : 978 81-7835-582-5

*Re*print 2016 in India by
Kalpaz Publications
C-30, Satyawati Nagar,
Delhi - 110052
Phone : 9212729499
e-mail : kalpaz@hotmail.com

Laser Typesetting at : Vinayak Printers, Delhi
Printed at : Salasar Imaging System, Delhi

Contents

Preface

Women Entrepreneurship in India
– *Some Facts and Prospects*

Entrepreneurship has acquired special significance in the changing economic scenario. Due to various changes taking place and impact of globalization and change in economic status of our country, entrepreneurship is being encouraged. Entrepreneurship in turn may lead to increased production and enhanced economic development of our nation. Although, women entering into the field of entrepreneurship is considered a new phenomenon, world over but women working in cottage industries and handicrafts or even in home-based productions like bee-keeping, sericulture, fisheries, mushroom cultivation or even masala, pickle, papad, making is centuries old small scale, home based enterprises in India.

In the present context, an Entrepreneur can be defined as "one who undertakes an enterprise, especially a contractor acting as intermediary between capital and labour" (Oxford English Dictionary).

In India, there is by and large, greater need for women to take up entrepreneurship as it would give them economic status. Economic status would further lead to social well-being and status. This is also necessitated on account of the fact that women constitute almost half of the Indian population and the old system of men being able to feed and look after the needs of their families completely cannot the possible in today's world of increasing prices and competition.

The scenario is changing in developing countries and in India also due to modernization, urbanization and development of education and business. Women are now seeking gainful employment in several fields in increasing numbers. Women are also spreading their wings in entrepreneurship. Today, we can find women entrepreneurs in the fields of manufacture of solar cookers, as in Gujarat, T.V. capacitors in promotion of technology and consultancy services for women entrepreneurs.

The two schemes offered by DST are –

TAAS – Technology Absorption and Adaptation
TATT – Transfer and Trading in Technology

Department of Science and Technology has been entrusted with the implementation of this grants - in - aid scheme for the development of Women Entrepreneurship in India.

Efforts put in by various organizations promoting entrepreneurship are well appreciated and will help in the development of this sector.

However, the role of academicians towards entrepreneurship development is also being recognized.

This book will help all those who were to venture into entrepreneurship development in India, especially the institutes promoting entrepreneurship. The responsibility of extension personnel and extension training institutes will also help towards this endeavour.

The Department of Science and Technology has actively engaged in evolving and implementing various programmes for Orissa. Further, in Kerala they are manufacturing traditional goods like embroidered items, toys, mats, etc.

Inspite of all these facts and figures, entrepreneurship for women can be planned and developed and the need for generating and providing appropriate awareness, skills and training and competencies amongst majority of them would prove helpful and would benefit and promote women entrepreneurship, which would be of vital importance.

Women today must supplement the family income, using their potential and skills that they possess. These skills and competencies may further be sharpened and tuned by way of training. Thus, women in India, no longer need to wait for employment outside home or with an organized sector. They can successfully start their self-employment ventures and earn their livelihoods.

The problems faced by women entrepreneurs may be, (some may be specific, some general)

- Problem of finance
- Scarcity of raw materials
- Stiff competition
- Limited mobility
- Family ties
- Lack of education
- Male-dominated society
- Low risk bearing ability
- Inadequate infrastructural facilities
- Shortage of electricity or power
- High cost of production
- Social attitudes
- Low need for achievement
- Socio-economic constraints

Introduction

Challenges of Women Entrepreneurship

Women have been regarded as the nuclei of nation and the builder and moulder of its destiny. It is an accepted fact that "when women move forward, the family moves, the city moves and the nation moves." Days are gone when women in India remained confined to four walls of their homes and their immense strength and potential remained unrecognized and unaccounted, now women entrepreneurs are an important input of economics development. A woman is a catalyst of development and with her we prosper, but without her we are poor.

Entrepreneurship happens to be one of the best ways towards self sufficiency and poverty alleviation for women in a country where employment is not guaranteed. The women entrepreneurs need not be highly educated. It is enough if they possess basic knowledge of a language, entrepreneurial skills and the knowledge of the system. And also entrepreneurship is a more suitable profession than regular employment in public and private sectors, since they have to fulfill dual roles. In emergence of nuclear families and diversification of labour activities has resulted in the non-availability of servants, limited baby care facilities at home and work is pushing women towards entreneurial activities. Women entrepreneurship is the process where women take lead and organize a business or industry and provide employment opportunities to others. Though women entrepreneurship is a recent phenomenon in India which came into prominence in late 1970's now more and more are venturing as entrepreneurs in all kinds of business and service sector. There are successful women entrepreneurs today heading enterprises like electronics, multimedia, garment, industry and so on.

The problems follow the women entrepreneurs like shadow. Women entrepreneurs have to struggle much more and face the following problems.

1. In a traditional society women have been trained to listen, obey and leave decision to men in the family.
2. Family environment is not generally helpful. Women entrepreneurs have to take time off from their household duties.
3. It is also difficult to find men prepared to work under women.
4. The women entrepreneurs suffer from a number of problems at the pre-investment stage, investment stage and post-investment stage. The problems mainly relate to finance, raw material and marketing. Getting finance is a big problem because women generally do not have property in their name. They cannot offer property as collateral security. Banks too consider women less creditworthy.
5. The rural women entrepreneurs particularly do not know how to synchronise their skills with the market requirements.
6. Inefficient management for marketing and sale.
7. Stiff competition.
8. Low mobility.
9. Social attitudes.
10. Low ability to bear risk.
11. Lack of education.
12. Low need for achievement.
13. Inadequate infrastructure.

The risks are even more for the women entrepreneur as she has to work in a male dominated area. The main drawbacks to women's success are lack of experience, and inaccessibility of resources to develop the entrepreneurial skills like independence, self confidence, assertiveness, drive. Development as entrepreneurs is a recently discovered phenomenon for women for which they need lot of motivation, training and family members support. Facilities are provided by governmental and non-governmental agencies to motivate and to impart training to develop entrepreneurial skills in women. But most of the women are kept away from such developmental programmes due to social norms, values and attitudes towards women.

If the women decide to go in for a small business the basic ability cannot really be in question. The issues relating to self-confidence, lack of knowledge and information and absence of role models can partly be solved by education and experience. Business risks can be minimized by careful planning and expert guidance. There are several specialized agencies, financial organs and voluntary organizations offering guidance and financial help. Increasing number of entrepreneurial development programme (EDP) is offered by these agencies which help develop project profiles, feasibility reports, personal counseling about one's unit, marketing skills etc. The EDPs range from general to industry – specific programmes which are product or process oriented. Some additional concessions are required. Banks and other financial institutions should come forward to give loans to women entrepreneurs without obtaining security from them and at low interest rate. Maximum possible assistance should be provided to women for completing documentation and other formalities. Lastly, to ensure women entrepreneurship development integrated efforts by various institutions and corporations are needed so that required assistance may be provided to potential women entrepreneurs.

Entrepreneurship would to a great extent solve two major problems – mass poverty and widespread unemployment. India will have to pay lot of attention and search for encouraging entrepreneurship especially in small sector, which involves low capital and high labour intensity.

It is rightly observed that small scale sector not only provides larger employment but also mobilizes local resources, skills, savings, and takes up industries for wider distribution of wealth.

It is also seen that in the past two decades, many attempts have been made to develop a network of small scale and cottage industries or micro enterprises. Many government efforts to design special programmes to promote entrepreneurship on scientific basis were also made. We have also witnessed many indicators and parameters to prove the worth of such efforts and programmes for achieving national goal. We all know that this problem of unemployment is enormous and is taking 'Gigantic Form'.

The effort of academicians, policy and programme planners should be to develop and train hundreds and thousands of women entrepreneurs to meet this ever growing challenge.

Entrepreneurs play a pivotal role in the economic development of any country. Entrepreneurs are considered to be the most important economic agents for the economic augmentation and growth of any country. They act as the owners, producers, coordinators, market makers, decision-makers, risk takers and innovators. They provide an improved allocation of resources for the best interest of their enterprises as well as the country. They are considered the economic pioneers initiating changes in the economy. They strive to increase productivity and improve the quality of output through the application of more efficient production technique, better plant layout and effective marketing policies. They ensure production of better quality of goods and services at lowest cost. They generate employment opportunities and arrange for the betterment of the standard of living.

Entrepreneurship is also considered a life moving force behind any economy. It is also believed that without entrepreneurial activities the process of industrialization is not possible.

List of Contributors

Varsha P. Jobanputra, *C.C. Home Science College, Jin Road, Limbadi- 363421, Dist.-Surendranagar.*

Shantaben Makawana, *M.Sc., F.N. M.A. (Home Science), Laboratory Assistant, C.C. Home Science College, Limbadi-363421, Dist.-Surendranagar.*

Nilamben V. Mandaliya, *Lecturer in Home Science, C.C. Home Science College, Limbadi-363421, Dist. – Surendranagar.*

Shailesh Vasavada, *Regional Officer, CED - Vadodara.*

Maithili T. Pathak, *Lecturer, Bhavan's Shri A.K. Doshi Mahila College, Jamnagar.*

Dinesh Awasthi and Manoj Mishra, *Entrepreneurship Development Institute of India, Ahmedabad.*

Mrs. Kamalamani Rao, *Lecturer, A.K. Doshi Mahila College, Jamnagar.*

Rajkumar Kamble and Ulka Shinde, *Department of Home Science, Rajaram College, Kolhapur, Maharashtra - 416 004.*

Bishnupriya Dasgupta, *Sr. Lecturer, F.R.M. Department of P.G.S.R. in Home Science, S.N.D.T. Women's University.*

Ms. Darshnini Durkal and Dr. Rameshwari Pandya, *Sr. Lecturer, Department of Home Science Extension and Communication, Faculty of Home Science, M.S. University of Baroda, Baroda.*

Manisha N. Khakhar, *Lecturer, Bhavan's Shri A.K. Doshi Mahila College, Jamnagar.*

Bhavna D. Ranch, *Lecturer, Bhavan's Shri A.K. Doshi Mahila College, Jamnagar.*

Varsha P. Chhichhia M.H.Sc., *Lecturer, Bhavan's Shri A.K. Doshi Mahila College, Jamnagar.*

Sucheta Singh, *Ph.D. Scholar – Resource Management, Department of Home Management, Faculty of Home Science, M.S. University of Baroda, Baroda - 390 002.*

Dr. Anjali Pahad, *Reader,* **Ms. Avani Maniar,** *Lecturer, Department of Home Science Extension and Communication, Faculty of Home Science, M.S. University of Baroda, Baroda.*

Dr. Shilpa Kapadia and Mrs. Shetal Barodia, *Centre for Continuing/Adult Education and Community Services, M.S. University of Baroda, Vadodara.*

Dr. Varsha Parikh, *Lecturer, Department of Home Science Extension and Communication, Faculty of Home Science, M.S. University of Baroda, Baroda.*

Bishnupriya Dasgupta, *Sr. Lecturer, F.R.M. Department, S.N.D.T. Women's University.*

Dr. Sarjoo Patel, *Lecturer,* **Ms. Vrushali Datar,** *Teaching Assistant,* **Prof. Veena Gandotra,** *Professor,* **and Ms. Sonia Thakur,** *Ph. D. Scholar, Department of Home Management, Faculty of Home Science, M.S. University of Baroda, Baroda.*

Dr. Asha Patil, *Reader,* **Ms. Dimple Kshatriya,** *Lecturer, Department of HSEC, Faculty of Home Science, M.S. University of Baroda, Baroda.*

Bharti V. Oza, *Lecturer, Bhavan's A.K. Doshi Mahila College, Jamnagar.*

Dr. Neerja Jaiswal, *Lecturer, Department of Home Management, Faculty of Home Science, M.S.University of Baroda, Vadodara.*

Shobha Nagnur, Channamma N., Geeta Channal.

B.N. Kalsariya, *Agricultural Officer, Sardar Smruti Kendra, GAU, Junagadh.*

M.N. Popat, *Professor and Head, Department of Extension Education, GAU, Junagadh.*

K.M. Karetha, *Agricultural Officer, Department of Horticulture, GAU, Junagadh.*

B.R. Karkar, *Assistant,* ***M.C. Dhaduk,*** *Extension Educationist*

B.N. Kalsariya, *Agricultural Officer,* ***N.D. Bharad,*** *Assistant Extension Educationist, SSK, GAU, Junagadh.*

Sangeeta Patel, *S.M. Patel College of Home Science, Vallabh Vidyanagar, Anand, Gujarat.*

Mrs. Kamalamani Rao, *Lecturer, A.K. Doshi Mahila College, Jamnagar.*

1

The Concept and Theories of Entrepreneurship

Medha Mehta

Introduction

Entrepreneurship is a process undertaken by an entrepreneur to augment his business interests. It is an exercise involving innovation and creativity that will go towards establishing his/her enterprise. The concept of entrepreneurship and of its related issues are analysed, discussed and deliberated.

Only of the qualities of entrepreneurship is the ability to discover an investment opportunity and to organize an enterprise, thereby contributing to real economic growth. It involves taking of risks and making the necessary investments under conditions of uncertainty and innovating, planning and taking decisions so as to increase production in agriculture, business, industry etc.

Entrepreneurship is a composite skill, the resultant of a mix of many qualities and traits – these include tangible factors as imagination, readiness to take risks, ability to bring together and put to use other factors of production, capital, labour, land, as also intangible factors such as the ability to mobilize scientific and technological advances.

The concept and theories of entrepreneurship evolved over more than two centuries have undergone major changes. Yet the concept of entrepreneurship is not clear. As the concept of entrepreneurship is complex in its content, it is influenced by not only economical aspects, but also by sociological, political, psychological, ethical, religious and cultural values. The concept also bears testimony to courage, creativity, determination, networking, hard working etc. over the years the social scientists have interpreted the phenomenon of entrepreneurship differently in accordance with their perception and economic environment.

Theories of Entrepreneurship

Theories of entrepreneurship are broadly classified into economic, psychological, sociological and cultural.

The static approach of the emerging Neo-classical school did not readily accommodate a concept with such dynamic connotations as entrepreneur. Alfred Marshall, for example, laid much more stress on the routine activities of management and superintendence than he did on the innovative activity of the entrepreneur.

The phenomenon of entrepreneurship development has been viewed, explained and interpreted differently by social scientists. Among those who have stressed on the routine activities of management and superintendence than he did on the innovative activity of the entrepreneur.

An Economic Theory

Mark Casson, in his book *The Entrepreneur – An Economic Theory,* presented a functional definition of the entrepreneur and considered why the entrepreneurial function is so valuable. He emphasized that the demand for entrepreneurship steams from the need to adjust to change, and that the supply of entrepreneurship is limited firstly, by the scarcity of the requisite personal qualities, and secondary, by the difficulty of identifying them when they are available. He suggested that there are four main qualities which are crucial for a successful entrepreneur of which one – imagination – is almost entirely innate. The other three qualities may be enhanced. The problems encountered in screening for these qualities, and in enhancing the ones that are deficient, have a number of important implications for the development of a successful entrepreneurial career.

Theory of High Achievement

McClelland identified two characteristics of entrepreneurship, namely, doing things in a new and better way and decision-making under uncertainty! He stressed the need for achievement or achievement orientation as the most directly relevant factor for explaining economic behaviour. This motive is defined as the tendency to strive for success in situations involving an evaluation of ones performance in relation to some standard of excellence. People having high need for achievement are more likely to succeed as entrepreneurs. McClelland explains the entrepreneur's interest in profits in terms of a need for achievement. People with high achievement (N-Ach) are not influenced by money rewards as compared to people with low achievement. The latter type are prepared to work harder for money or such other external or such other external incentives. On the contrary, profit is merely a measure of success and competency for people with high achievement need.

Theory of Profit

Knight identifies the entrepreneur as a recipient of pure profit. Pure profit, according to him, with regard to the entrepreneur, is bearing the costs of uncertainty. He identifies uncertainty with a situation where the probabilities of alternative outcomes cannot be determined either by a prior reasoning or by statistical inference. A prior reasoning is simply irrelevant to economic situation involving a unique event.

Knight argues that business uncertainty can be reduced through consolidation. Consolidation is to uncertainty what insurance is to risk; it is a method of reducing total uncertainty by pooling individual instances. The elasticity of the supply of self-confidence is the single most important determinant of the level of profit and the number of entrepreneurs.

Theory of Adjustment of Price

The adjustment of price is the main role of the entrepreneur. If the wrong price prevails in the market, then an opportunity for profit is created somewhere in the market if a frustrated buyer or seller is willing, respectively, to pay a higher price or accept a lower one. Then, again, if different prices prevail in the same market, there is scope for profitable arbitrage between the two segment of the market.

Alertness to disequilibrium is the distinguishing characteristic of an entrepreneur. Alertness enables some individuals to intervene in the market by changing the price while other individuals simply respond by changing their buying and selling plans in lieu of the new price.

Theory of Market Equilibrium

Hayek's main contribution to entrepreneurial theory is to point out that the absence of entrepreneurs in Neo-classical economic in intimately associated with the assumption of market equilibrium. According to Hayek, the equilibrium postulate is equivalent to a postulate of full information; not full information in the sense of a complete information theory about every conceivable thing, but full information in the sense that no further information is needed in order to modify anyones decisions.

For him, the empirical content of economics relates to the process of adjustment towards an equilibrium. This process involves the acquisition and communication of knowledge. He visualizes a world in which there is a continuous process of discovery. Markets help people to communicate their discoveries to others and learn of discoveries, thereby moving towards a sale of equilibrium.

Modern Concept

The term entrepreneur in the modern sense came into usage in the late 18th century with the advent of the Industrial Revolution in England. It was during this period that people developed inventions and made an appreciable amount of discoveries in a variety of productive occupations. Their innovative behaviour engaged them in doing new and useful things or old things in an improved way. The invention of colour photography and colour television, for example, were the responses of innovative efforts of the individual who conceived the idea, developed it and pursued it to its ultimate success. These innovators came to be known as entrepreneurs.

Conclusion

All the theories ascribe a functional role to the entrepreneur in the productive process and entrepreneurial rewards are explained by the degree of success attained by fulfilling that function, rather than by a purely proprietary claim on income by virtue of mere asset ownership. Again, all the theories have been grounded against the backdrop of a capitalist society and as such the functional roles performed by the entrepreneur is determined within the capitalist paradigms of production and distribution. The varied theories evolved over more than centuries have thrown up the concept of intrepreneur as a logical evolution of entrepreneurship in corporations. The intrapreneur is a professional with entrepreneurial skills. The concept of entrepreneurship will certainly undergo a change with the advancement of technology, information technology in particular. The evolution of entrepreneurship is a continuous process.

References

King's Book – Management of Small Scale Industries Entrepreneurship.

Vasant Desai – Dynamics of Entrepreneurial Development and Management.

Syed Vazith Hussain – Small Scale Industries in the New Millennium.

2
Issues and Problems in Women Entrepreneurship

Varsha P. Jobanputra

Introduction

Who is this woman entrepreneur? What are her Qualities?

She is a woman of commitment, who is not relevant, independently employed. She has a close relationship with her father and, after obtaining an undergraduate and subsequently a graduate degree in some area of liberal arts, marries, has children and starts her first significant entrepreneurial venture in the service area in her late 30s or early 40s. Her biggest problems at start up and later in the venture reflect a lack of business training generally in the financial area.

Why women entrepreneur were less in India?

Women were always ready to adjust, accept, accommodate and be dependent on men for support. This was hardly conducive to the development of self-confidence, initiative or willingness to take risks; characteristics absolutely essential for entrepreneurship. These values and attitudes also meant that girls were often given less education than boys and even when girls were educated up to school leaving or beyond, the aspirations of the parents and even of the girls themselves were lower both as to educational attainments and future prospects. For a young girl marriage and children were considered the only life long activity and education was imparted either to make her a better wife and mother to secure a better husband, since husbands preferred educated wives.

Basic Problems of Women

The basic problem or difficulty of a woman entrepreneur is that she is a woman - this pertains to her responsibility towards her family, society and work. With joint families breaking up, many women simply do not have the support of elders. Women have been confronted by such dilemmas ever since they started leaving home for the work place. On the other hand, the attitude of society towards her and constraints in which she has to live and work are not very conducive. In spite of the constitutional equality, in practice the attitude of men is not only tradition-bound but even of those who are responsible for decision-making, planning and research is not of equality. They still suffer from male reservations. This attitude of reservation creates difficulties and problems at all levels, i.e. family support training, banking, licensing and marketing. Women in rural areas have to suffer still further. They have to face not only resistance or reservation from men but also from elderly women who are ingrained in the attitude of inequality. In rural areas joint families are still the norm. The overbearing presence of elders restrain even young men from venturing out; so one can imagine how much a young girl needs to put up to become economically independent. Though in rural areas women are working along with men since times immemorial, their contribution in monetary terms remains unaccounted, or if at all accounted, it is given a very low value. They are mostly engaged in low-paid, back-breaking agriculture activities or act as helpers in handicrafts.

Problems of Women Entrepreneurs are as below

1. *Need for achievement, Economic Independence and Autonomy are absent:* Need for achievement, economic independence and autonomy are the basic ingredients required in a successful entrepreneur but these basic requirements are absent or found in negligible quantities in a women in India. She is held back by her own pre-conceived notions of her role in life. She sees herself only in the image of a perfect mother, wife and house-

maker. She is proud to bask in the glory of her husband, father, son etc. this results in a conflict which inhibits achievement, independence and progress. Therefore, when the very urge is absent, how can she be motivated to be an entrepreneur?

2. *No Risk Bearing Capacity:* All throughout her life time, she has led a protected life dominated by the family members. In her childhood, she relied on her parents or elder family members. In her adulthood, she relied on her husband and in-laws and again in her old age, she depended on her husband and sons, i.e., at no time has she faced the risk of life all alone. Therefore, she has no confidence to bear the risk all alone. Then how can she be an entrepreneur, when business is nothing but a risk-bearing enterprise?

3. *Lack of Education:* The overall literacy percentage among females is only 39.3% in India. A woman is discouraged to learn more than the male members of the family. Due to this lack of education, she is unaware of technological knowledge, marketing knowledge etc. Moreover, whatever bookish knowledge she gathers is not sufficient to meet the various problems in the business field.

4. *Family Involvement:* In India, it is almost only a woman's duty to look after the children and other members of the family. Man plays secondary or an insignificant role. Her involvement in family problems leaves very little energy and time to come out of her shell and play a significant role in economic development.

5. *Male Dominated Society:* Equal treatment to men and women is absent at the family level and social level. When a women steps into the middle management or top management level, she has to face hostile reactions from her male colleagues, especially from those who are subordinates or at par with her. The male superiority ego complex creates a barrier in the pathway of success. This situation is found sometimes even between a

husband and wife and usually under such circumstances, a woman feels pressurized by male domineering ego.

6. *Lack of Information and Experience:* The lack of information and experience makes it very difficult for her to select technology, market and location and also to tackle problems related to labour and finance. The Government realizing the need and importance of women entrepreneurs' participation in the contribution to the economy has offered some assistance, thereby trying to create a favourable climate for woman entrepreneurs to play a significant role in the rapid development of India.

7. *Finally, the problems of liquidity and easy availability of finance:* About half of all the informal sector small enterprises world wide are run by women, access to bank credit is vital for them, as few women have personal savings available for investment.

Awareness

1. More awareness programmes should be conducted jointly by development agencies and voluntary agencies like AWAKE.

2. The age limit of Forty five years for training in [EDPs] Entrepreneurship Development Programmes should be raised to Fifty years as many women start their enterprises late in their life at least at this point of time.

3. The employment clause of Fifty per cent women should be removed from the definition of women entrepreneurs.

4. Preference in Government purchase should be accorded to women entrepreneurs, especially items of downstream supplies.

5. A majority of women entrepreneurs are from the middle class families, have low technical education, less family responsibilities (owing to the joint family system) but desire to become entrepreneurs. This potential should be identified and trained.

Conclusion

The problems of entrepreneurs are multidimensional. These can be solved by the co-ordinated efforts of entrepreneurs, coordinated functioning of promotional agencies, and governmental assistance without red tape or bureaucratic delays. The entrepreneur has to be educated; and she should have a proper training in acquiring the necessary skill in running an enterprise. In fact, the entrepreneur is the kingpin of the industrial spectrum.

Today, there is a greater awakening among women. Given an opportunity, they will deliver the results. In education, they have not only excelled but also become top makers. Likewise, in office and industry, many have shown brilliant results. Even in rural India with education, women have shown better performance. Educating women is absolutely essential in the development and straightening her personality. The need of the hour is to provide an opportunity in a conducive atmosphere free from gender differences to promote women entrepreneurship.

References

Desai, Vasant – Dynamics of Entrepreneurial Development and Management.

King's – Management of Small Scale Industries and Entrepreneurship.

Mitra, Joyati – Women and Society.

Sharma, D.D. and S.K. Dhameja – Women and Rural Entrepreneurship Development.

3

Awareness about Factories Acts for Women Entrepreneurs

Shantaben Makawana

Introduction

The basic objective behind the whole process of regulations is to ensure that the results of operation conform as closely as possible to established standards of goods, specified procedures, or instructions. The small-scale industry has to develop as an important segment of society; as such it has to adhere to the rules of the land, i.e., it has to be subjected to the various regulations. Regulations governing the small-scale industry are of two types: *Protective and Promotional.* Protective regulations are in the nature of various safeguards, while promotional regulations are in the nature of giving a push to the small-scale industry, i.e., they are growth-oriented.

The Small Scale Enterprises are being regulated and governed by the following acts

Factories Act, 1948

1. *Definition of a Factory:* Section 2 (m) of the Act defines a factory as any place wherein ten or more persons are working and in which manufacturing process is carried on with the aid of the appropriate power machinery and infrastructure, premises in which power is not used come under the term of a factory if twenty or more persons are working in them, this definition brings a greater

number of place under the purview of this Act that was the case under the Act of 1934.

2. *Employment of Children*: The Act fixes the maximum age of persons who can enter a factory for work at 14 years, it prohibits the employment of children up to the age of 13.

   The Act further lays down that a qualified surgeon must certify that a person has completed the age of 14, such certificates must be obtained by a factory *by a factory* manager and must be available for inspection by a factory inspector.

3. *Hours of Work for Children*: The Act reduces the hours of work for children between the ages of 14-17 years from 5 hours a day to 4½ hours a day. It also prohibits children from doing night shift.

4. *Hours of Work for Adult Female and Male Workers*: The Act prohibits employment of women in factories between 6 P.M. to 7 A.M. It reduces ten hours of work for adult men and women workers from 54 to 48 per week and from 9 hours to 8 hours a day.

The Payment of Wages Act, 1936

The payment of wages to factory workers in a particular form and at regular intervals without any unauthorized deductions is the objective of this Act.

Scope of the Act: The provisions of the Act are applicable to workers engaged in factories as defined by the Factories Act of 1948, and to persons employed on any railway by contractor or sub-contractor. The State Government may, after giving three months' notice of its intention of doing so by a notification in the official Gazette, extent the provisions of this Act to any class of persons employed in any industrial establishment. The provisions of this Act are applicable to those persons whose wages do not exceed Rs. 400 per month.

The Employees State Insurance Act, 1948

Experience in the working of the Workmen's Compensation Act of 1923 revealed that the benefits conferred by it upon factory workers in many cases, did not reach them. This was due to various reasons. Firstly, a claim for compensation for injury had to be filed in an ordinary court of law and the lack of finance often made it impossible for a worker to file such a suit and fight it out. Secondly, armed with expert legal advice, it was often possible for an employer to prove that the accident either did not arise out of and in the course of employment or that it was due to the worker concerned being under the influence of drink or drug at the time of the accident, or that it was due to his negligence or his disobedience of safety rules. In such conditions, workers were generally unwilling to go to court of law, and preferred to accept whatever compensation employers chose to pay out of a sense of pity or charity. The Employees' State Insurance Act of 1948 was framed to prevent such victimization of the worker by the employer.

The Employees Provident Fund Act, 1952

The Act provides for the institution of a contributory provident fund in establishment in which 20 or more persons are employed. The contribution, which shall be paid by the employer to the fund, shall be 80 per cent of the basic wage and the dearness allowance payable to each employee, while the employee's contribution shall be equal to the contribution payable by the employer.

The Indian Electricity Act, 1910

The Act relates to the supply and use of electricity energy.

Issue of licence: A State Government may, on an application made in the prescribed form and on the payment of the prescribed fee, grant a licence to supply energy in any specified area also to lay electric supply lines for the transmission of energy.

Conclusion

Rules and regulations governing Small-Scale Enterprise Act as a governor ensuring steady growth of the industry as well as the environment (ecosystem) and the labour force. It ensures both healthy growth and rapid growth. The basic objective of these rules and regulations scale is to ensure that the results of operations confirm as closely as possible to established standards of goods, specified procedures or instruction. The need for rules and regulations are meant to put these SSIs [small-scale industries] on the successful track.

They are the directions for excellence, growth and development. And, regulation is a monitoring mechanism of rules. Since, small-scale enterprise is concerned with land, environment, goods, people and consumer, rules and regulations have been formulated to safeguard these varied interests.

References

Syed Vazith Hussain - Small Scale Industries in the New Millennium.

Desai, Vasant - Dynamics of Entrepreneurial Development and Management.

King's - Management of Small Scale Industries Entrepreneurship.

4

Women Entrepreneurship Information about Financial Facility

Mandaliya Nilamben V.

Introduction

During the pre-independence period, financial constraints had hampered the rapid development of industries in the country. After independence, the Government built up a network of specialized financial institutions with a fairly big capital base to provide financial assistance to all types to industries, including small-scale industries.

A growing economy needs the support of a financial structure which is responsive to the needs of development. In India, in the process of financial deepening, commercial banks had to shoulder special responsibilities for meeting the financial needs of diverse sectors of the economy, at various stages of development. In the process, they have evolved various modes and instruments of financing, fashioned various organizational innovations, moved away from traditional commercial banking and evolved into development banks, responsive to socioeconomic needs.

Finance is now made available to entrepreneurs on a totality basis by commercial banks, except in cases where the State Financial Corporations and other similar financing agencies step in to meet their medium-term requirements. An appropriate type of credit is granted for the construction of the factory building, the purchase of plant, machinery and equipment, and for working capital requirements. In deserving cases, loans are advanced for the expansion, renovation and modernization of plant and machinery. Banks and financial institutions provide the export finance needed by small industries for letters of credit, issuance of guarantees and extension of pre-shipment and post-shipment credit facilities. The interest rate structure is generally graded on a slab basis, with a favourable bias towards the smaller loans. Institutional support and economic factors are stimulating entrepreneurial activity and thus generating more robust economic development.

Financial Institutions

1. ***Industrial Finance Corporation of India (IFCI)***
   Incorporation and Purpose

The Industrial Finance Corporation of India (IFCI) was established in 1948 under an Act of Parliament with the object of providing medium and long-term credit to industrial concerns in India. IFCI transform into a corporation from 21st May, 1993 to provide greater flexibility to respond to the needs of the rapidly changing financial system.

2. ***The Industrial Development Bank of India (IDBI)***

The Industrial Development Bank of India (IDBI) was established on 1st July, 1964 under the Industrial Development Bank of India Act, as a wholly owned subsidiary of the Reserve Bank of India. In terms of the Public Financial Institutions Laws (Amendment) Act, 1975, the ownership of the IDBI has been transferred to the Central Government with effect from 16th February, 1976. The most distinguishing feature of the IDBI is that it has been assigned the role of the principal financial institution for coordinating, in conformity with national priorities, the activities of the institutions engaged in financing, promotion or developing industry. The IDBI has been assigned a special role to play in regard to industrial development.

3. ICICI

(The Industrial Credit Investment Corporation of India)

The ICICI (The Industrial Credit Investment Corporation of India) was conceived as a private sector development bank in 1955 with the primary function of providing development finance to the private sector. Its objectives now include:

Assisting in the creation, expansion and modernization of such enterprises;

Encouraging and promoting the participation of private capital, both internal and external, in ownership of industrial investment and the expansion of investment markets.

Apart from its head office at Mumbai, the ICICI has four regional offices located at Mumbai, Kolkata, Chennai and New Delhi.

Financial assistance is being provided by ICICI in the following forms:

- Rupee and foreign currency terms loans
- Underwriting of share and debenture issue
- Direct subscription to equity
- Guarantees
- Soft loans
- Lease financing
- Financial Indo-US joint ventures in research and development.

In practice only such projects costing in excess of Rs.300 lakhs are considered for financial assistance by the ICICI. However, for purpose of foreign currency loans, no minimum project cost restriction is imposed.

4. The National Bank for Agriculture and Rural Development

The preamble to the National Bank for Agriculture and Rural Development Act 1981, sets out the objectives for establishing the new institution. To quote, 'An Act to establish a bank to be known as the National Bank of Agriculture and Rural Development for providing credit for the promotion of agriculture, small-scale industries, cottage and village industries, handicrafts and other rural crafts and other allied economic activities in rural areas with a view to promoting integrated rural development and securing prosperity of rural areas, and for matters connected therewith or incidental thereto.

5. *The Small Industries Development Bank of India (SIDBI)*

The idea of setting up Small Industries Development Bank of India (SIDBI), in response to a long-standing demand from the small scale sector as an apex-level national institution for promotion, financing and development of industries in the small scale sector, embodied an opportunity to set up a proactive, responsive and forward looking institution to serve the current and emerging needs of small scale industries in the country. As a precursor to the setting up of the new institution, the Small Industries Development Fund was created by Industrial Development Bank of India (IDBI) in 1986 exclusively for refinancing, bills rediscounting and equity support to the small scale sector. The outstanding portfolio of the order of Rs. 4200 crore from IDBI was transferred to SIDBI in March 1990. SIDBI started off from a strong base: percentage of IDBI, backing of a special statute - the Small Industries Development Bank of India Act of 1989, a large capital base of Rs. 450 crore, availability of experienced manpower endowed with development banking skills carved out of IDBI's professional staff and ready availability of a vast network of institutional infrastructure and enduring financial linkage with State Financial Corporations (SFCs), commercial banks and other institutions; all these augured well for the growth of the nascent institution. SIDBl became operational on April 2, 1990.

6. *Khadi and Village Industries Commission*

The Khadi and Village Industries Commission (KVIC), established by an Act of Parliament in 1956, is engaged in the development of Khadi and Village Industries in rural areas. It has under its purview 26 village industries besides khadi. After amendment to the KVIC Act in July 1987, the scope for coverage of activities was widened and as a consequence 70 more new village industries were identified and brought under its fold for implementation. The main objectives of the KVIC are providing employment in rural areas, skill improvement, transfer of technology, building up of strong rural community base and rural industrialization. The significant characteristics of khadi and village industries under the purview of KVIC lies in their ability to use locally available raw materials, local skills, local markets, low per capital investment, simple techniques of production, which can be easily adopted by the rural people, short gestation period and above all production of consumer goods. KVIC activities serve the poorest of the poor comprising Scheduled Castes, Schedules Tribes, women, physically handicapped and minority communities in difficult, inaccessible hill and border areas.

7. *National Small Industries Corporation Ltd.*

The National Small Industries Corporation Ltd. (NSIC) was set-up by the Government of India in 1955 with the objective of promoting and developing small-scale industries in the country. Various activities undertaken by NSIC include supply of indigenous and imported machines on easy hire-purchase and lease terms, marketing of the products of small industries on consortia basis, export marketing of small industries products, developing export worthiness of small-scale units, enlistment of small-scale units for participating in Government stores purchase programme, development and modernisation prototypes of machines, equipment and tools, supply and distribution of indigenous and imported raw materials, training in various technical trades and co-operation with other developing countries in setting-up of small-scale projects on turn-key basis.

8. *State Financial Corporations*

State Financial Corporations (SFCs), operating at the State-level, form an integral part of the development financing system in the country. They function with the objective of financing and promoting small and medium enterprises for achieving balanced regional socio-economic growth, catalyzing higher investment, generating greater employment opportunities and widening the ownership base of industry.

Conclusion

Financial management is an integral part of industry and ranks equally in importance with other key components like production and marketing. Capital and finance form the bed rock foundation of industrial development. They are provided by a number of financial institutions. The saga of industrial development in the post-independence period is the story of these core institutions as well as market participation.

References

Syed Valith Hussain – Small Scale Industries in the New Millennium.

Sharma, D.D. – Women and Rural Entrepreneurship in India.

Desai, Vasant – Dynamics of Entrepreneurial Development and Management.

5

The Challenges, Prospects and Problems to Women Entrepreneurs

Shailesh Vasavada

Socio-economic and religious barriers have confined women within four walls of their house due to social systems developed since its inception. Upliftment of women became a matter of great concern since long, but women's participation in major economic activities becomes a matter of prime concern only after World War II. There is no doubt that role of women entrepreneurs in economic growth of all the developed countries is very significant. But still there is a large gap to attain equality in all the major fields of economic development in the world. In India women entrepreneurship is comparatively new and recent phenomenon activated since last two to three decades. India is a very large country having extreme differences state-wise, location-wise, social condition-wise and economic condition-wise.

It is very difficult to generalize Challenges, Prospects and Problems for women at large in India, inspite of this vast variance it is a matter of great concern that a Successful Indian Women Entrepreneurs are no way different in terms of their personality, cognition, achievement motivation, dependence and other related attributes. As per the Economic Survey in 1990 women own 10% of SSI, it was also expected to reach up to 23% by 2010 though it has not reached to that level and attained 14%. It is estimated, expected and planned to reach 20 to 25% by the year 2020.

Scenario of Gujarat

India is very large country varying greatly in Socio Economic developments. Gujarat is one of the most developed states of India ranked as number two in industrial growth. As per the economic sensus 1998 (EC - 1998 there were 1915000 - Small enterprises in non-agricultural sector have employed 4159000 lakhs persons out of that only 469000 were female. Surprisingly in rural area this portion is 15.27% is against 9.7 in urban area. According to statistical reports on "industries in Gujarat (1997)" number of women entrepreneur were 459 (3.65%) in 92-93, which is raised to 896 (6.44) in 95-96. This increasing trend suggest that by 2005 it is expected women entrepreneur will reach 12%. Even though this proportion is very low and required to be improved. The main constraint in Women of Gujarat is found to be social barriers and poor institutional support. Women of Gujarat have contributed to almost all the sectors like Engineering, Plastic, Garments, Textiles, Chemicals and Food Industries.

Entrepreneurship Development for Women

ED = $f(E_t, O_p, S_k, P_r, F, I_f, E_n)$

Entrepreneurship Development is a function of entrepreneurial traits, opportunities, skills, Project Plan, Finance, Infrastructure, and Environment. To Study Challenges, Prospects and Problems of Entrepreneurship above factors should be taken into consideration. Women at large can be further classified according to following criteria

- Age
- Education
- Marital Status
- Occupational History
- Geographical Location

- Income Level

Challenges, prospects and problems of women entrepreneur vary from target to target. We shall be studying challenges, prospects and problems of "Educated Unemployed Urban and Semi Urban Women". Further to understand their problems and prospects.

Following is the SWOT Analysis of a Typical Unemployed Educated Urban / Semi Urban Women" SWOT Analysis

Internal

Strengths

- Have Hard Working
- Have Commitment
- Able to Handle Situations
- Have Dual Responsibility
- Good at Public Relation
- Can Get Sympathy and Support

Weaknesses

- Have Family Responsibility
- Are Emotional
- Have Low Technical Knowledge
- Have Many Cultural and Social Barriers
- Lack of Self Confidence
- Low Risk Takers

External

Opportunities

- Govt. incentives
- Competitive Economic Situation
- Increase in the Participation of Women in Entrepreneurial Activities
- Women Economic Development Bank

Threats

- Marriage in Case of Unmarried
- Have Responsibility of Children
- Face Family Resistance
- Resistance from Support System Agencies
- Face Social Barriers

From the above SWOT Analysis, it is evident that lots of strength and opportunities are being suppressed by weakness and threats.

(a) The threat portion is the challenges to women entrepreneurship, Govt. and Non-Govt. Agencies should formulate policies to eliminate these threats and making easy entry to women entrepreneurer.

(b) Weakness portion of the SWOT relates to problems to Women Entrepreneurer. Designing Training Programms, Awareness Camps, and Seminar will reduce these problems. Also developing a support system for women is also desirable.

(c) Strength and opportunities combines together determines the prospects for Women Entrepreneurs.

The Challenges for Women Entrepreneurship can be categorised as under:

- To sensitize financial institutions and development agencies on women credit needs.
- Extending marketing support including marketing outlets, design support and assistance in maintaining quality control of product and process.
- Providing Technical Support.
- Enhancing Women's participation in policy making process.
- Global Challenge like effect of WTO.

Problems to Women Entrepreneurs

- Lack of Confidence and Low risk taking ability.

- Lack of Technical exposure to some sectors like Engineering and Fabrication.
- Being emotional cannot overcome procedural resistance and resistance from support systems, family resistance etc.
- Networking among Women Entrepreneurs is absent.

Prospects to Women Entrepreneurs

- Immerging Social need to engage Women to Economic Activities.
- Immerging opportunities in many industrial sectors for women, e.g. Service Sector, Tourism Ind., IT.
- Govt.'s emphasis on WEDP.
- Banking Sector needs Honest and Efficient Borrowers.
- Many state level as well as national NGO. Associations and Federation are working for WEDP. e.g. SEWA [Self

Approach Model for Challenges

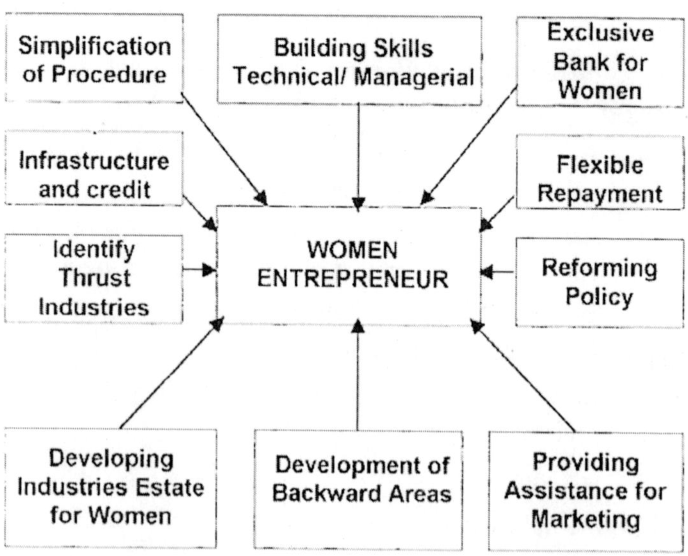

Approach Model for Overcome Problems

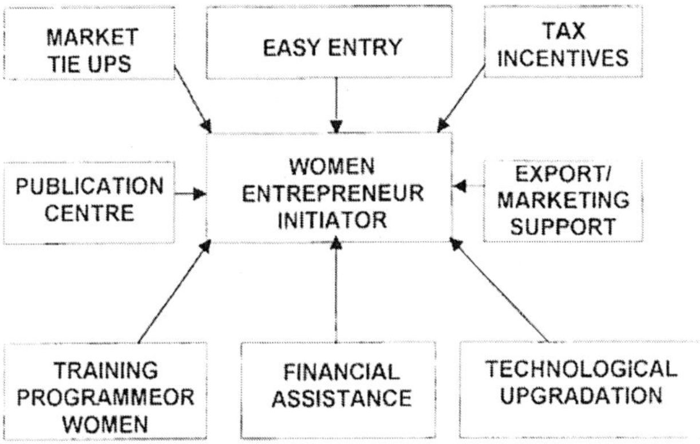

Programme Module

Session		
Day	*I*	*II*
Ist Week		
1	Registration and Inauguration	Programme objective and strategy Microlab
2	Entrepreneurship traits and competency	Enterprise Building Planning and Evaluation
3	Govt. Policy, Incentives and Institutions	Schemes and assistance from DIC
4	Schemes and Assistance from SFC	Schemes and Assistance Bank
5	Expericence sharing with women entrepreneur	Business opportunities, identification process
IInd Week		
1	Local Business opportunities	Selection of product Brain Storming
2and 3	Achievement	Motivation Training
4	Market Survey	Exercise/Video Role Playing
5	Market Survey Break	Counselling for Market survey
IIIrd Week		
1	Financial Management	Costing - Financial ratios
2	Managing a small business	Marketing Management
3	Project Report and Appraisal	Loan Application Bank/SFC
4	Working Capital Management	Finalisation of scheme Counselling
5	Successful Entrepreneur experience sharing	Project Appraisal Role playing and validiction

Employed Women Associations] Gujarat and FIWE New Delhi, I Create Inc.

In addition to the above Module more subjects are being added as per the requirements and size of the project.

6
The Encouragement Provided to the Women Entrepreneurship

Maithili T. Pathak

Introduction

Entrepreneurial development is a complex phenomenon. Productive activity undertaken by him and constant endeavor to sustain and improve it are the outword expression of this process of development of his personality. An entrepreneur is one of the important segments of economics growth. Basically he is a person responsible for setting up a business or an enterprise. In face he is a person responsible for setting up a business or an enterprise, in fact he is one who has the initiative skill of innovation and who looks for high achievements. An urge to exercise power over things and objects persists among all human beings. The urge may vary in degree from person to person.

The entrepreneur is an important input of economics development. He is a catalyst of development with him we prosper, without him we are poor.

The term "entrepreneur" is defined in a variety of ways

- ***Joseph A. Schumpeter***

Person who introduces innovation, changes, is an entrepreneur. He has treated entrepreneur as an integral part of economic growth. According to him, the fundamental source of equilibrium was the entrepreneur.

- ***Martin Luther King***

I have a dream, and thousand followed in spite of overwhelming obstacles. In order to establish a successful new business venture the entrepreneurial leader must have a dream and work against all obstacles to achieve it.

Women entrepreneurship in India out of total 940.98 million people in India in the 1990's females comprises 437.10 million representing 46.5% of the total population. There are 126.48 million women workforce but as per 1991 census, only 1,85,900 women accounting for only 4.5% of the total self-employed persons in the country were recorded.

The entrepreneurial qualities are to some extent innate. But not all of them are entirely innate. Some can be enhanced by training, or simply by experience. For example, analytical ability and computational skill can be enhanced by education at school and university, while practical knowledge and foresight skills can be enhanced by the general experience of everyday life. Entrepreneurial careers will be strongly influenced by the desire to enhance qualities which are scarce, yet difficult to obtain through delegation because of the problems involved in screening for them. Of the two indispensable qualities of the entrepreneur, imagination is almost entirely innate, while foresight can be enhanced by a varied experience. Imagination and foresight are the scarce qualities which are difficult to analyses and quantify. Delegation skill and organization skill, though not essential, are highly desirable whenever large-scale decision-making is involved. These are qualities which can be enhanced through experience.

Many women, in society, do various business for which they do get encouragement from their children, husband, family members and relatives, society and from the nation.

They are as follows –

1. ***Children***

It is seen that children are always helpful to their mother physically as well as mentally. Each child helps mother for example, if she is tying then 'bandhani' then the child gives her mental support at least by tying two or three knots in the cloth. They also try to do their own work by themselves. Moreover, they avoid troubling their mother while working. In this way every mother is seen getting help from her children.

2. *Husband*

Husband and wife are the two wheels of their conjugal life. If they don't get cooperation for any work, then success is impossible. Particularly for a wife. When she gets help from a husband she feels very encouraged and gets inspiration to do the work in a good way. To women the help of then husbands by helping in household chores, by participating in the work concerning kids, some outdoor work like purchasing, works relating to bank and post office, and paying all types of bills. A housewife can only do her business well if the husband is taking interest in, how to develop her business more, how to get finance or credits and subsidies, and how to manage the payment of installments.

3. *Family Members and Relatives*

Family members are always seen helping the women in different ways for her business. In certain families other people like friends, cousins and their sons, every one irrespective of the ages, are seen helping in some way or the other.

4. *Society*

Women entrepreneurs get a lot of encouragement from the society also. Some women run such industry which is directly useful for the working women, for example, making of 'Khakhara, Thepla, Papad', etc. The working women get helped by purchasing regularly from them. The producers provide quality goods and are very sincere about the satisfaction of the consumer. The society helps such entrepreneurs by recommending their goods to others. Some groups of society are sympathetic to women entrepreneurs and are constantly guiding and suggesting then in thier progress.

5. *Nation*

The financial resource are unavoidable for any economic activity and it is particular for the starting of new industry because for any business venture four "M" are important.

1. M = Machine
2. M = Men
3. M = Material
4. M = Money

From the above four sources Money is such a force by which we can gain the other three sources 'Man', 'Machine', and 'Material'. Therefore Money is called the "Lubricant" and the "Blood of the Business".

Some National Financial Institutions for Entrepreneurship Development are –

- IDBI - Industrial Development Bank of India.
- SIDBI - Small Industries Development Bank of India.
- IFCI - Industrial Finance Corporation of India.
- ICICI - Industrial Credit and Investment Corporation of India.

Some State Financial Institution for Entrepreneurship Development are –

- GSFC - Gujarat State Financial Corporation
- GIIC - Gujarat Industrial Investment Corporation
- GSIC - Gujarat Small Industries Corporation
- GIDC - Gujarat Industrial Development Corporation
- All other National Banks and Private Banks and Co-operative Banks.

Result–Discussion

Result of Questionnaires at a Glance

No.	Point of Questions	Result	Yes	No
1.	High Price	95%	Yes	No
2.	Business Guidance	20%	Yes	No

Contd...

Table Contd...

3.	National Facilities	10%	Yes	No
4.	Training	60%		
5.	Reason for Starting Business	High Price, of the Financial Growth of family	Yes	No
6.	Help from Husband	95%	Yes	No
7.	Source of Capital	Family Member and Friends	Yes	No
8.	Help from Others	Physical Help		
9.	Society/Children	98%	Yes	No
10.	Knowledge about Loans	90%	Yes	No
11.	Why Industry at Home	Responsibility of Home	Yes	No
12.	Able to satisfy the need of Husband and Children	95%	Yes	No
13.	Financial support to the Family	95%	Yes	No
14.	Appreciation not going out	95%	Yes	No
15.	Facing Difficulty	Very Little	Yes	No
16.	Envy from other Women	100% Negative answer	Yes	No
17.	Mental Satisfaction	70%	Yes	No
18.	Two Work Trouble	90% Family Realized	Yes	No
19.	Comparison of Out-Door Work	70%	Yes	No
20.	Objection against Customer Treatment	100%	Yes	No
21.	Obstruction from Neighbors and Guests	95%	Yes	No
22.	Vacation, Leave	Sadness Expressed	Yes	No
23.	Physical - Mental care	Everybody	Yes	No

Discussion

Women of Jamnagar running small scale industry were the respondents out of which some do 'tie and die work' (Bandhani work), cutting bettle-nut, doing brass-pot work, miscellaneous sewings work etc. Such women have started home industry only with the reason of ascalating prices of goods and commodities. Many such women had not got adequate guidance for their business. Though they resided in city but in slum areas, they had not got knowledge about facilities offered by our country. They have collected the funds for their venture from their friends and relatives. Only four women had an idea about government policies for giving loans to entrepreneurs.

All the women had got physical and mental encouragement from their children, husband, family member and friends, society and nation. Such women are not the victims of envy of other women. The women had complete job satisfaction regarding their business ventures.

The most painful matter was that such women were not able to take care of their own mental or physical health and particularly in brass-pot work. When there is a power-cutoff or recession in the market the work is not provided for women at their homes which causes lot of mental and physical discomfort.

Conclusion

Women staying in slum area of Jamnagar were the responding who were running small scale industries like 'bandhani work', brass-part work, cutting of bettle-nut and miscellaneous sewing work. They got very good help from kids, husband, family members and society. No doubt the help from government is very well provided such as organizing training camps, awareness regarding financial scheme, and information through medium of propaganda of all such helps and schemes of government but the larger class of our country is illiterate and hence proper information does not reach to these women entrepreneurs and the society surrounding them are not also able to provide any type of information. So the government should revitalize all the efforts that they do for the benefit of women of slum areas to help then become successful entrepreneurs.

These small scale women entrepreneurs are justifying their both duties in a very fine manner. They also get full job satisfaction and support their family financially. But it is a matter of regret that they are not able to take care of their own health and hygiene. It is thus suggested that, the government should set a scheme for the health of small scale entrepreneurs of going door to door for their check-up every three months.

The another of this article is thankful to –

- Principal Prafulbhai Chhapia for encouragement and inspiration.
- Prof. Vasuben Trivedi (M.L.A.) for warmth and guidance.
- Prof. Varshaben Chhichia (Syndicate Member Dean, Head of Department for guidance and administrative facilities).
- Rtd. Principal Bharat Chhaya for wider information of the subject.

References

Desai, Vasant, Dynamics of Entrepreneur Development and Management.

Desai, Vasant, Entrepreneurial Development.

C. Jamnadas, Fundamentals of Entrepreneurship.

7

Capacity Building - Means and Ends Towards Economic Empowerment of Women

Dinesh Awasthi and Manoj Mishra

Introduction: The Context

Empowerment as a concept is multidimensional and not easy to define. Empowerment of women is widely used in the development literature recently - but in different ways by different agents. United Nations Development Programme attempted to create a GEM (Gender Empowerment Index) in 1995 and focused on participation-economic, political and professional. Each of these is measured by one yardstick the income earning power, share in parliamentary seats, and share in professional and managerial jobs. The obvious assumption is that these three things can empower a person; it is true that these are important pathways to the empowerment of women in general. But, as critics rightly ask, can these achievements actually solve the problem of institutionalised power structure, which are the main factor behind women's subordination? For example, although it is undeniable that income confers power, power relation within the families, which again gets carried over to the workplace and to the broader social framework, are so complex that income-earning women enjoy less control over their earnings than men in the same position. For poorer women, income earning becomes such a compulsion that it may imply less empowerment instead of more! Conceptualising power and women's empowerment entails understanding its multidimensional nature, the complex ways in which women experience subordination, and the ways they negotiate or manage the state of affairs.

The United Nations (UN) Conference on Women, held in Beijing in 1995, placed considerable emphasis on practical actions, which could contribute to the economic empowerment of women. In addition, the Women Entrepreneurs' Summit (Paris 1997) hosted by the Organization for Economic Cooperation and Development (OECD), brought together a large number of women entrepreneurs from around the world. Together they have drawn attention to the potential and opportunities, as well as the barriers and constraints, relating to women's entrepreneurship development.

This chapter attempts to look at women's entrepreneurship development from the perspective of contemporary approaches to gender and development issues, as well as from systematic approaches used in micro enterprise development. The chapter endeavours to bring these two approaches together.

In order to understand the reality facing women entrepreneurs, one needs to develop a conceptual framework which encompasses a number of well-defined concepts, as well as distinct spheres and arenas within which the barriers, constraints and opportunities facing women entrepreneurs are analysed (Finnegan & Danielsen, 1997). A better understanding of the women entrepreneurs as a group is also needed, as there are quite a few misunderstandings about them with reference to their role dualities. These factors are likely to enter into the calculus of women entrepreneurship programmes.

A thorough understanding of the disadvantages and the continuing disempowerment they have been subjected to have to be complemented by recognition of the positive role of women as agents of social change. The key determinant of women's role, as a force for their empowerment, is their ability to gain the necessary bargaining power to effect change in discriminatory agendas. After all they need to influence the norms that affect their day-do-day relationships in various spheres of social transaction.

In order to assess the different constraints and the capacity building needs of micro enterprises led by women, one has to take into consideration the typologies of women entrepreneurs.

Typologies of Women Entrepreneurs

The nature of capacity building needs will vary with their level of operation. One could divide self-employed, or are in the employer category, into three broad typologies.

1. ***Microentrepreneurs**:* Women, earning low incomes in rural and urban areas by engaging themselves as home-based workers (producers), small vendors, petty traders and hawkers, producers and suppliers of services and cultivators, etc. could be defined as micro-entrepreneurs. They are mostly illiterate, are from lower strata of society (in terms of caste and communities), have very low level of skills, mostly learnt a part of their household work (cooking, knitting, bamboo basket weaving, textiles, handicrafts and so on); and have no or very little work experience. They enter into micro-enterprise sector out of economic compulsions, to supplement family income; and in case of women headed households, to earn livelihood for the family (Perera, 1995). Because of their background they stand little chance to get wage employment in organised sector. Most of them operate from their own homes (if they have one); use low (or no) technology and cater to the local and lower end of the market segments; and micro enterprises are mostly their part-time occupation, characterised by irregular hours of work (Renenyi, 1991). These businesses are almost wholly funded from family savings and small loans from informal money tenders (Liedholm and Mead, 1987). They mostly operate outside the legal net of the governments, as in general is the case with this sector, which sometimes has also been labelled and illegal sector as *"[it is] virtually impossible for poor.... to live and work legally..... the cost of remaining legal are overwhelming"* (de Soto, 1987, p.2). As a result they are also deprived of most of the Government support, which unequally favours the large, organised sector (Levitsky, 1993, pp. 5-12).

2. ***Small-Scale Entrepreneurs:*** This segment belongs to urban middle and upper middle class women entrepreneurs who have relatively easy, access to the government support infrastructure. They are better qualified, have better exposure to market and most of the times have better business networks through their family members and friends who may be in business. It has been observed that most of them enter into business at the middle age (35-45 years), after their children have grown-up and they have more time at their disposal (Awasthi and Jose, 1996, pp. 163-175). A study of 45 women entrepreneurs conducted by Entrepreneurship Development Institute of India provides convincing evidence of the women's capabilities as entrepreneurs, who successfully set up and manage their enterprises in a 'Man's World Environment' of industry which is complex and hostile to women. They also manufacture better industrial products involving better technology, have higher investment (in the range of Rs. 1.0 Lakh to Rs. 10.00 Lakh) and employ on an average 5-8 workers (Kanitkar and Contractor, 1992). They are not just self-employed but are well-groomed entrepreneurs. The characteristics associated with entrepreneurship such as 'ambition', 'self-confidence', 'risk taking', 'resolutions', 'assertiveness', 'high achievement motivation', etc. are more pronounced among them compared to those operating in the subsistence sector.

   It has, however, also been argued that, by the time they are free from their familial responsibilities, some of them have hardly any scope to get appropriate employment in the organised sector. For, despite being qualified, they lack adequate and relevant experience to make inroads in the employment market at a desired level. In order to channelise their energies and give a vent to their creativity they take up entrepreneurship as a career option. It means, this shift is because of the push factors that some of them become entrepreneurs rather than by choice or because of the pull factors. That is why probably Patel (1986) calls them forced entrepreneurs.

3. ***Women Owners of Large Businesses***: These women entrepreneurs, by and large, come from wealthy class of the social strata, mostly from business houses or from the families of senior bureaucrats. This is a minuscule minority in the women's business world. Mostly they become entrepreneurs through inheritance and/or division of large business houses. They have access to the corridors of power and all those who matter. They are altogether in a different league of business operations, which has hardly anything in common with women micro and small-scale entrepreneurs, except their gender.

We argue that despite these differences, they face constraints of various kinds in operating their businesses because of the gender bias, which cuts across the size of business operations and the typologies.

Why Women-operated Micro-Businesses do not grow?

Women often state future of their children and the stability of their family as priority. Moreover, the behavioural pattern of women is that of modesty, coupled with hesitation and lack of articulation, which is often misinterpreted as a reflection of their incompetence and lack of entrepreneurial qualities. Moreover, difficulties in raising sufficient capital limits the type of enterprises women tend to launch. Inadequate investment capital coupled with low levels of skills compels them to adopt low technology based production process; and the inadequacy of working capital forces them to buy raw material in smaller quantities, making it costlier. All this affects their cost of production adversely. This also limits their ability to experiment or introduce new products or designs (Howarth, 1993). Local market oriented production, determined by the customers, who are also poor, leads to restricted pricing at the cost of their profit margins, as most of the WMSEs cater to the low price, low quality market segment of wage goods (Renenyi, 1991). These businesses are mostly self-funded and the income generated out of these enterprises is hardly ploughed back into business, as it has to meet the family requirement. This also puts a constraint on the growth.

Women's business thus tend to be smaller - and grow slower-than men's. They are more likely to be home-based and to be in sectors that are technologically unsophisticated and overcrowded to the point of market saturation". (The World Bank, 1994, p. 50).

In this chapter we will attempt to discuss the spheres within which women entrepreneurs operate. The overall context of Women Entrepreneurs can be described in terms of:

(a) the macro environment within which women entrepreneurs create and develop their enterprises;

(b) the meso sphere (or the intermediary and institutional sphere) within which women entrepreneurs can operationalize their enterprises, and

(c) the micro sphere (or family and household sphere) within which the gender specific division of labour and decision-making power shape women's multiple identities, including her potential identity as an entrepreneur in a given cultural and ideological context. These three different but interconnected spheres are depicted in diagram 1.

(a) The Macro Sphere

The macro environment within which all entrepreneurs (including women) develop and grow comprises of many interconnecting structures and dynamics, that include;

- laws and regulations.
- the economy.
- competition.
- international trade, including market liberalization and globalization.
- availability of finance and credit.
- the labour market.

Diagram 1

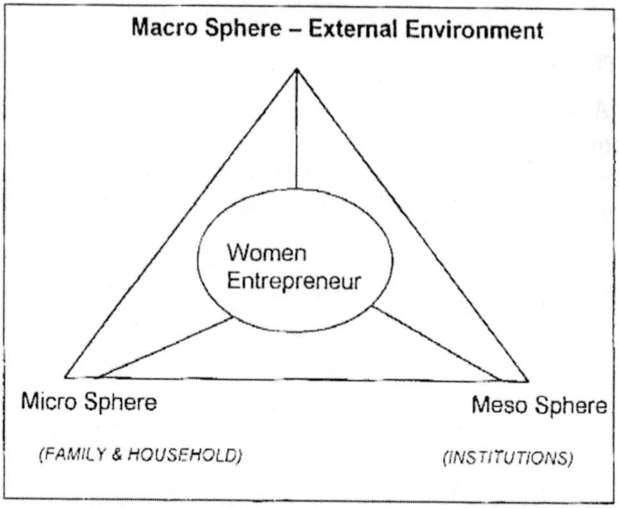

- human capital resource.
- technology.
- physical infrastructure.
- natural resources.

While macro environment influences enterprises, both large and small entrepreneurs, both women and men, there is enough evidence to indicate that women are more disadvantaged than the men in relation to the opportunities and barriers arising from these structures and dynamics. Why is this so? We argue that it is because of women's ability to bargain in the labour market, as in other spheres of negotiations, is critically constrained by gender bias. Bargaining takes place over wages, conditions of work and workers' rights. However, women's bargaining power in the workplace as compared to that of men, is constrained not only by gender gaps in skills and education, but also by employers' assumptions regarding women's abilities, work commitment, efficiency and needs, which is further exacerbated by the unequal sharing of family responsibilities in the micro context.

Therefore, the world of work and the way in which it treats, classifies and discriminates women and men, including the operation of formal and informal labour markets, significantly contributes to the process of disempowerment of women.

(b) The Meso (Institutional Sphere)

A large number of organizations are involved in extending support services to entrepreneurs. However, for a variety of reasons many of these organizations tend to act as barriers when it comes to providing assistance to women entrepreneurs. In some cases this can be attributed to a lack of awareness about women's concerns and sensitivity towards gender issues. At the meso level many organizations implement policies and operationalize programmes, for women entrepreneurs, even they contribute to the continuing process of women disempowerment.

The gender sensitivity of the organizations is determined, to a great extent by the structures and dynamics of the macro environment described earlier. However, presence of a conducive or enabling macro environment is not a guarantee of gender sensitive practices. While the state might formulate gender-progressive laws and policies, the resistance offered by the government bureaucracy, judiciary, and other such official organs might hinder the implementation of these measures. (UNDP, 2001 a)

These meso level organizations that support / promote women led micro enterprises could be classified in a number of different ways. We have adopted a organizational based classification.

I. The Stakeholder Focussed organizations:

- Government organizations;
- Non-governmental organizations, including international NGOs, community organizations, private sector organizations, donor-assisted agencies, cooperatives.

II. The client / member focussed organizations

- Women entrepreneur specific organizations; (such as women producer's organizations);
- Small enterprise development or entrepreneurship development organizations;

- Cooperatives;
- Mainstream organizations, such as employer's organizations, worker's organizations and government agencies.

III. The Support organizations

- Providing access to credit;
- Providing access to markets;
- Providing access to business skills;
- Providing access to technical skills;
- Providing broader economic support;
- Improving bargaining power;
- Empowering on socio-political fronts;

IV. The activity focussed organizations: Organizations engaged in:

- Business skills training;
- Technical skills training;
- Business support services;
- Credit and finance.

V. Organizations focusing on issues related to women in development. These organizations could focus on one or a combination of more than one issues:

- Equity;
- Anti-poverty;
- Efficiency:
- Empowerment;
- Gender and Development.

(c) The Micro Sphere

In India, women experience an unequal power relationship with men, which are often reflected in persistent intra-family inequalities in the distribution of tasks, in access to and control over resources, as well as in intra-household bargaining power, which typically also weakens a woman's extra-household bargaining power. This amounts to deprivation of influence at all levels. Gender relations also determine the ascription to men and women of different abilities, attitudes, desires, personality traits, behaviour, etc. - factors which are seen to be important in entrepreneurship development.

More often than not, women's work is neither given due recognition nor valued in monetary terms. The work in home is unpaid, and many working women (including those in formal as well as informal sector occupations) are in marginal and lowly paid jobs (Agrawal Bina, 1994).

However, it should be stressed that the term "women", or "women entrepreneurs" for that sake, are not uniform categories or homogeneous entities. There could be very fundamental differences among women entrepreneurs, for example in terms of level of poverty or wealth; skills level; educational and literacy level; experience of work or business; age; family commitments and family support, and so on. Existing gender relations interact with other dominant structures of social hierarchy also such as class, caste and race. These interactions of course, vary over time and space. Women's interests and needs are reflected in multiple identities according to the interaction of the above structures. For example, poor women fight subordination in at least three roles and identities; (i) as a worker, where the issue of job security is important; (ii) being poor, where basic survival needs have to be ensured; and (iii) being a woman, where gender inequality is evident.

Constraints faced by Women Entrepreneurs

The women entrepreneurs face lack of right business linkages, access to credit schemes, identification and selection of viable project, preparing, understanding and monitoring business (project) plans; and, training (Tuladhar, 1996). Enterprises thus face the disadvantages both of size and location; and, women entrepreneurs suffer from "triple disadvantage", due to the additional constraints they face as "women", in terms of their compulsions to combine household and enterprise activities, social constraints to mobility and lack of access to and control over resources, they face a variety of problems (Choudhury, 2000). In fact, entrepreneurship is a function of four interrelated systems viz. Self Sphere System; Social Sphere System, Resource Sphere System; and, Support Sphere System. Women suffer on all these accounts (Mali, 1991).

Enterprise-based activities, however, involve access to and mobilization of productive resources, new technologies and inputs from outside the household production system and access to marketing information and to markets; and, women, particularly mountain women, are often not able to take up these activities due to such handicaps as lack of ownership and control over productive resources, such as land and capital, and, for that reason, lack of access to credit, lack of time to move out to acquire inputs and services due to over work in household and framing activities, and restrictions on their social mobility due to traditions and lack of education and consequence back of exposure to markets and access to market information __________ in traditional societies like India and Pakistan, their performance is ______ to the mark due to restrictions on mobility and lack of business and _____ skills (Ibadat, n.d.).

Constraints Faced by Women Entrepreneures

1. ***Self Sphere System***
   - Lack of Education
   - Lack of Managerial Competencies
   - Lack of Self Confidence and Motivation
   - Lack of Skills
   - Lack of Decision Making Skills and Attitude
   - Low Social Security
2. ***Social Sphere System***
   - Triple Responsibilities (Productive, reproductive and Societal_____)
   - Lack of Mobility
   - Gender Bias
   - Male Domination
   - Lack of Family Support
3. ***Resource Sphere***
   - Lack of Property Rights

- Lack of Financial Resources
- Lack of Collateral
- Low Exposure to Business
- Lack Access to Market Information
- Lack of Access to Inputs

4. ***Support System Sphere***

- Lack of Access to Channels of Credit
- Lack Access to Training
- Lack Access to Infrastructure
- Limited Access to Appropriate Technology
- Lack Access to Business Networks

INTEGRATED–CONTEXTUAL MODEL–A model of factors

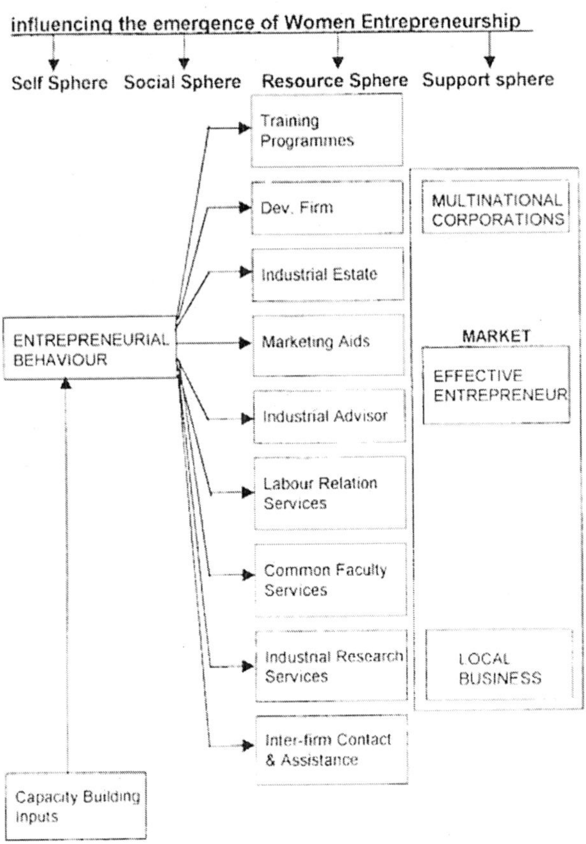

They have low level of confidence and their families have little confidence in their capability. Social perception towards women is narrow. They are considered as weak and passive. Religious beliefs are also not favourable to women. Women cannot travel out of home for a long period of time. Women are looked as consumers and spenders rather than as producers and bread earners. They lack access to credit, training and education. Family does not support women in their enterprises. When in business, they mostly concentrate on traditional types of activities that are easy to enter but are very competitive and less profitable, such as handicrafts, hosiery, garments, restaurants and teashops. Moreover, lack of time due to excessive household responsibilities, social restrictions on mobility, narrows down the enterprising potential.

The Situation of Women Entrepreneurs

As discussed earlier, gender differences occur in each of the three spheres. A consequence of these differences is the disempowerment of women, as reflected in their poor level of participation in small and cottage industries and micro enterprises.

Women Entrepreneurship and Support Activities

The above stated conceptual framework for Women Entrepreneurship activities, which leads to economic empowerment, provides stimulus to devise a systemic input structure for mitigating the constraints.

Constraints of Potential Women Entrepreneurs and Development Inputs

	Constraints	*Inputs*
1.	Low self-image and confidence	Motivational inputs, unfreezing and experience sharing by successful local entrepreneur
2.	No faith on others including friends	Group building experiences
3.	No exposure to industry/ business	Field visit to factories and big markets

Contd...

4.	Whom to contact for starting a venture what formalities and procedures are to be followed	Information inputs on procedures and formalities
5.	No idea of business	Business Opportunity Identification and Guidance
6.	How to know whether identified business is a viable and sound proposition?	Market survey, and project report preparation
7.	How does one carry out bank operation?	Training in simple banking procedures like filling-up deposit and withdrawal slip etc.
8.	How to manage the business?	Basic management orientation through simulation exercies
9.	How to read and write accounts?	Functional and numerical literacy. Simple accounting in terms of writing income and expenditure
10.	Almost no technical skills (except-in the case of artisans)	Technical Training (on-the-job training)

Sequencing of MEDP Activities and Inputs: A Brief Outline

- Identification of the area
- Liaison with Government agencies
- Identification of opportunities
- Survey of the area/village
- Promotional campaign - Handbills, meetings and drum beating
- Application screening
- Selection through FBEI/GET Test
- Unfreezing
- Entrepreneur from local area
- Exposure to industry, agriculture and market
- The real enterprise experience

- Opportunity Guidance
- Information Inputs - Bank operations
- Communication skills
- Market Survey Techniques
- Market Survey
- Survey report by the Entrepreneur
- Comments on Market Survey and feasibility by bank officials
- A.M.T.
- Communication
- Management Inputs
- Business accounting/arithmetic
- Procedural and legal aspects like sales tax, registration, etc.
- Finalisation of product
- Technical Training
- Business Plan Preparation
- Submission of Loan Applications to Bank
- Follow up phase (organising the first follow up meeting)
- Preparation of the Documentation Report and submission of the same to the sponsors and own organisation for records.
- Follow up to two year
- Submission of the final reports and audited statement of accounts to the sponsors and closing the programme after final documentation.

Institutional Capacity Building - Meso Sphere

A second major thrust in promoting women's entrepreneurship development is to develop and enhance the capacity of key organizations to enable them to integrate gender concerns into the work of their organization and play a more

---

* Though the traditional method of imparting AMT as followed more explicitly it may be mentioned that small doses of motivational inputs had to be given time and again, in order to maintain its effectiveness upon the trainees.

comprehensive role in supporting women. A logical sequencing of these capacity-building activities, grouped into several clusters, is shown below :

- Development of the organization or system and improving its management;
- Promoting effectiveness in dealing with gender issues and increasing gender sensitization, as well as developing skills in mobilising and organising women in recognition of women's potential as agents for social change;
- Improving the training skills and business development services, including credit support services;
- Developing public relations skills to positively influence attitudes and promote positive and reinforcing images of women entrepreneurs on the one hand, and combat limiting stereotypes of women entrepreneurs on the other;
- Enhancing the prospects for sustaining the capacity of the institutions and agencies, as well as the improved status of the individual women entrepreneurs, including the development of supportive linkages and networks;
- Improving monitoring and evaluation skills, as well as impact assessment.

Market Segmentation and Product Differentiation

As mentioned earlier, it should be well understood that not all women entrepreneurs are the same, nor do all support agencies have identical needs. The cost-effectiveness of support programmes aimed at individual women entrepreneurs and women led enterprise supporting organisations can be greatly enhanced by identifying specific "segments" which share relatively similar characteristics, and by providing client-specific solutions to meet their needs. The following are classifications which can be used in segmenting client groups - whether they are organizations or women entrepreneurs.

- Intermediary support agencies can be segmented based on the identification of their ultimate target groups and their respective needs.

- Entrepreneurs can be segmented by the stage of development of the enterprise - establishment; launch; consolidation; growth; diversification.
- Enterprises can be classified as "subsistence" or "growth" enterprises, each with their respective needs.
- Segments can be identified based on the needs and interests expressed by the women entrepreneurs themselves.
- Further segmentation can take place according to the features and characteristics of the enterprise, as well as its products and services.
- Market features can also be used as a means of classifying enterprises.

Provision of Specialist Support

A range of "differentiated products and services" can be effectively provided within the WED approach to meet the needs of various segments of women entrepreneurs. Several of these specialist support services can be accessed through mainstream small enterprise agencies; others may be designed with the specific needs and circumstances of women entrepreneurs in mind. In any event, it is essential that all of these services take the gender factor into account in order to ensure that they are accessible to women entrepreneurs on the one hand, and that they are relevant and cost-effective mechanisms for contributing to the further economic empowerment of women through micro and small enterprise development on the other.

Conclusion

As the title of this paper implies, we have intended to examine women's entrepreneurship development from a number of different perspectives. We have put forward the question: "Is Women Entrepreneurship Development an end in itself or is it a means to a more wide-reaching end?" In presenting Women Entrepreneurship Development in the context of both gender and development" and conventional "small enterprise development" perspectives, we are of the opinion that Women Entrepreneurship Development needs to be examined and assessed in a wider context. To be truly effective, Women

Entrepreneurship Development needs to be placed in the context of critical and relevant gender issues on all levels - from the micro to the macro level. It should be noted that there is no guarantee that "women only" programmes are necessarily sensitive to gender issues and, rather than promoting equality of opportunity, they may lead to reinforcement of gender bias and perpetuation of women's disempowerment. The economic empowerment of women through Women Entrepreneurship Development needs to give substantial emphasis to the development to women's bargaining power at all levels, as well as a highlighting a perspective that ensures the breakdown of limiting gender stereotypes and recognises the importance of women's agency. In other words, Women Entrepreneurship Development should be seen as a means towards achieving economic empowerment for women, ultimately leading towards a more holistic empowerment of, women at the social, political and economic levels.

References

Agarwal, Bina (1994). A Field of One's Own: Gender and land rights in South Asia, Cambridge University Press, Cambridge.

Awasthi, Dinesh N. and Sebastian Jose (1995). Evaluation of Entrepreneurship Development Programmes, New Delhi, Sage Publications.

Belandres, Lolita F.B. (1996). Factors affecting women entrepreneurship in small and cottage industries in the Philippines (draft report), ILO-SAAT, New Delhi.

Carr, Marilyn; Martha Chen and Renana Jhabvala (1997). Speaking out: Women's economic empowerment in South Asia, Vistaar Publications, New Delhi.

Choudhury, Hira Neog (2000). Women Entrepreneurship in Assam: Problems and Prospects, in Mali, DD (ed), Entrepreneurship Development in North East, Guwahati, Indian Institute of Enrepreneurship.

De Soto, Henvando (1987). "Constraints on People: The Origin of Underground Economies and Limits to their Growth", a Book review of Otrosendrew (The other Path), ILD, Lima Peru, p. 2.

Finnergan & Danielsen (1997). "Promoting the development of Women Entrepreneurs - means and ends in Women Entrepreneurship Development" ILO - SAAT, New Delhi.

Howarth, Rhona (1993). "Women's Micro enterprise - Lessons: for Enterprise Support Agencies", Indian Management, - February-March, pp. 21-25.

Jayaweera, Swarna (1996). Factors affecting women entrepreneurship in small and cottage industries in Sri Lanka, ILO-SAAT, New Delhi.

Karim, Nilufer Ahmed (1997). Factors affecting women entrepreneurship in small and cottage industries in Bangladesh, ILO Area Office, Dhaka and ILO-SAAT, New Delhi.

Mehler Gisela (1997). Women Entrepreneurs at the Micro Level: Some observations and thoughts. Paper, prepared for ASEED MED Summit, Colombo, August 1997.

Mali, D.D., (1991). Developing Entrepreneurship Among Women, The Assam Tribune, 18th March.

Kanitkar, Ajit and Contractor Nalinee (1992). In Search of Identity: The Women Entrepreneurs in India, Ahmedabad, Entrepreneurship Development Institute of India.

Levitsky, Jacob (1994). Financing of SMEs, New Delhi, WASME Publication.

Leidholm, Carl, and Meed, Donald (1987). Small-Scale Industries in Developing Countries: Empirical Evidence and Policy Implications, MSU International Development Paper No. 9, East hansing: Michigan State University.

Misra, S.P. (1996). Factors affecting women entrepreneurship in small and cottage industries in India, ILO-SAAT, New Delhi.

Obhasanond, Prani (1996), Factors affecting women entrepreneurship in small and cottage industries in Thailand (draft report), ILO-SAAT, New Delhi.

Papola, T.S. (1991). Industry and Employment: Recent Indian Experience, ISID Foundation Day Lecture, Delhi.

Patel, V.G. (1986). "Issues in Women Entrepreneurship Development", keynote address delivered at the Fifth National Convention of Women Entrepreneurs under Aegis of Women's Wing of NAYE, Gujarat Chapter, Ahmedabad, India, February 6-8, 1986.

Perera, Lakshmi (1995). "Women in Small-Scale Enterprise Development in Sri Lanka", in Dignard and Havet (eds.), 1995; pp. 101-116.

Shaikh, Perveen (1997); Women entrepreneurship in small and cottage industries in Pakistan (draft report), ILO Area Office, Islamabad and ILO-SAAT, New Delhi.

The World Bank (1994). Enhancing women's Participation in Economic Development, (A World Bank Policy Paper), Washington, IBRD.

Tuladhar, Jyoti (1996). Factors affecting women entrepreneurship in small and cottage industries in Nepal, ILO-SAAT, New Delhi.

UNDP (2001). Decentralization process in India – beyond 73rd and 74th amendment, an article by UNDP, New Delhi.

8
Women Entrepreneurs in Lower Middle Class Families and Their Problems

Kamalamani Rao

Introduction

The dream of becoming the owner of her own business is no more a vision in the lower middle-class women entrepreneurs in this changing society, even though this field is no bed of roses to her and that the society is still not ready to accept woman in a separate entity as an entrepreneur, which makes her life more different. This has not barred the younger and older woman to start some or the other small scale or house industry in the field of education or any field in which they are interested.

In carrying on her enterprise, the woman has not for while working in their enterprise women need to maintain cordial relationship among the family members. Time management also becomes one of the main responsibilities of a women entrepreneurs of any field along with income earning, then only she can discharge their dual role of an entrepreneur, as a wife and mother.

By working hard they have proved that they are at par with men folks and have raised their standard in the eyes of the society and wiped out the dependency syndrome, at the same time to tide over the problem of "male ego", an atmosphere of co-operativeness and humility need to be established in the home so that there are no ego-battles.

This has encouraged me to do the survey of women entrepreneurs in lower middle class families in Rajkot and problems faced by them.

Material and Method

A Survey was carried on Women Entrepreneurs in lower - middle class families by using a questionnaire in Rajkot and the sample size being 25 women entrepreneurs and grouped in three categories according to their nature of work. The questionnaire can be seen in appendix –

On the basis of data collected by way of questionnaire the three groups include number of women entrepreneurs according to their nature of work.

GROUP I	GROUP II	GROUP III
Education (Tuition and Playhouse)	*Health and Physique* (Beauty Parlour)	*Miscellaneous* Household industries, Tailoring and Embroidery, Artificial and Fancy Jewellery making
7	6	12

Results and Discussion

The data obtained is presented in Table 1 and Graph I and II.

Table – 1
Findings of the Survey of 25 Women Entrepreneurs in Lower Middle Families and their Problems

General Information	Group I	Group II	Group III
	Education	Health and Physique	Miscellaneous Industries
	Tuition, Playhouse	Beauty Parlour	Household Inds. Tailoring and embroidery, Artificial fancy Jewellery
Women Entrepreneurs in %	28	24	48
(C) Background			
Age (years)	32-40	31-44	18-40
Education	Graduate	Graduate	Undergraduate
Family size	2-6	3-4	5-6

Contd...

Table Contd...

(D) Period of Business (years)			
(E) Reasons for Starting the Business			
(B) Big Family Size	As a Hobby Some as to meet family needs	For Livelihood As a hobby and for mental peace To avoid loneliness	Due to single male earner Disability of male earner
(C) Death of Husband			
(D) Disability of Income earner			
(E) Others			
(F) Marketing and sales			
(C) Income – Rs./month	2000-2900	1300-3000	900-2250
Local	Nearby Children, of friends and working women	Customers from nearby area, friends	To shops, friends, Relatives and nearby people
Outside			
	Education	Health and Physique	Miscellaneous Industries
	Tuition, Playhouse	Beauty Parlour	Household Inds. Tailoring and embroidery, Artificial fancy Jewellery

Graph 1 Percentage Women Entrepreneurs having Different Enterprises

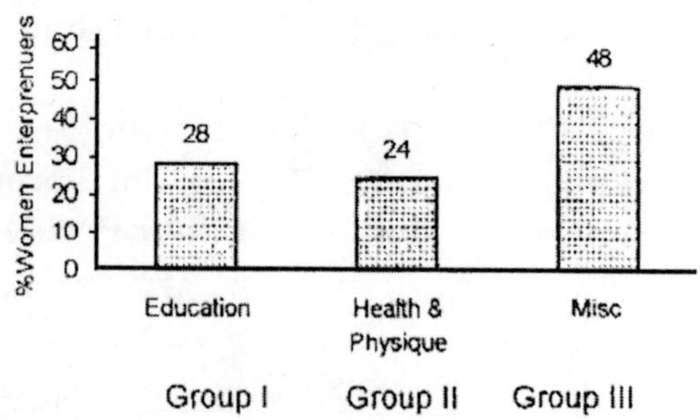

General Information	Group I	Group II	Group III
E Problems faced during the work			
1. Arrangement of finance	Self finance, Relatives, friends, advance payment	Self finance	Self finance Part Advance Payment

Contd...

Table Contd...

2. Arrangement of material	From local market	From local market	From local market
3. Availability of market	Friends, Relatives and Neighbour	Nearby area, Friends and Relatives	Shops, friends and Relative, local people
4. Work Space	Sufficient with equipped facilities	Well equipped rooms	Limited space
5. Publicity	Month to Month Pamphlets	Mouth to mouth Pamphlets	Unawareness Cannot afford advertising
6. Collecting payment	Advance Cash	Advance Cash	Advance against order balance cash payment
F. Attitude and Cooperation of			
1. Husband	Full Cooperation From everybody Few husbands do not cooperate	Full Cooperation From everybody Few are teased by in-laws and relatives	Full Cooperation from everybody
2. Family members Relatives and Neighbours			
G. Contribution to society/ family by you			
1. Work satisfaction	Satisfied, feel they are training children	Satisfied, get mental peace	Satisfied, want to expand business

Discussion

Regarding the socio-economic profile of these women, the data indicates that women entrepreneur who are graduates is Group–I (28%). The data therefore proved that a good educational background helps to be a successful entrepreneurs. In Group–II (48%) women entrepreneurs were undergraduate but had good skill in their work and practical experience.

Age-wise Group-I was in the age of 32-40 years, Group-II 31-44 years and Group-III between 18-40 years when they started their, enterprise. This further proves that there is no age bar to start ones own enterprise, by women entrepreneurs.

Some women entrepreneurs of Group-I started business as hobbies, while others to meet family needs whereas Group-II started to avoid loneliness, for mental peace and as a livelihood. Group-III started business to meet family needs due to large family size, disability of male earner and career to renders then disable to earn the livlihood for their families.

Group-I shows earning of Rs. 2000-2900/- month, Group-II 1300-3000/- month and Group III 900-2250/- month. Women entrepreneur of all groups had self-financed for starting their enterprise and not borrowed from friends or relatives to start and continue their enterprise.

The survey also showed that most women entrepreneurs received better cooperation from all members. Few women entrepreneurs in Group-I and II were humiliated by in-laws or did not get any help or co-operation.

Conclusion

It is clear from the survey that women entrepreneurs are efficient, hardworking, follow a disciplined routine and effectively discharge the dual role of a family responsibility and entrepreneur. They should solicit love and cooperation from family members being tactful and wisely diplomatic.

Acknowledgement

I thank all women entrepreneurs of Rajkot for their kind response and cooperation during the survey.

Reference

Sharma, D.D., Dhameja, S.K. Women and Rural Entrepreneurship in India.

9
Scope of Women Entrepreneurship through Home Science Curriculum in Traditional University

Kamble Rajkumar and Shinde Ulka

Introduction

The process of human evaluation goes parallel with the education of the human beings as is evident from the history of civilization. Home science education has become an important integral part of our education system and has tenets in the community all over the country. Home science is a dynamic profession with a richly diverse range of practice, theories, research and skills, which the qualified practitioners can adopt in so many problem solving situations. There is a great need that Home Science education should be focused on the knowledge objectives, attitude objectives and skill objectives. However, this implementation is rarely possible in the home science education under social science in traditional university. Hence, there is an emerging need to establish the training center of women entrepreneurship for the professional approach and wide identity of Home Science students.

By comparison of these 10 characters social science stream has less opportunities in economically self reliant and professional identity in wide range. Hence, these students do not get, viable and reliable exposure after graduation. Therefore, the training centre of women entrepreneurship will provide a platform to these students for the development of self confidence, self expression, motivation to run small scale business, able to earning at early age while learning and independent professional identity.

Comparison of Home Science Education between Science Oriented and Social Sciences Stream

Sr. No.		*Science oriented*	*Social science oriented*
1.	Knowledge coverage areas	More	Less
2.	Examination system	Semester	Annual
3.	Duration of degree course	Four years	Three years
4.	Research areas	As per specialization	General
5.	Extension Work	As per specialization	General
6.	Motivation for the subject	As per specialization	General
7.	Acquiring knowledge	More, each semester offers different courses	Less, students are having option to choose the other subject papers also
8.	Percentage for higher studies (i.e. PG, M.Phil., Ph.D.)	More	Less
9	Percentage of passing NET, SET qualifying examination for lecturership and research Scholarship	More	Less
10.	Professional exposure and job settlement	More	Less

Entrepreneurship Through Home Science Curriculum

In the three year degree course student covered at least one paper from five specialization areas of Home Science. Hence, they get basic knowledge or idea about each specialization. By using this knowledge students will be able to boost themselves as entrepreneur through training centre. There is wide scope of entrepreneurship training areas like traditional and novelty areas such as :

Sr.	*Traditional areas*	*Sr.*	*Novelty areas*
1.	Ideal planning and preschool management	1.	Gardening, flower preservation and bouquet center windows treatment.

Contd...

Table Contd...

2.	Dietetic counseling center start independently or consultant with other medical hospitals.	2.	Bakery Unit with emphasis on high fibre bread, biscuits etc.
3.	Traditional textile and dress designing including embroideries, paithani, narayan pethi, batik, tie-dye etc.	3.	Formulation of weaning mixes and supplementary foods and their marketing
4.	Interior decorator – Independently or collaboration with architect in home, hotels, hospital, executive offices.	4.	Cultivation of vegetable and fruits with soil fortification of minerals or constancy with farmer or cultivators.
5.	Cultivation and preservation of mushroom and its marketing	5.	Project management organizational structure, leadership development and use of advanced technology.
		6.	Communication, marketing, profit margin and linkages with agro based industries, village industry, food processing and preservation industries, textile designers, national-international organizations and NGO's dealing and co-operation techniques.

On the whole it can be concluded that, Home Science graduate students acquire basic knowledge during their course work but they are unable to implement their gained knowledge into professional and in practical utility. There is a wide scope to the Home Science student to develop as a good entrepreneur if their parent institutions provide a platform of apprenticeship through entrepreneurship training centers and modification of curriculum according to the new trends, technology and need base.

10
Entrepreneurial Motivation: A Comparative Study on Male and Female Entrepreneurs

Bishnupriya Dasgupta

Abstract

A total of 108 owners and managers of the cosmetic industry selected and divided equally on the basis of their venders from the manufacturing and service industries, matched in terms of sign (Small scale) experience (year group of establishment) and location were studied to identify and assess their motivations to entrepreneurship. Five care related entrepreneurial dimensions were identified through factor analysis, entrepreneurial care, social care, economic care, work care, and individual care. The entrepreneurial care dimension leading to entrepreneurship was the strongest dimension with no distinguishable difference between the genders in both categories. The motives to be independent and have a preferred work style and life style in the individual care were also very strongly felt needs among both male and female entrepreneurs without exception. The finding implied that the factors to entrepreneurship for males and females were same and if females were not on the entrepreneurial same as much as males (as the case in India even today) it was because the items identified within the entrepreneurial dimension and individual dimensions were not instilled in them strongly to take action.

The term motivation refers to any orgasmic state that mobilises activity that is selective or directive with respect to the environment. Entrepreneurial Motivation is described as a socio-psychological drive among the people that leads to economic development of a country. Lessons from the developed nations make it abundantly clear that entrepreneurship is a vital ingredient for economic development. So the question is "what is it that makes the people of countries more or less entrepreneurial than others"? B. Murthy et. al.[10] believe that different countries are at varying levels of economic development because the people of these nations are placed in different socio-economic settings and have different attitudes.

With a presence of virtually half the population in a society, women represent a vast potential contributor to the society's development process. There is ample support from the Government observed in its development-oriented plans and policies framed around women. Yet, even today, entrepreneurship remains the most important bastion of male dominance in most countries and women everywhere are far, far from entrepreneurial pursuits. Up until 1970, in all countries including the United States, the presence of women on the entrepreneurial scene was only 5.7%, (Bird & Bush, 2000)[11]. The closest any country has come to equalizing, is the United States of America which registered 38% women entrepreneurs in the year 2000. Today the claim is 50%. Where lies the problem? Why were women on the entrepreneurial scene so conspicuous by their absence? A study was thus taken up to identify and assess the motivations felt by males and females that led to entrepreneurship.

Unlike most studies in which motivation and personality traits have been used interchangeably, in this study some distinction has justifiably been made between the two. "Entrepreneurial motivation" has been treated as a separate entity, distinct from "personality characteristics". Motivation is the willingness to exert high levels of effort towards achieving organizational goals to satisfy individual needs, it is a person's response to an internal or external stimuli and results. From an unfulfilled need (V.Vijaya & T.J. Kamalanabhan). Personality traits are predispositions to behave in certain ways, they cannot be summed up as consequences arising from a "need". They are genetically determined and are shaped by environmental influences, they get crystallized over time and last a life time. "Motivational stage" is a temporary phase as its strength usually decreases as the need is fulfilled or object is attained.

"Personality traits" are well-established patterns of behaviour, more or less permanent, unless affected by strong environmental variables. People with same personality traits can have different motivations and people with same motivations have different personalities. Peter Drucker,[12] – the noted author, consultant and management guru found that the much discussed "Entrepreneurial Personality" was present only in a handful of entrepreneurs in the last 30 years of his career, yet he knew many other people like surgeons, journalists, scholars, sales people, even musicians did have them without being the least bit entrepreneurial, (Havard Business Review, 1985).

She Birely and David Muzyka (1997)[13] in an attempt to find out what sort of people entrepreneurs were like reassuringly found that there was no such things as 'identikit' entrepreneur. Those who took the entrepreneurial path were 'marvellously heterogeneous'.

Methodology

Having established the presence of few women entrepreneurs in the cosmetic manufacturing industry through a survey, and keeping in view the comparative nature of the study, the respondents, Male and Female owner managers were purposely selected and matched in terms of size; (small scale) experience, (year group of establishment) and locality. The sample size was restricted to the number of available Female Manufacturers (27) a total of 108 respondents comprised the sample. The scale developed by V. Vijaya and T.J. Kamalanabhan (1998, IIT Madras) to assess entrepreneurial motivation was applied after having established its reliability and validity. The scale helped in establishing and understanding patterns of entrepreneurial motivation among the genders, identifying the differences in motivational strengths between men and women entrepreneurs and also variances between the different classes of entrepreneurial ventures namely manufacturing and ______ The strength of the motives was ______ by using the Liker type five point rating scale.

I. Entrepreneurial Core						
2. Get complete job satisfaction	3.63	3.41	3.33	3.85	1.261	0.292
3. Be a leader	2.93	2.33	2.96	3.52	3.299	0.023**
5. Utilize my keen business sense	3.44	2.81	2.96	3.74*	3.934	0.011
6. Be an employer never an employee	3.00	3.81	3.33	3.70	2.037	0.113
7. Get best monetary return for my talent	3.70	3.93	3.37	3.78	1.379	0.253
8. Exploit my innate talent and potential	3.78	3.52	3.52	4.00	1.455	0.231
11. Do some thing creative	3.70	2.63*	3.81	3.67	8.762	0.000
12. Show that I am inferior to more.	3.07	2.67	2.89	2.78	0.568	0.637
Something that others usually do not	3.86	3.22	3.93	3.78	2.393	0.073
26. Utilize my decision making problem solving skills	3.52	3.59	3.30	3.33	0.558	0.644
Total	**37.81**	**35.18**	**36.84**	**39.71**	**1.597**	**0.195**
II. Social Core						
9. Attain high social status	3.11	2.85	2.33	2.78	1.741	0.163
10. Acquire lots of wealth for self	2.52	3.07	1.81*	2.56	5.467	0.002
21. Earn the respect of people	3.56	4.41*	3.04	3.00	6.859	0.000
22. Enjoy the best luxuries of life	3.19	2.96	2.56	3.07	1.833	0.146
27. Compete with others and prove to be the best	2.74	3.52	3.22	3.07	1.480	0.224
Total	**15.12**	**16.81**	**12.96**	**14.48***	**3.600**	**0.016**
III. Economic Core						
1. Get over shortage of money	2.52	4.22*	2.15	2.89*	13.700	0.000
4. Make my family rich	3.11	3.52	2.78	3.37	2.081	0.107
13. Supplement the family income	3.15	3.96*	2.93	3.19	3.783	0.013
16. Ensure financial stability of children	3.19	4.22*	3.15	3.45	3.810	0.012
Total	**11.97**	**15.92**	**11.01**	**12.90**	**9.098**	**0.000**
IV. Work Core						
18. Provide good service or product to community	3.70	3.33	4.00*	3.07	5.091	0.003
19. Make money to clear debts.	2.70	2.15	2.00	2.07	1.561	0.203
23. Get over monotony experience change	2.85	2.52	3.30*	2.04	5.726	0.001

Contd ...

Table Contd ...

24. Help people by providing employment	2.74	1.85	3.41*	2.93	9.656	0.000
Total	**11.99**	**9.85**	**10.71**	**10.11**	**5.373**	**0.002**
IV. Individual Core						
17. Be Independent	3.33	4.11	4.11	3.96	2.118	0.102
20. Have my own preferred work style and life style	3.81	3.48	3.74	3.52	0.464	0.708
25. Utilize concessions or loans from Govt.	1.63*	1.04	1.70	1.44	2.856	0.041
Total	**8.77**	**8.63**	**9.55**	**8.92**	**0.897**	**0.446**

Findings

Five core motivations were identified with the help of factor analysis by the principal components method. Five core factors that emerged out of the analysis were Entrepreneurial core, Social core, Economic core, Work core and Individual core.

Entrepreneurial core dimension was found to be strongest motivational force for all the respondents irrespective of their gender or category of industry to which they belonged. The motivation to take up entrepreneurship as a profession came from this factor. The felt needs in this dimension were to exploit their innate talent and potential, to achieve what others could not, to fulfill a creative ability, innovate and bring about change. They wanted to be leaders, decision makers and employ people rather than be employed. The strong urge to take risks and do business. Most importantly to get complete job satisfaction. The indication was that their needs and wants were not getting fulfilled, they were dissatisfied with whatever they were doing which finally lead to the entrepreneurial path.

The strength of the Individual core was also equal among all the respondents irrespective of gender or industry to which they belonged. The need to be independent was the strongest felt motive among all the identified motives, the freedom to work and live the way one wanted to came from this factor. Surprisingly neither the males nor the females [who were especially given so many incentives] had the urge to utilize concessions or loans from government, an indication that these incentives really did not help in motivating people to take the entrepreneurial path.

The Social core and the Economic core dimensions were found to be stronger among the males in both the categories, but significantly so for males in the service industry only. To gain social recognition, earn respect of people through acquisition of wealth. To get over shortage of money, become rich, financially secure and stable, came through in these dimensions. The need for acquiring wealth was particularly low among females. The Work core motive was stronger in females, more significant in case of the female manufacturers whose intense desire to get over the monotony of their existence and be useful to society by providing employment to people, good service and product to community made them take up entrepreneurship.

None of the entrepreneurs in any of the groups took up entrepreneurship with the desire to utilize government loans offered as an incentive; even women to whom they were specially offered.

Conclusion

The strength of the Entrepreneurial Core factor responsible for taking up entrepreneurship as a profession was equal for both male and female entrepreneurs in both the industries and there was no significant difference in this core dimension, therefore, it could be convincingly concluded that needs felt by the males and the females leading to entrepreneurship were similar in the case of both the genders and they took the entrepreneurial path because of the same reasons. The individual motivations in the entrepreneurial core dimension were the causative factors to entrepreneurship for all persons irrespective of the gender to which they belonged. And if women were not on the entrepreneurial scene it was because fewer of them as compared to the males felt the motives identified under the entrepreneurial core dimension. If things have to be changed then these identified needs have to be instilled in women from the beginning in their formative years of growing up as they were done in the case of males.

The Individual core factor was also found to be equal among both the sexes with the need for independence emerging as the strongest motivating factor for all, this preference for individual work style and life style which got fulfilled through having ones own enterprise was thus responsible for individuals taking up the entrepreneurial path. Those who did take up the challenge of entrepreneurship felt these urges deeply. It was because fewer women had the desire to be independent and have ones own preferred work style and life style they were not on the entrepreneurial scene convincingly. Women were in the past, and are even today expected to be dependent on the male members of the house [fathers, brothers, husbands and sons] for everything. The aim of most parents for the daughters was and even today is to get them married and settled, and for the sons to take up responsibilities independently. The outcome is obvious, women in general do not feel the need to be independent and most do not have the desire to change the type of work they are doing and the life they are leading, so they are not visible on the entrepreneurial front.

The Social core and the Economic core dimensions were stronger among the males, implying that they became entrepreneurs because they felt the need to get social recognition and create wealth. The *Work core* dimension was stronger among females indicating that it was the change in the work front that they were seeking which led them to entrepreneurship. Government policies and subsidies did not motivate individuals to take up entrepreneurship, and few if at all took the loans and concessions offered.

Implication

At a time when Tony Blair is talking about kidpreneurship, it is important for the parents, educators and trainers to realize the importance of instilling the individual motivations identified in the entrepreneurial core dimensions among the populace right from school, i.e., in the teenage itself, specially for the girl child. The motivations are then needed to be tended and kept alive through various programs and public channels till such time when action results and the entrepreneurial plunge is taken. It was time to realize that government subsidies were in motivations at all for women to take up entrepreneurship, the entrepreneurial need had to be felt strongly for women to take the entrepreneurial path.

Bibliography

- Anna, V., Pillai, N.C. "Women Entrepreneurs in Kerala" Social Change, June, 1990. Vol. 20, No. 2, pp. 61-69.
- Agarwal, R.C. Women power - The Neglected Factor in Development in Kalbagh C. (ed.) Women and Development, 1992, p. 48.

11
Training Women to Start Day Care Centres in Baroda City

Darshnini Durkal,
Rameshwari Pandya

Introduction

Traditionally, our history and also as depicted in our mythology, women have been the moral force of the society. They have held prime positions in the families and have developed the culture and soul of our Indian civilization.

In recent years, the percentage of women beneficiaries in development programmes is increasing. Thus, in self-employing women, the need to train them is also increasing.

Women can be successful entrepreneurs and self employed, as women get a higher economic status through self employment. This is the basic requirement for raising their status, otherwise women in labour force, inspite of their contribution to the family income are undervalued. Only women themselves can change this situation. Self employment will give them money, power and status, both in the family and in the society. For those women, who would like to remain at home and earn, having self employment opportunities in the home premises will serve the purpose. This self employment promotes the idea of flexible working hours, helping them to work in hours suitable to them and giving them a chance to do something other than household work, which can make the lives of many women pleasant and satisfying.

Since the past three or four decades, employment of women is becoming an important issue at national level in India. This trend has made it more essential for women with potential to develop certain skills, get the right kind of training to join the work-force with full confidence and faith. So only with the help of training, women's earning power can be increased. Training programmes provide training in selected vocations to women with skills which would enable them to earn through self employment.

Women from time immemorial have been participating in economic activities. Traditionally women worked at home or in the farms, with the children being cared for by other family members or themselves as a concurrent activity. But with increasing emphasis on women's education, changing social norms, increase in cost of living, women were forced to work out of homes. Employment thus changed the pattern of women's employment at least in some sectors.

This change as well as changes in the structure and the functioning of the Indian family has influenced the allocation enactment of child rearing responsibilities. One would presume that the process is linked to extension and modification of the women's house-wife-mother role. Such change calls for concurrent alternations in the distribution of responsibilities both in the household as well as at community and societal levels. Wherein others pitch in to share some primary responsibilities of women, thus offering some support.

Child Care Training: Why do we Need?

Children services today are considered to be vital not only for children's wellbeing, women's development empowerment but also to release families from the vicious cycle of poverty and underdevelopment. Childcare services are therefore a necessary input to ensure healthy overall development of children, release girls and older siblings for education and an avenue for training and employment for women. Although in the last two decades there has been a rapid expansion and extension of childcare facilities but their reach as well as quality continues to suffer.

Women have a dual value system, one pertaining to home and other to job. This value system creates many problems specially for educated housewives who have multifarious responsibilities thrust upon them. The tension is experienced when these mothers have to leave the children at home in the care of untrained and unreliable maid servants or relatives. Absence of appropriate arrangements for looking after of children in absence of working mother is another source of role conflict and tension, though the phenomenon of relying on support from various sources is not a new one.

When we think of a working woman with young children, two pictures emerge : (a) one of a harassed woman who always has to rush to manage several roles and is not able to pay enough attention to any of her duties, (b) the other who has support from the kin and non-kin members and therefore is able to delegate to and share her responsibilities with others. This to an extent enables her to perform her roles more efficiently.

Both these are realistic pictures and we are aware that they are accurate in varying degrees. However, the questions that would automatically arise are : (a) what kind of dispositions do the modern middle class working women have? (b) What supports are available to them? (c) What is the influence of these social ties on the performance of their parental roles?

The vast majority of child care in this country is unlicensed, unregulated, "underground". Child care workers are among the lowest paid workers in our society. Many prefer to be paid in cash to avoid paying even a small amount to the government in taxes. In such cases, parents may not be able to substantiate child care costs to claim tax credits.

In a broad sense the term "day care" means simply that some person other than members of a child's family takes care of a child during part or a good part of a child's day. The care can be administered in the home or out of the home in some other setting. Day care has been used traditionally by working mothers from poor families, but it has also been used by working mothers and non-working mothers from other than poor families.

In the field of child welfare, the concept of day care implies services for a child during the day that a parent cannot perform because of economic, health or social conditions affecting the home. Day care in the field of child welfare is distinguished from nursery schools or other socio-educational activities for young children by its emphasis on the need of the parent to seek help in caring for the child.

The idea of programmes that aid a mother in handing over her job of mothering to a day care facility has been highly controversial, because it has been traditionally thought that the primary responsibility of women with young children is that of giving suitable care to their children in their own homes. However, although the Aid to Families with Dependent Children programme would enable many of them to reject outside employment and stay in their home, the right to work must also be recognized for those who do not wish to be dependent upon society or to live at a subsistence level.

The care of a child in a family other than his own serves many needs which cannot be met by other types of care. Care in a foster home is also particularly useful for the child from two to six years of age if his family lives far away from nursery schools of day care centres, then a good foster home near the child's own home eliminates long trips to such schools or centres. In addition, certain small children who, because of emotional, physical or mental disabilities, are unable to adjust happily to group care find the individual care and homelike atmosphere of a good foster family day care most beneficial.

In the other type of individual care, supervised homemaker service, the child receives care in his own home, so that he remains in known surroundings and has a sense of security not always afforded by other forms of day care. A carefully selected homemaker, actually a visiting foster mother, is placed in the home to care for the children when the mother is temporarily incapacitated or absent from the home, or when the child of a working mother is temporarily ill, or when the child or children of a working mother do not fit into a group care programme.

The main considerations are not under which auspices day care services should be operated and from what source funds should be obtained, rather it is important for each community to determine what child care services are needed to supplement what the home and school together can make available.

Importance and Need of Child Care Services

During the decade from 1981-91 the total number of female workers in India reached the figure of 9.1 crores, showing an annual growth rate of 2.39% (Census 1991). In the present changing social scenario, with nuclearisation of families and more and more women joining the workforce outside homes, the need for child care services to take up the role of providing quality care of the children while parents have gone for work, is increasing day by day. The expansion of the cities into far off suburbs has created vast distance between home and work place. Young couples are compelled to make their homes in suburbs and with no kin network, they are dependent on services from the community. One of the grave problems that these young couples face, be it educated working women, women in unorganized sector or self employed women, is the care of their children.

It is a fact that education and training play an important role in delivering quality child care services. But ironically, the low status of child care as a profession does not attract highly educated women. Besides, training facilities hardly exist, creating barriers for developing professionals in the field of child care. Therefore, trained professionals is a must for child care services. The need and importance of child care services is not only present in India, but throughout the world, the feeling of independence that children seek during the early childhood years is often shared by parents. A mother who gave up her job when the baby was born may decide to return to work when she feels the child is able to adjust to the care and attention of someone else. Sometimes, parents realize that their money situation calls for both of them to work. Many single-parent families may never have had a choice about who would care for their children while they worked.

Such situations are so common that day-care centres and pre-schools have taken on new responsibilities to children. To meet these new responsibilities, people are specially trained in child care and in early childhood education The centres and pre-schools try to meet the needs a child may have.

There are various types of day-care and these go under different names. They are nursery school, pre-basic school, Balwadi, Balmandir, Creche, Kindergarten, extended school programmes, etc. The purpose of all these programmes is to provide day care to the children of the working mothers but in India the emphasis has been on the educational aspect, rather than on the care aspect. With more and more employment opportunities for women in this country, there is a need to have more day care centres. Therefore, hereafter the emphasis should be on day care rather than on education although there has to be some element of informal education in a day care centre. The purposes of day care centres are different from those of preschools. Young children are sent to day care centre because there is no one to take care of them at home.

Day Care Centres help the young child's development in the following ways :

- *Good Health* : By balancing activity and rest and making sure that all children have medical checkups and are immunized against certain diseases.
- *Skills* : By improving skills already learned and teaching new ones under the teacher's guidance and supervision.
- *Speech* : By making children's vocabularies larger and widening their interests.
- *Emotions* : By teaching children to express their emotions in socially approved ways.
- *Social behaviour* : By teaching socially approved behaviour patterns.
- *Social Attitudes* : By teaching children to be tolerant of those who are different to add to the group, and to be good sports, good followers, and good leaders.
- *Creativity* : By encouraging children to express their creativity in ways that will please them.
- *Discipline* : By teaching children, through consistent and

fair disciplines, to obey rules and respect those in authority.

- *Self Concept* : By stressing self-confidence, and feelings of self-worth.
- *Easier adjustment to school* : By teaching skills that are basic to school work.

In day care centres, taking care of the children's physical needs is a major concern. Often young children receive most of their toilet training in the day care centre. They also learn many of their self-help skills, such as self-dressing and self-feeding.

Day-care centres can be thought of as second homes for children. The caretakers can be thought of as substitute parents. Children go to the centres from early morning until early evening five days a week. They are usually taken there each morning as parents are on their way to work. Parents must trust the caretakers at the centre with the child. The child's basic physical and psychological needs are taken care of by people other than parents.

Physically, children thrive in well-run day care centres. Many children eat two or three meals there. They are given the right food for their age and level of development. Since the children are there all day, they eat, rest, and play according to a schedule that meets their needs. Centres are usually well equipped for indoor and outdoor play. Medical attention is on hand in case a child has an accident or is ill.

Socially, children learn to deal with people outside the family, especially other children. They have a chance to share toys, play games, and take part in activities. They learn how to cooperate with each other. When caretakers are specially trained in early childhood education, they guide and encourage children in their learning experiences. This helps develop the child's intellectual abilities.

Choosing a Day-Care Centre

Ideally, children's basic needs are met in well-managed day care centres. Unfortunately, not all centres are well managed. It is a good idea for parents to look into centres before choosing one for their child. They will need to use both their own judgement and the advice of other more experienced people before making a decision. When parents decide that they want to send their child to a day care centre, they may get useful advice from other parents, teachers, clergy, or social service agencies. These sources may know more about the child care centres in the area and can give parents needed facts.

It may also be helpful for parents to visit the different day care centers. In some cases, it may be helpful to send the child to the centre for a few weeks as a trial period. This gives the child time to adjust to the new environment. It also gives the parents time to make changes if they are needed.

What parents should think about when choosing Day-Care Centres

- Is the centre licensed and regularly checked by the government authorities?
- What is the cost of each child?
- How old is the child? Are there other children the same age for companionship?
- Is the centre near enough to the parents' place of work so it could be quickly reached in an emergency?
- Is it well equipped for activities?
- Do they act as though their task is just to baby-sit, or do they encourage the physical and psychological development of the children?
- Are there enough teachers and aides to give each child individual attention?
- Is there careful supervision of all children at all times?
- Is the food well prepared, of good quality, and suited to the age of the children?
- Is the environment relaxed and happy? Or do the children seem bored and irritable?

Justification of the Project

Department of Home Science Extension and Communication has conducted several researches, action projects and community development programmes for helping women in income generation in order to uplift the status of women. This project will also contribute in this effort of changing women's status through training for self employment.

While conducting survey, project worker found that there were many day care centres in Baroda city, but their staff members were not trained, and many of them wanted to start their own day care centres.

Urban Basic Service and Urban Corporation Development (UBS/UCD) workers of Baroda Municipal Corporation also had approached the project worker for training women for child care centres. The serious need for training and efforts to organize it at various levels had become imperative.

1. *Need for Income Generating Activities*

Income generating activities not only help in motivating, but also in sustaining their interest in continuing with the women's empowerment programme. This is one way by which women can contribute to the family income. These activities enable women to earn and add to the income of the family. These activities thereby :

- Improve women's social status.
- Make them economically independent.
- Can make them fight against the ill-treatment rendered towards them by the family and society.
- Will be able to utilize their leisure time more productively and avoid boredom.

2. *Need for Self Development*

A fruitful and purposeful utilization of leisure time is necessary for making life happier and fuller. There is the need to initiate the work of organizing people for self development through better utilization of their time. The society and family still does not expect women to be socially active in the community affairs or civic problems and prefer that women should remain confined to their homes.

Such training will enable women to work collectively in groups and make them socially active. It will bring them out from the confines of their homes and make them financially independent, giving them immense self confidence and also earn the respect of their husband's and in-laws when they pool in additional income into the family income.

3. *Recommendations of symposia on 'Role of Banks in Empowering Women' (Sponsored by NABARD - Ahmedabad)*

Symposium on 'Role of Banks in Empowering Women' was organized by Centre for Continuing Adult Education and Community Services, the M.S. University of Baroda, Vadodara on 4th and 5th January, 2002, it being the year of women empowerment.

This project has been designed considering the above justification of promoting women and providing opportunities for vocational development. The main purpose of this project was not only to give training for starting day care centres but also to help women in establishing their own day care centres.

It was observed that majority of women faced economic problems, therefore the project titled, "An Action Project for Training Women to Start Day Care Centres in Baroda city in the year 2002-2003" was conducted.

Major Objective of the Project

To help women in starting Day Care Centres.

Specific Objectives of the Project

1. To organize training programmes for starting day care centres.
2. To help women in developing project proposal for starting day care centres.
3. To help women in availing loans from banks for starting day care centres.
4. To collect reactions of the women regarding the training programme.

Methodology

The project was carefully planned so that it was completed in time and achieve the set objectives. The steps which were followed during the project are discussed under the following sections :

1. *Feasibility Study*

The project worker surveyed ten day care centres of Baroda city. The purpose of the feasibility study was to find out the functioning of day care centres, to understand the initial problems that one may face while starting a day care centre.

The project worker observed as well as interviewed people who were running the day care centres.

Major Findings of the Feasibility Survey

1. Majority of the day care centres had female owner (90%), only one day care centre was owned by a male.
2. Most of the owners of the day care centres were graduates.
3. Main purpose behind setting up of the day care centres was to become economically independent and provide services to the working parents.
4. Most of the person's incharge of day care centres did not have any special training for starting day care centres. But they were interested in providing training to their staff members.
5. Most of the day care centres used their own funds for starting their business.

2. *Selection of the Content*

As most of the owners of day care centres of Baroda city did not have any special training for starting day care centres, it was decided to plan a training programme, in such a way that women could gain knowledge on how to start their own day care centre and run it effectively.

The content of the training programme was decided by referring to different books, consulting experts and visiting various day care centres.

3. *Contacting Resource Persons*

The project worker contacted resource persons from different areas for conducting the training programme. The project worker invited the resource persons for their expert advice, suggestions and valuable tips.

Experts were invited from the different departments for conducting the following sessions :

Topics	*Name of the Department*
• Activities for children. • Day care center and needs of children • Guiding young children and role of day care worker • Transition from home to preschool. • Develop skills for working with children. • How to evaluate day care centers.	Department of Human Development and Family Studies
Nutritions food safety for children	Department of Foods and Nutrition
Health for children	Doctor, Health Centre, MSU
Advertisements for day care centers	Department of Home Science Extension & Communication
Anganwadi Programme	Project Officer from ICDS
Role of Banks in starting day care centers	Planning Manager, BOB
Role of District Industrial Centre in getting loans from banks	Planning Manager, DIC
Management of day care centers	Credit Manager, DIC
Experience shared by people running day care centers	Owners of the Day Care Centres

4. *Preparation of Teaching Aids*

The project worker visited different libraries for referring books on day care centres, for preparation of the teaching aids. To make any training programme successful, use of variety of teaching aids is very important. Teaching aids helps the learners to understand the concept easily.

The project worker prepared different types of teaching aids for the training programme, like :

Teaching Aids	*Topics*
Poster Charts	• For publicity of training programme • Planning for day care • Ideal points for a day care center
Flip Charts	• Things to be remembered while developing child's food habits. • Bank schemes.
Flash Cards	• Points that should be kept in mind while playing • Qualities of day care worker. • Techniques of reaching out to parents.
Handouts	• Children's songs • Bank schemes • DIC schemes

5. *Preparation of Booklet*

The booklet on day care centres was prepared with the following purposes :

1. To act as a manual for starting day care centre.
2. To act as reference material for future.

Different books were referred to make a complete and sound booklet. The booklet was prepared in Gujarati. The following topics were covered in the booklet :

1. Planning for day care centre – long term and short term goals.
2. Setting up and running the day care centre – Place, Materials, Workers, Registers.
3. Reaching out to the parents – Parent's meeting, Newsletters, Celebrations.
4. Role of day care worker.
5. Preparation of indigenous materials for children.
6. Nutrition for the children.

7. Children songs.

6. *Selection of Target Group*

The project worker wanted maximum number of women of Baroda city to take advantage of this training programme. For this purpose, she approached various institutions like - Vikas Jyot Trust, UBS/UCD Beneficiaries from Baroda Municipal Corporation, Integrated Child Development Schemes Worker (Anganwadi worker).

The purpose behind visiting these institutions was to collect the names of women who were interested in getting training for starting their own day care centre.

The project worker also approached friends and relatives and informed them regarding the day care centre training programme, so that these friends and relatives could further encourage other friends and relatives of theirs to take part in this training programme. In this way, the project worker did word of mouth publicity for the training programme.

7. *Publicity through the Newspaper*

The project worker gave press notes in local newspapers so that people could read it and take part in the day care centre training programme. The project worker gave press notes in the 'Gujarat Samachar', 'Indian Express' and 'Sandesh' dailies.

8. *Implementing the Training Programme*

The project worker implemented the programme as per the plan for the training programme. The project worker collected the background information of all the participants.

9. *Schedule of the Training Programme*

The training programme was divided into fifteen sessions as the training programme was for fifteen days. The training programme on day care centre was planned from 9th December, 2002 to 24th December 2002 from 12 to 2 p.m.

Different experts were invited to conduct the training programme.

10. Place for Conducting the Training Programme

The project worker selected 'Pragati Centre' of the Department of Home Science Extension and Communication, Faculty of Home Science, M.S. University, Baroda, for conducting the training programme on Day Care Centre. This centre was selected as it had all the facilities of space and physical arrangements like electricity, water and facilities of audio-visual aids.

11. Certificate and Booklet Distribution to the Participants

The project worker organized a function for the distribution of certificates at the 'Pragati Centre' of the Department of Home Science Extension and Communication, on 24th December, 2002.

The criteria for getting the certificate and the booklet was announced in advance in the class to the participants, i.e., hundred percent attendance in the training programme.

12. Availing Loans from Banks for Starting Day Care Centres

- ***Development of Project Proposal***

The project worker guided the women individually on the preparation of the project proposal for availing of loans. The project worker helped the women in collecting documents like quotations with registration numbers on it. The project worker also helped the women in calculating expenses for running the day care centre, for example : the expenses required for toys and furniture for the day care centre. The project worker helped the women to visualize the profitability of the enterprise.

- ***Forms for Availing Loans***

The forms for loan application were collected from the District Industrial Centre, Narmada Bhavan, and Baroda. The project worker guided women in collecting the required documents like light bills, school leaving certificates, quotation of toys and furniture and project proposal. The project worker also helped the women in filling up the forms and also checked the complete application forms.

Evaluation of the Project

Evaluation is an essential step in the extension process. It is through the process of evaluation that one arrives at judgements and conclusions that will aid in decision making. It also helps in finding out the shortcomings of the programme, which in turn can be though of for the next programme planning. This section presents the evaluation of the project in the following :

1. Reactions collected through structured tool

A reaction scale was developed in Gujarati as well as in English to collect the reactions of the participants, regarding day care centre training programme. The reaction scale consisted of :

1. Background information
2. Reactions of women regarding the training programme

1. Background information

Table 1 indicates that nearly twenty-nine (28.6%) of the respondents belonged to the age group of 16 to 31 years. The table further shows that 25 percent of respondents were between the age group of 32 to 39 years, whereas few of them (12.5%) belonged to the age group of 48 to 55 years and about, five percent (5.3%) of the respondents belonged to the age group of 40 to 47 years.

Table 1
Percentage Distribution of Respondents According to the Age

N = 56

Sr. No.	*Age in years*	*%*
1.	16 – 23	28.6
2.	24 – 31	28.6
3.	32 – 39	25.0
4.	40 – 47	5.3
5.	48 – 55	12.5

Table 2
Percentage Distribution of Respondents According to their Educational Level

N = 56

Sr. No.	*Educational Level*	*%*
1.	Illiterate	1.8
2.	Upto Primary	3.6
3.	Upto Secondary	17.8
4.	Upto Higher Secondary	14.3
5.	Upto Graduation	62.5

Table 2 indicates that majority (62.5%) of the respondents were educated upto graduation level. Around eighteen percent (17.8%) were educated till secondary level and fourteen percent were educated upto higher secondary level.

Table 3
Percentage Distribution of Respondents According to Work Experience with Children

N = 56

Sr. No.	*Work Experience*	*%*
1.	Having work experience	39.3
2.	Not having work experience	60.7

Table 3 indicates that majority (60.7%) of the respondents had no work experience with children, but were interested in developing the ability to work with children, whereas, thirtynine percent of the respondents had work experience with children.

Table 4
Percentage Distribution of Respondents According to their Marital Status

N = 56

Sr. No.	*Marital Status*	*%*
1.	Unmarried	51.7
2.	Married	48.3

Table 4 indicates that little more than half (51.7%) of the respondents were unmarried girls and fortyeight percent of them were married women.

Table 5
Percentage Distribution of Respondents According to Reasons for Attending the Training Programme

N = 56

Sr. No.	*Reasons for attending the training programme*	*%*
1.	To become economically independent	48.2
2.	Interested in working with children	41.1
3.	To utilize free time	10.7

Table 5 indicates that majority (48.2%) of the respondents reported the reason for attending the training programme was to become economically independent by starting their own day-care centre. Interest in working with children was the reason reported by nearly fortytwo percent of the respondents. Only few of them (10.7%) reported the reason for attending the training programme to utilize their free time.

Table 6
Percentage Distribution of Respondents According to the Information about the Training Programme

N = 56

Sr. No.	*Information about training programme*	*%*
1.	Through Newspaper	48.2
2.	Through neighbours, relatives or friends	21.4
3.	Through VNM News	16.1
4.	Through NGOs and Gos	14.3

Table 6 indicates that majority (48.2%) of the respondents got information about the training programme through the newspaper. Twenty one percent of the respondents got the information about the training programme through neighbours, relatives and informed personally by the project worker. However, few of them (14.3%) got the information through non-government organizations or government organizations. About sixteen percent (16.1%) of the respondents got the information about the training programme through local television telecast on VNM News.

Table 7

Percentage Distribution of Respondents According to Opinion about Satisfaction about the Training Programme

N = 56

Sr. No.	*Satisfied with training programme*	*%*
1.	Satisfied	100
2.	Not satisfied	0

Table 7 indicates that all the participants (100%) reported that they were fully satisfied with the training programme.

Table 8

Percentage Distribution of Respondents According to Reasons for Liking Training Programme

N = 56

Sr. No.	*Reasons for liking the training programme*	*%*
1.	Information was useful	60.7
2.	Each class was properly guided	23.2
3.	Talks were interesting	16.1

Table 8 indicates that majority (60.7%) of the respondents reported that the reason for liking the training programme was that the information was useful to start their own day care centre. About one-fourth (23.2%) of the respondents reported that each class was properly guided. Only few of them (16.7%) reported that the talks were interesting.

Table 9

Percentage Distribution of Respondents According to the Information about the Training Programme

N = 56

Sr. No.	*Arrangements of training programme*	*Yes*	*No*
1.	Place of training programme	100	0
2.	Seating arrangements	100	0
3.	Time	85.7	14.3
4.	Duration of training programme	67.9	32.1

Table 9 indicates that all the respondents (100%) reported that they were satisfied with the physical arrangements for the training programme, which included the suitability of the place and the seating arrangements.

The table further shows that more than eighty percent (85.7%) of them were satisfied with the time of the training programme. Some of the respondents (14.3%) were not satisfied with the timings of the training programme, because they were working women. Nearly sixty-eight percent (67.9%) of the respondents reported that they were satisfied with the duration of the training programme. However, more than thirty percent (32.1%) of the respondents were not satisfied with the duration of the training programme and wanted it to be for a longer period.

Table 10
Percentage Distribution of Respondents According to their Opinion towards the Language Used by the Experts in the Training Programme

N = 56

Sr. No.	*Language used by experts*	*%*
1.	Could understand the language	100
2.	Did not understand the language	0

Table 10 indicates that all the respondents (100%) reported that they were able to understand the language used by the experts. All the participants were knowing Gujarati and Hindi. The language for training programme was mainly Gujarati and Hindi.

Table 11
Percentage Distribution of Respondents According to Opinion towards Teaching Material Used in Training Programme

N = 56

Sr. No.	*Understanding about teaching material*	*%*
1.	Could understand the teaching material	100
2.	Did not understand the teaching material	0

Table 11 indicates that all the respondents (100%) reported that they were able to understand clearly the teaching materials used by the instructors. All the teaching materials were prepared in Gujarati and had many colourful illustrations. It helped the participants in planning activities for children and in preparing kits for children.

Table 12

Percentage Distribution of Respondents According to their Opinion Regarding Time Allotted to Each Session

N = 56

Sr. No.	*Understanding about teaching material*	*%*
1.	Satisfied with the time allotted	75.0
2.	Not satisfied with the time allotted	25.0

Table 12 indicates that majority (75%) of the respondents were satisfied with the time allotted to each session. However, it was found that nearly one-fourth (25%) of the respondents were not satisfied with the time allotted, as they wanted more time for each session.

Table 13

Percentage Distribution of Respondents According to their Opinion towards Usefulness to Training Programme

N = 56

Sr. No.	*Usefulness of training programme*	*%*
1.	Developed good confidence for starting day care centre	71.4
2.	Was a complete guide for starting day care centre	28.6

Table 13 indicates that majority (73.4%) of the respondents reported that the experience of the training programme developed in them good confidence for starting their own day care centre, whereas, more than twenty-five percent (28.6%) of the respondents reported that the experience of the training programme was a complete guide for starting a day care centre.

Table 14
Percentage Distribution of Respondents According to their Opinion about Starting their Own Day care Centre

N = 56

Sr. No.	*Understanding about teaching material*	*%*
1.	Able to start their own day care centre	85.7
2.	Unable to start their own day care centre	14.3

Table 14 indicates that majority (85.7%) of the respondents reported that due to this training programme they would be able to open their own day care centre. However, it was found that few of them (14.3%) reported that they would not be able to open their own day care centre due to family problems.

Table 15
Percentage Distribution of Respondents According to their Opinion to Others about this Type of Training Programme

N = 56

Sr. No.	*Positive advice to others regarding this training programme*	*%*
1.	Gave positive advice	100
2.	Did not give positive advice	0

Table 15 indicates that all the participants (100%) reported that they would give advice to others to join this type of training programme in future.

Table 16
Percentage Distribution of Respondents According to their Liking of Sessions in the Training Programme

N = 56

Sr. No.	*Most liked session*	*%*
1.	Activities of children	58.9
2.	Guiding young children and role of day care worker	14.3
3.	Visit to day care centres	15.0

Contd ...

Table Contd ...

4.	DIC role in getting loan from bank	5.0
5.	Bank role in starting day care	3.3
6.	Nutrition for children	1.7

Table 16 indicates that majority of respondents (58.9%) liked the session of activities for children. Less than fifteen percent (14.3%) of the respondents liked the session of guiding young children and role of day care worker. Fifteen percent of the respondents liked the session on DIC role in getting loans from banks. Few of them (3.3%) liked the session on role of banks in starting their own day care centre. Only one respondent liked the session on nutrition for children.

Overall looking at these tables it is clear that all the respondents were on the whole, satisfied with the day care centre training programme to a great extent.

Suggestions given by the Participants

1. Increase the duration of the training programme from 15 days to 1 month.
2. Include more practical experiences.
3. More visits to day care centres should be arranged.
4. During the day care visits, participants should be allowed to participate in the activities of the day care centres like managing the children.
5. Advertisement of the training programme should be given in advance.
6. Include more activities like
   - Open group discussion
   - Activities for children
7. The experts should evaluate the participants and give them some grading, whether they are eligible to run a day care centre or not.

Problems during the Project Work

The project was undertaken with the objective of training women for starting their own day care centres. While working with these women and during the training programme, problems faced are listed below :

A. *Problems Faced by the Project Worker*

1. It took a lot of time to locate women who were interested in starting their own day care centre.
2. Based on previous experience, banks were not ready to provide loans to some of these women.

The project worker had to spend a lot of time in persuading the bank officer to sanction loans to these women.

B. *Problems Faced by the Women Participants*

1. Though the women were keen and interested in starting their own day care centre, due to family problems many of them were not in a position to start their own day care centre.
2. The attitude of the bank officers was not very encouraging.

Conclusion and Recommendations

The following conclusions can be made after the completion of the project:

1. Such type of project gives opportunity of self development to the women.
2. The project helped women to start their own day care centres.
3. Women got an opportunity and experience to deal in government offices and banks in order to receive loans.
4. Such type of training programme gave them an opportunity to interact within groups and thereby helped them in learning to cooperate with one another.

Recommendations

1. Such training programmes can also be taken up for day care workers.
2. Same project can be taken up in rural areas.
3. A study can be undertaken on the following topics:
   (a) Parent's opinion about their day care centre.

(b) Problems faced by the parents while choosing a day care centre.

4. Comparisons of various kinds of child care facilities available to employed mothers.

Bibliography

- Abernathy, V.D. Social network and response to the maternal role. International Journal of Sociology of the Family. Vol. 2(1), 1973, pp. 86-92.
- Adolf, B. and Rose, K. The employers guide to child-care: Developing programmes for working parents. New York: Prager, 1985.
- Arora, C., Children's services in Baroda city. Plans and Prospectus. Dissertation. (M.Sc.), Department of Human Development and Family Studies, Faculty of Home Science, M.S.U., 1979.
- BOB loans to women entrepreneurs, Bank of Baroda, Mandvi Branch, Baroda 2000.
- Chaturvedi, T.N., Administration for child welfare. Indian Institute of Public Administration, New Delhi, 1979.
- Condran, J.G. and Bode, J.G. Rashomon, working wives and family division of labour: Middleton. Journal of Marriage and the Family. Vol. 44(2), 1980, pp. 421-426.
- Desai, M. and Patel, V. Indian woman change and challenge in the international decade. Popular Prakashan, Bombay, 1985.
- Devi, U.L. Status and employment of women in India. B.K. Publications. New Delhi, 1982.
- Elizabeth, B. Hurlock. Child development, 6th edition, Tata McGrawHill Publishing Company Ltd., New York, 1978.
- Hazel, F. and Mulligan, R.A. The child and his welfare. W.H. Freeman and Company, San Francisco, 1972.
- Human Welfare and Prime Minister Rojagar Yojana, District Industrial Centre, Baroda, 1998.
- Indira Gandhi National Open University School of Continuing Education. Organizing child-care services, Block No. 7, Indira Gandhi National Open University, 1994, pp. 6-10.

12
A Study of Small Scale Enterprises (Industries) Training Centre by N.G.Os. for Women Entrepreneurs

Manisha N. Khakhar

Introduction

Even till date there is no single definition of "Entrepreneur" which can be fully accepted universally and applied across the nation.

The word entrepreneur can be defined as "A person who undertakes an enterprise or business, with the chance of profit or loss". The definition of an "Entrepreneur" is not gender specific as an entrepreneur can be a male or a female.

Specific role requires specific skills, women are no longer confined to conventional fields like embroidery, knitting and tailoring, pickle, paper and powder making, but are now venturing in modern technological fields popularity known as energy, electricity and electronics. They are making a mark in the areas of consultancy, advertising, garment making, beauty care etc.

A question that arises about Entrepreneur's what makes his/her an Entrepreneur? Several factors go into the making of an Entrepreneur. Individuals who initiate, establish, maintain and expand new enterprise constitute the entrepreneurial class. It is myth that Entrepreneurs are born. Entrepreneurs can be developed by planned training to develop the desired attitudes which are identified to be present in a person to become an entrepreneur. Some additional qualities are required which can be developed through appropriate training programmes and these qualities are termed as entrepreneur attitudes.

All individuals have a need for training new recruits; need induction in to the rationale and objectives of their jobs besides being trained in specific skills and routines. New professional staff may need to undergo additional programs of training to enable them to improve their professional qualification. Certain individuals may need training for a specific purpose, the development of a new service taking on a new role in the organization.

The importance of training employees has the following advantages.

It makes sure the availability of skilled workers at all levels of management. It increases the potential abilities of workers and this improves their performance at the maximum attainable level.

- Training reduces fatigue.
- Training improves the relation between employees and management.
- New techniques can be easily adopted through trained employees. Training enables employees to occupy higher position of authority.
- To build the necessary skills of new entrepreneurs and workers.
- Basic Knowledge.
- Skills.
- Effective.
- Vision (Future plan).

Small-scale industries in India suffer from various handicaps. One of the most important among these is the non-availability of technical and managerial personnel of the required caliber. The small industrialist cannot afford to employ workers and supervisors having a sound educational background and the requisite experience in production and in trade out of the 2 million small-scale units existing in the country. Women handle 7% of these units. In addition women will also be given preference on other management training programs.

Various agencies of government and non-government, like National Small Industries Corporation, Small Industries Development Bank of India - N.G.O.'s - Non government Organizations - EDI, Entrepreneurship Development of India - EDP etc. have evolved special assistance scheme to encourage women entrepreneurs in a big way.

Any training programme should not only proper entrepreneurial motivation and skill but should also ensure that entrepreneur are able to develop their enterprises well by scientific, managerial techniques and contents in various fields of management – financial management, marketing management, production management and inventory control.

Objectives

1. A study of three types of training centre.
2. Methods of Training Centre.
3. To plan, conduct, skill development and evaluate the modern technology used in the training centre.
4. Problem faced by the training centre.
5. To know the future plan of the trainees.

Material and Method

The information was collected using a questionnaire. The sample size was 50 trainees from different Training Centre of Jamnagar city. After collecting the filled in questionnaire, discuss with trainees and their instructors were held.

Table -1

Name of training centre

1. Garment making (Stitches and Embroidery) - Small Scale categories manufacturing.

2. Handicraft and Home-Decorative Item (Small Scale Category Manufacturing.
3. Beauty Care Clinics (Small Scale Categories Personal Services)

Table – List and Participants in three different Training Centres

Sr. No.	*Training Centre*	*Trainees*	*Total*
1.	Garment making (Stitches and Embroidery) – Small Scale categories manufacturing	20	20
2.	Handicraft and Home-Decorative Item (Small Scale Category Manufacturing)	15	15
3.	Beauty Care Clinics (Small Scale Categories Personal Services)	15	15
	Total	**50**	**50**

The above table, three different training centres are listed, indicating the number of participants. All the participants were given a set of questions.

Result and Discussions

Results obtained in the survey presented in Table - I, II and III.

Table I

Garment making Training Centre

Sr. No.	*Area of observation*	*Results*
1.	Time adjustment	75% trainees could make the time arrangement while 25% trainees were unable to do so.
2.	Skill development	Skill development was done in all training centre.
3.	Used to modern technology and equipment	28% trainees used modern technology in the training centre while 78% trainees did not do so.
4.	Problem in training centre	60% trainees had no problems while 40% trainees had problems in time adjustment modern technology useful to.
5.	Take the help of extra knowledge	28% trainees took the help of books, magazines and experts after training 72% trainees did not consult.

(contd.)

Table I Contd.

6.	Knowledge of theory before practical	75% trainees had theoretical knowledge first and conducted the practical afterward. 25% trainees have only practical knowledge without theoretical knowledge.
7.	Aim of the Enterprise Business	12% trainees took training to kill their time. 18% trainees took training to improve the standard of the enterprises. 70% trainees took training to improve their economic standard.
8.	Money arrangement	20% trainees made the money arrangement by their savings. 80% trainees made the arrangement of money by taking loan from the banks.
9.	Future plan of Trainees	30% trainees wanted to do Garment making training class (Centre) 52% trainees wanted to make Garment according to the order placed by the shopkeepers. 18% trainees wanted to do their fashion shop and readymade Garment Store.
10.	Marketing	50% trainees wanted to do the marketing through advertisement or pamphlets on door to door. 50% trainees wanted to do marketing through selling their products to the Garment shops.
11.	Need for Achievement and Development for Business	70% trainees want to do hard work. 13% trainees wanted to develop their enterprise through public relation. 17% trainees wanted to give satisfaction to the customers by using good materials.

During discussion with their training instructors, it was clear that more than 70% trained persons have started their own work and are successful in their trades. The establishment of the venture on the basis of this training does not need huge

Table II

Handicraft and Home Decorative Items

Sr. No.	*Area of observation*	*Results*
1.	Time adjustment	80% trainees could make the time arrangement while 20% trainees were unable to do so.
2.	Skill development	Skill development was done in all training centre.

(contd.)

(Table II contd.)

3.	Used to modern technology and equipment	58% trainees used modern technology in the training centre while 42% trainees did not do so.
4.	Problem in training centre	62% trainees had no problems while 38% trainees had problems in time adjustment and modern technology useful too.
5.	Take the help of extra knowledge	58% trainees took the help of extra knowledge. 42% trainees did not consult.
6.	Knowledge of theory before practical	70% trainees had theoretical knowledge first and practical after-ward, 30% trainees had only practical knowledge without theoretical knowledge.
7.	Aim of Business	18% trainees took training to kill their time. 18% trainees took training to improve the standard of the enterprises.
8.	Money arrangement	20% trainees made the money arrangement by their saving. 10% trainees made the money arrangement by their pre plan. 70% trainees made the arrangement of money by taking loan from the bank.
9.	Future plan of Trainees	42% trainees wanted to conduct good carreer. 32% trainees wanted to start their enterprise. 26% trainees wanted to start their gift shop and art gallery.
10.	Marketing	72% trainees wanted to the marketing through advertisement. 28% trainees want to make decorative item according to the order placed by the shopkeepers.
11.	Need for Achievement and Development for Business	70% trainees wanted to do hard work. 30% trainees wanted to give satisfaction to the customers by using good materials.

finances to start with. One can start his work with amount less that 30 to 50 thousand rupees, most of these trainees, preferred to run their business from their own houses.

During the discussion with their training instructors, it was found that people ask for attractive items of less expenditure, therefore the instructors have to do this type of production and train the trainees for same and the training period is small and also the demand is less due to the small city.

- Training period is less.
- Less demand due to small city.

Table III

Beauty Care Clinic (Training Centre)

Sr. No.	*Area of observation*	*Results*
1.	Time adjustment	75% Trainees could make the time arrangement while 25% trainees were unable to do so.
2.	Skill development	Skill development was done in all training centres.
3.	Used to modern technology and equipment	52% trainees used modern technology in the training centre while 48% trainees did not do so.
4.	Problem in training center	67% trainees had no problems while 33% trainees had problem in time adjustment and using modern technology.
5.	Take the help of extra knowledge	52% trainees took the help of book, magazines and experts after training 48% trainees did not consult.
6.	Knowledge of theory before practical	Theoretical knowledge is given in all training centres before practical knowledge.
7.	Aim of the Business	70% trainees took training to improve their economic standard, 20% trainees took training for development of personality. 10% trainees took training to utilise their time.
8.	Money arrangement	40% trainees made the money arrangement by their savings. 60% trainees made the arrangement of money by taking loan from the banks.
9.	Future plan of Trainees	80% trainees wanted to start Beauty care clinic, 10% Home-services, 10% work as beauticians

(contd.)

(Table III contd.)

10.	Marketing	By Advertisement
11.	Need for Achievement and Development for Business	20% to find out new scheme 30% trainees want to give satisfaction to the customers by good services. 50% trainees wanted to do hard work.

During the discussion with their training instructors, it was realised that there are excess of beauty clinics in all the streets therefore this enterprise is not a success.

There is a Lack of interest in beauty clinic in local clinics.

There are different method are used in different beauty clinics.

Instructors have to be alert according to the change of time, otherwise the number of trainees decreases.

Conclusion

It can be concluded that 80% only ordinary training centre have for their to trainees, without any special training for the future development of their entrepreneurship. Women entrepreneurs need more attention and constant follow up and special treatment.

Suggesions

So some of the suggestions based on the conclusions drawn are:

Training serves not only the purpose of motivation and skill development but should also ensure that entrepreneurs are able to develop their enterprise well by scientific managerial techniques and contents in various fields of management and financial management production management.

The level of training should be high, it must be comprehensive and the participants should be made familiar with the latest trends in production technology.

Over and above the training centres are suggested to: –

- Give training by using technical method with lectures.
- Performance of work by using demonstration.
- Give Practical training as a group wants.
- To provide Individual training with special and complicated work.

At the end of this stage a detailed discussion, with trainee is held to ascertain his or her future plans and plan finance facility, guided by Banks, Government agencies and other organization and voluntary agencies.

Acknowledgement

The author of this chapter are thankful for kind co-operation from Mrs. Meenaben Dasani and Naynaben from "Khoobsurat Beauty Care Clinic", Naynaben Chhapiya from Stitching, Embroidery Training Classes and Garment making centre, llaben Bhatt from Handicraft makers and Home Decorative Items training classes and centre and all the trainees for giving their proper information and spacing precious time.

Special information from voluntary agency named "Sava" and other information from District Industrial Centre, Jamnagar, was obtained.

References

Desai, Vasant, Dynamics of Entrepreneurial Development and Management, Himalaya Publishing House, pp. 161-179.

Sharam, D.D., Daneja, S.K., Indian Entrepreneurship, Theory and Practice, pp. 27, 33, 38, 93, 150-152.

Sharma, D.D. and Dhaneja, S.K., Women and Rural Entrepreneurship in India, pp. 119, 121, 174-175.

13

A Study of the Attitude of New Generation Girls Regarding Entrepreneurship

Ranch Bhavna D.

Introduction

The entrepreneur has been defined in various ways – an innovator, a risk taker, a resource assembler, an organisation builder and so on. An entrepreneur is the entire of above combined into one. He identifies opportunities, available in his own environment, exploits, it/them to his best advantage introduces new ideas, carries new activities, innovates, co-ordinates the factors of production and efficiently manages the business. Hence, an entrepreneur can be safely defined as a person who identifies the opportunities in his environment and responds to it in innovative way so as to make economic surplus by engaging himself in efficiently exploiting the environment and opportunities it offers.

Quesnay recognised a rich farmer as an entrepreneur who manages and makes his business profitable by his intelligence and wealth.

The small entrepreneurs are the backbone of any economy as entrepreneur is regarded as fourth factor of production. Empirical studies have shown that small scale enterprises are the important vehicles for meeting the growth and equity with social justice objectives of developing economics. In this age majority women run small enterprises. So our government emphasizes to develop entrepreneurship in women and introduced many schemes and subsidies to develop entrepreneurship in women and introduced many schemes and subsidies for women entrepreneurs. So, it will be proper to study the attitude of our new generation girls who have got the limitless opportunities which are before them.

Recently our Prime Minister Shri Atal Bihari Vajpayee has advised our youth not to go after service but to start their own enterprise. Because we live in the age of globalization.

The importance of entrepreneurship development in the country is increasing day by day. The students should be encouraged to choose self-employment and entrepreneurship as career option. If 5-10 percentage of total student population is directed towards becoming Entrepreneurs, it will be a substantial contribution in solving the massive unemployment problem in our country and at the same time it will have a positive impact on the Nation's Economy.

Now, it is universally accepted that entrepreneurs are not born - they can be developed and promoted through scientifically organized training programmes. However, certain attitudes are necessary to become a successful entrepreneur.

Everybody cannot become an entrepreneur. Some additional qualities are required which can be developed through appropriate training programmes and these qualities are termed as entrepreneurial attitudes.

Therefore, a good deal of thought and research was carried out to utilize the potential and talent of such young girls for economic growth and development of the country.

Methods and Materials

In order to know the attitudes of our new generation girls on the subject of entrepreneurship, discussion alongwith questionnaires methods were used. For this cause girls from various colleges across Jamnagar studying in S.Y. and T.Y. (Science and Home Science) were given the questionnaires and discussions were arranged in their classroom in 2003-2004 to know their attitudes on the subject.

Result and Detailed Interpretations

Following are the results obtained from the questionnaires. The reasons and their respective percentage, the new generation girls want to indulge in the enterprise, are as follows:

Sr.No.	*Reasons*	*Percentage*
2.1	Because of self interest	92%
2.2	Because I have taken training	56%
2.3	For self development	72%
2.4	To keep pace with the society	72%
2.5	To acquire an economic-social position in the society	76%
2.6	For upbringing of family's economic condition	50%
2.7	Because it is difficult to get job now-a-days	56%
2.8	Because the limits of job it is unacceptable	30%

From the result and discussions it was evident that majority of them wanted to do service in order to cope up with the domestic responsibilities. At the same time rather than upbringing of economic, self-interest, keeping pace with society as well as to acquire a socio-economic place as the reasons to indulge in enterprise.

Their inclination for the enterprises and in beginning finance needed according to them are as under:

Sr. No.	*Enterprise*	*Sample size: 50 Percentage (%)*	*In beginning finance needed according to them*
1.	Tuition classes	22%	Rs. 20,000 to Rs. 20,000
2.	Laboratory (patho)	4%	Rs. 50,000 to Rs. 60,000
3.	Sewing and computer job work	12%	Rs. 2,000 to Rs. 50,000
4.	Beauty parlour	18%	Rs. 5,000 to Rs. 50,000
5.	Various classes	22%	Rs. 200 to Rs. 3,000
6.	Production and sale of various stuff	22%	Rs. 2,000 to Rs. 76,000

Various classes, sale of each stuff chosen are ladies related. Besides these, they listed various handicraft items, art - concerned classes, starting of women association, nursery, food products, readymade garments, boutique, cutlery items production and sale.

In reply to the question about the source of finance Fifty four per cent of them would seek finance from banks and various government plans, Thirty six per cent from the family members and personal savings and Ten per cent did not have a clue or believe that finance is not required.

Thirty per cent girls knew more or less about the government schemes. But they were not aware that bank loans are available for starting an enterprise.

They predict that in the beginning the monthly profit could be nil or Rs. 200 to Rs. 5000.

They believe marketing is more important than raw materials and management for that advertisement through friend circles, T.V., newspaper, pamphlet, etc. could be thought of for marketing.

Problems of finance and space are predominant. Else, different problems regarding marketing are faced for respective enterprise. Ten per cent of them are unaware of the problems.

Seventy six per cent of them believe that proper training is necessary for starting any enterprise.

They would be assisted in their enterprises by their family members such as father, mother, brother, sister and husband (if married). They also hope that they will be able to contribute separate time for enterprise and family and easily make adjustment for both.

It was found from the discussion that because of the uncertainty regarding marriage, it is not feasible to invest large amounts in the enterprise.

Conclusion

From this discussion, we may conclude that present generation girls want to earn by one means or other. They do not want to be just a housewife but want to contribute to both responsibilities, so that they could achieve self-development and improve their socio-economic standards.

But there is a larger section of girls preferring jobs instead, so that no investment is required, still a decent income, care-free life, less responsibilities are there. This will ease them to adjust domestic and job responsibilities.

Those girls waiting to indulge in the enterprise owing are very few in number. Their enterprises include women regarding services, sale, production, and so on. They prefer enterprises where minimum financial investment is required viz. tuition classes, other classes, beauty parlour, various handicrafts and household items. They want to start at small scale and then, if successful; gradually want to expand it.

On the other side, still many of them do not have an idea of other enterprises, training, governmental schemes, marketing enterprises related items and problems and financial aspect of the enterprise.

They are required to mentally prepare themselves for all these. They must be frequently informed with new enterprises and their exclusive details in different ways.

For these some suggestions are as follows:

1. To give perfect training for all kinds of enterprises.
2. To arrange lectures for new ideas about the enterprises.
3. To organize some fairs in every city.
4. To communicate for other ideas for developing enterprises through websites etc.
5. To give information in details about financial needs for an enterprise, and many schemes of the government, some special offer for women, subsidies etc.
6. Some TV shows and programmes which encourage women to open enterprises should be organised.

Acknowledgement

The author of this chapter wants to thank all girl students who had given answers to the questionnaires and discussion.

References

Anitha, H.S., Entrepreneurship Development, Mangla Deep Publication, Jaipur.

Sharma, D.D. and Dhaneja, S.K., Indian Entrepreneurship, Abhishek Publications, Chandigarh.

14

Problems Faced by Women Entrepreneur and Importance of Training in their Enterprise

Varsha P. Chhichhia

Entrepreneurs are the backbone of nation's economic progress. They organize land, labor and capital and provide the much needed goods and service to the society. Therefore, they are sometimes referred as a fourth factor of production. They create wealth and give employment to a large section of society.

Peter F. Drucker, defines "An entrepreneur as one who always searches for change responds to it and exploit it as an opportunity. He has aptly observed that innovation is the specific tool of entrepreneurs that means by which they exploit change as an opportunity for a different business or a different service."

E.E. Haggen "Entrepreneur is an economic man who tries to maximize his profit by innovations. Innovations involve problem solving and the entrepreneur gets satisfaction from using his competition capability in attacking business".

In short, entrepreneur means innovator, a risk, a resource assembler, an organizer and builder or trainer, it means, "entrepreneurs are made not born" by experience and training. In 21st century women entrepreneurship movement has become started in India. It is cordial to industrial development as any other economic factor. It has got added relevance due to massive unemployment of both educated and uneducated women. At present time women have gradually changed their attitudes and orthodoxy. Women are very much conscious of their cordial to industrial development as any other economic factor. It has got added relevance due to massive unemployment of both educated and uneducated women. At present time women have gradually changed their attitudes and orthodoxy. Women are very much conscious of their existence and their rights.

Today major problem for educated unemployed girl is to find a job. So, with the help of (economic and training) of government and N.G.O's. they started their own enterprise by using their skill talent's, knowledge, ability and provide job opportunity to group.

We saw so many successful women entrepreneur from our society, e.g., Shehnaz Hussain, world famous beautician; Ravina Raj Kohli, President in Star News; Bhanu Athaiya, famous dress designer; Vidya Chhabanya, Chairman of Jumbo group and so many.

Above all life for a women entrepreneur is not a bed of roses but they face endless problems. Out of 2 million small scale units existing in the country women manages hardly 7% of these units. Small industry development organization (S.I.D.O.) wants to give a impetus to the training of women entrepreneur for more accelerated growth of the economy, in particular, more number of product / process oriented training programs are proposed to be undertaken during 8th plan.

Such training programs are for the following enterprises –

- Readymade garment
- Food Processing
- Leather Utility articles
- Screen Printing
- Lens grinding
- Beauty Care

Whether in small industry or in large, problems always exist. The problems of industries whether in the small sector or in organized sector are almost identical. The organized industry is financially very strong and its resources are large so it can face its problems more effectively. Because of its week financial structure the resources of small unit is limited. While the large sector can employ trained and experience workers.

The problems of entrepreneur are Multinational. These can be solved by co-ordinate efforts of entrepreneurs, coordinated function of promotional agencies and government assistance red-tape of bureaucratic delays. The entrepreneur has to be educated and she should have a proper training in acquiring the necessary skills for running an enterprise. In fact the entrepreneur is the "King Pin of Industrial Spectrum."

Method and Material

The information was collected through by questionnaire. A sample of 40 women entrepreneurs of different field of Jamnagar related to brass industry, fashion world, beauty world, and handicraft and hospitality business were selected. Duly filled questionnaires were collected from the respondents which followed discussions.

Result and Discussions

Whether man or women both have to face similar difficulties and obstacles for development of enterprise but women entrepreneur face more difficulty due to their equal share of responsibility towards family and also due to the attitude of Indian Society towards Indian women entrepreneur.

Result obtained in survey I shown in Table – I

Table I

Sr. No.	*Fields of information*	*Answers*
1.	Type of problems faced by women entrepreneur	- 79% women entrepreneur said they had a family responsibility and had a financial pressure. - 46% said marketing is difficult. - 91% said lack of availability of training center government training center are not keen enough to show fare interest in training, while private training center provide much better training.

(contd.)

(Table I contd.)

		- 54% women entrepreneur said time spend does not give worthy outcome of money. - 35% women entrepreneur said that need of modifications from time to time are essential to survive. - 93% women entrepreneurs have lack of exposure of facilities like internet. - 72% women entrepreneur said in beginning years we have to struggle more to survive in the market but once success is achieved. Survival is not a big issue.
		- 3% women entrepreneur had complete organized computer set up in their factory and they made efficient use of internet marketing to develop their enterprise. - All the entrepreneurs claimed that their standard of living and respect in society is lifted up as they form the earning group of society and they had all satisfied that they are the reason for survival of many other families working under them.
2.	Steps taken by government to solve above problems	- Spread education through campaigning open training centre which runs efficiently and gives sufficient proper training. Remove corruption from its root. - The license authentication it should be made compulsory in all the enterprises. - Different schemes run by government should be exposed by media and campaigning.
3.	Effect on social life	- 90% women entrepreneur said due to work load some times they can not attend social and religious ceremonies.

(contd.)

(Table I contd.)

		- All said they get respect from society and elder people of family.
4.	Effect on Family life	- In the initial years their life is disturbed due to imbalance between work and family, but as routine is set up after passage of time everybody in the family adjusts and their proper balance between work and family. - Due to increase in income the need of children can be fulfilled well.
5.	Effect on Personality	- Confidence is increased - Continuous encouragement for something to do new. - Remain updated with current trends of world - Life become very active. - There is a constant feeling of being different from others.
6.	Opinion about expansion of enterprise	- By making more and more use of current technology they wish to expand their enterprise. - To remain updated with the knowledge of newer and enhanced version of machines to build up strong marketing policy. - To give training to more and more number of labourers.
7.	How many trained person in their enterprise	- 3 to 30 well-trained permanent persons are present in their enterprise. At place where there were no trained employees they were providing them with sufficient training.
8.	Are they flexible or not	- They said the need of flexibility time-to-time change. For example in marketing and planning out holiday schemes for workers and in profit loss adjustment and for family.

(contd.)

(Table I contd.)

9.	Do you wish government should run training centres and for which type of industry	- **Yes, training centres run with full honesty in type of jobs which have less money investment.** - **It should be planned for less educated people.** - **Training centre should provide sufficient technical and practical knowledge along with theoretical knowledge.**
10.	Their opinion about making training compulsory	- **100% said yes as the quality of their manufactured goods is enhanced.**

- Forty women entrepreneurs whom I met during my study were smart, intelligent, highly qualified and well experienced. They have invested from 2 lakhs to 15 lakhs of Rupees in their enterprise.
- According to them there is a strong need for a change in educational strategies, B.A. and B.Com. degree is not enough for getting a handsome job, so technical education should be entered in their courses.
- With changing trends female gets the freedom to work and explore in their field but government policies heavy taxes and corruption become obstacles in their progress.
- Government schemes do not reach to common people some times. So for less educated and low income group of women, training centre should be established which help them to start a new enterprise with low investment.
- They say that women have enough management skills, caliber and sincerity to progress in their field but they only lack some experience. With some amount of experience they can progress in any enterprise.
- In society and family they are looked up with high respect despite all this they feel that their husbands are reluctant to mould themselves in house keeping tasks.

I would like to present my views of survey after discussion

with some successful and extraordinary talented women entrepreneurs.

I met a widow lady of Darbar community who runs bead casting factory (age 33 years). She told me that I come from a very respectable, restricted and rigid community, but I fulfill my duties towards work at the same time also take care of my responsibilities and maintain my self respect. She was a woman of substances and took care of marketing, money management, labour management very skillfully. She has the responsibility of survival of 25 labor families. She does marketing in region around 500 to 700 km through self driving. According to her she has progressed so much through the support of her family and community so can other women too.

Urmi Pau who is finance director and manufactured window covering items (age 32 years) in her factory say's that for efficient training of women along with government, NGO's, Mahila Media, Chamber of Commerce Corporation and Panchayat should also make some efforts in this direction.

Mrs. Bindiya Toliya my student who runs a beauty parlour, health centre and beauty training centre (age 37 years) gave me one cutting which was about two women who were specialist in chemistry. They wanted to establish a plant to manufacture Zinc Sulphate. They approached a bank for seeking help, the bank did not provide any loan and did not even mention any concrete reason.

Mrs. Ralisa Vithlani manufactured sanitary plastic pipe (age 46 years) said entrepreneur women play's double role in her life and thus they face so many hardships. Women have to face many obstacles in enterprise and cannot progress at a faster rate as a man entrepreneur. Women entrepreneur have sufficient skill but they only lack necessary training to enhance their skills. Indian women are comparatively more responsible towards their family. So, sometimes they cannot concentrate more on development of enterprise.

Conclusion

The results of my study have been very interesting so far.

With reasonable discussion I found that today's women are very much alert and smart along with efficient home-management. They can also perform economic management of their enterprise with intellectual skills.

There has been a spectacular change in women, empowerment, skill, self confidence and self respect.

They are satisfied with the feeling that they provide survival to numerous other families. They have strong desire of knowing and teaming something new at each phase. They give equal importance to their enterprise as much as they give to home.

With efficient time management they have learned to adjust in home, society and enterprise. They make constant efforts for their own achievements too along with family.

__________ their complains were that women are not alert to improve their skills by training. They said sometimes government policies are very unclear and bank also not give sufficient support as we are women.

References

Anitha, H.S., Entrepreneurship Development, pp. 1-3.

Sharma, D.D. and Dhaneja, S.K., Indian Entrepreneur Theory and Practice.

Desai, Vasant, Dynamics of Entrepreneurial Development and Management, pp. 695-700.

Sharma, D.D. and Dhaneja, S.K., Women and Rural Entrepreneur in India.

15
Handicrafts and Entrepreneurship

Veena Somani

Introduction

As per the Indian ethos and tradition it was responsibility of a man to earn for family while woman was supposed to cook, to do household chores and rear children.

But after the industrial revolution, women also started moving out for work. In today's world, the stereotype division of work no longer exists. Man and woman both work together in all the fields of economy. Women have entered even in those area of work which were once considered as man's bastion from driving a vehicle, to joining the armed force, women have started contributing their mite, and carve a niche for themselves.

With changing attitude in society concept of gender equality also started gaining foothold admits rapid expansion of economic horizons, triggered by scientific and technological revolutions. That is why, perhaps the list of three basic necessities food, shelter and clothes have become endless.

Newer avenues have been explored in each of the basic necessities to meet the aspiration and need of the class which has climbed the ladder of prosperity.

Textile, for example, has no longer remained a basic necessity. There is much more than the demand to cover and protect the body. A piece of cloth or an outfit is looked beyond it's basic value. Value addition on basic product is infact, the key that opens up new vistas.

Clothing and textile too have witnessed major change from the viewpoints of producers or manufacturers and end users. From individual weaver to a textile mill, the manufacturing process has become complex.

There is also a group who provide only inputs. Women always played a lead role since centuries in cloth making. There used to be a single economical, social class called weavers, who used to inherit the skill of weaving. They were the master weavers and this skill has remained their bastion. Machine could not replace them. Patola is one of them which is still woven by weavers.

This research paper tried to find out the economic implications of Patola, by weaving.

Materials and Method

Kadam mahila handicraft and industrial manufacturing and sales cooperative, Rajkot was selected for this purpose because of its traditional method of weaving Patola by hand. This unit offered employment to Sixty women workers specializing in different aspects of Patola making like bleaching, grafting, dying and weaving. Various parameters like pattern of Patola, production, selling and current fashion trend in Patola were studied by a set of questionnaire and personal interviews. Working pattern of women in such a unit was determined by questionnaire and personal interview at their residence.

Table 1
Labour Charges

Bleaching/ kg.	*Corn/Weft Yarn/kg.*	*Worp Yarn/kg.*	*Grafting and Dyeing Per Piece*	*Weaving/ piece*
100	50	200	400	500 per two person

Table 2
General Information about Women Entrepreneurs

Sr. No.	*Topic / General Information*	*Yes*	*No*
1.	Family Business	60(100%)	-
2.	Work Satisfaction	60(100%)	-
3.	Weekly Leave	60(100%)	-
4.	Bonus	-	60(100%)
5.	Additional Economic Benefits	-	60(100%)
6.	Production by order	23(38.18)	37(61.42)
7.	Occupation associated physical hazards	14(23.24)	46(76.36)

It can be seen from Table 2 that :

- All the workers had family history of Patola making. They had work satisfaction and enjoyed weekly leave.
- There was no additional government subsidy or bonus for the workers.
- Less number of families did production with prior orders.
- Occupation associated physical hazards were less.

Table 3
General Information Regarding Work Pattern

No.	*Type of work*			
1.	Bleaching 17(28.22)	Grafting & Dyeing 30(49.80)	Weaving 13(21.58)	Others (00.00)
2.	Period of training			
	3 months 09(14.94)	6 months 49(81.34)	9 months 02(3.32)	Others (00.00)
3.	Working hours			
	6 hrs. 10(43.56)	8 hrs. 43(71.38)	10 hrs. 24(39.84)	Others (00.00)

(Contd.)

(Table 3 contd.)

4.	Duration of work			
	5 yrs. 08(13.28)	7 yrs. 28(46.48)	10 yrs. 24(39.84)	Others (00.00)
5.	Place of work			
	At home 55(91.30)	Sub centre 01(1.66)	Main centre 04(6.64)	Others (00.00)
6.	Use of income			
	Personal (00.00)	Family expenditure 08(13.28)	Savings 52(1.66)	Others (00.00)
7.	Investment			
	Post Office 24(39.84)	Bank 35(58.10)	LIC 01(1.66)	Others (00.00)
8.	Income by			
	Per Piece 01(1.66)	Per kg. 54(89.64)	Per hrs. 05(8.3)	Others (00.00)

It can be seen from Table 3 that

- Maximum number of women did grafting and dyeing followed by weaving and bleaching.
- Maximum period of training required was six months, working at homes were 8 hours and duration of work was seven years.
- Women worked from home in maximum numbers followed by main centre and sub-centre.
- Income generated was mainly channelized for saving in banks.

Table 4
General Information about Production and Customer Demand (present fashion)

Types of production							
Sari		Dress/Dupatta		Chaniya Choli/Dupatta		Others	
Prod.	Customer Demand	Prod.	Customer Demand	Prod.	Customer Demand	Prod.	Customer Demand
36(59.76)	19(31.54)	28(46.48)	22(36.52)	06(9.96)	19(31.54)	00.00	00.00
Types of Sari [Patola]							
Small Border		Lagdi Border		Tissue Border		Others	
Prod.	Customer Demand	Prod.	Customer Demand	Prod.	Customer Demand	Prod.	Customer Demand
19(31.54)	13(21.58)	11(18.26)	20(33.2)	30(49.80)	27(44.82)	00.00	00.00

Contd...

(Table 4 contd.)

Colours							
Traditional		Modern		Both		Others	
Prod.	Customer Demand	Prod.	Customer Demand	Prod.	Customer Demand	Prod.	Customer Demand
14(6.64)	10(16.6)	11(18.26)	27(44.82)	45(74.7)	23(38.18)	00.00	00.00
Types of Design							
Borderbutti		Plain and Pallu		All over		Others	
Prod.	Customer Demand	Prod.	Customer Demand	Prod.	Customer Demand	Prod.	Customer Demand
(14.94)	08(13.28)	25(41 .05)	26(43.16)	28(46.48)	26(43.16)	00.00	00.00
Types of Material							
Resham fibre		Complete Golden fibre		Mixed		Others	
Prod.	Customer Demand	Prod.	Customer Demand	Prod.	Customer Demand	Prod.	Customer Demand
(64.74)	41(68.06)	00(00.00)	00(00.00)	21(34.86)	19(31.54)	00.00	00.00
Selling Cost							
200/-		2800A		3500A		Others	
Prod.	Customer Demand	-Prod.	Customer Demand	Prod.	Customer Demand	Prod.	Customer Demand
(29.88)	21(34.86)	38(63.08)	33(54.78)	04(6.64)	06(9.96)	00.00	00.00
Motif							
Bird & Animal		Natural		Human		Others	
Prod.	Customer Demand	Prod.	Customer Demand	Prod.	Customer Demand	Prod.	Customer Demand
(34.86)	30(49.80)	25(41.05)	08(13.28)	14(23.24)	22(36.52)	00.00	00.00

It can be seen from Table 4 that

- Production and customer demand for dress and dupatta were maximum.
- In sarees tissues borders and all over designs were preferred.
- Modern as well as traditional colours are used almost equally in Patola making.
- Only resham fibre is preferred by customers.
- Cost of sale preferred was ranges from Rs. 2800 to Rs. 3500.
- Natural motif were the most preferred motifs followed by birds and animals and humans.

Table 5
General Information about Selling

1.	Advertising			
	T.V.	Hording	Pamphlets	Others
	02	01	56	-
	(3.32)	(1-66)	(92.96)	(00.00)
2.	Type of Selling			
	08	31	21	-
	(13.28)	(51.46)	(34.86)	(00.00)
3.	Methods of Selling			
	Fair organized by Government	Fare organized by Private Organization	Exhibition/Sale	Others
	01	02	57	
	(1.66)	(3.32)	(94.62)	(00.00)
4.	Dead Stock Clearance			
	Sale	Sp. Discount	Gift/Coupon	Others
	15	22	23	-
	(24.9)	(36.52)	(38.18)	(00.00)
5.	Place of selling			
	Local Level	National Level	International Level	Others
	57	- 03	00	-
	(94.62)	(4.98)	(00.00)	(00.00)

It can be seen from Table 5 that

1. Selling was maximum through advertising followed by pamphlets.
2. Wholesale selling was maximum.
3. Exhibition-cum-sale was most preferred method of selling at local level.
4. Dead stock clearance was by special discount and gift coupons.

Conclusion

From the present study following conclusions can be made:

1. Rajkot Patola were comparatively cheaper than original patan Patola because of printing only in weft yarn.
2. Women workers carried out work at home with good working condition but less financial rewards.

3. Production increased over the years. Type of garment, colours, design and motifs were chosen as per customer demand.

References

Cockett, B.R. (1964). Dyeing and Printing, London, Sir Issac Pitman and Son Ltd.

Story Joyce (1979). Manual of Dyes and Fabrics, London, Thames and Hudson Ltd.

16

Pioneering Innovative Women Entrepreneurs' Classifications and their Problems

Sucheta Singh

Introduction

Entrepreneur according to Oxford English Dictionary (in 1987) is "the director or manager of a public musical institution; one who "gets up" entertainments, especially "musical performance". Not until its supplement appeared in 1933 did the dictionary recognize that the word had a place in business, and would mean "one who undertakes an enterprise especially a contractor.....acting as intermediary between capital and labour".

The first published reference to entrepreneurs was probably in the year 1723 and it focused on the fact that entrepreneurs buy goods for factors of production at a fixed price to sell them later and elsewhere at an uncertain price. They hire and combine various factors of productions and they also bear the risk.

Entrepreneur is the person who tries to create something new, organizes production and who undertakes risk and handles economic uncertainty. He is a potentially enterprising individual, endowed with special ability to innovate of imitate and for decision making, interacted in advancing technology and willing to assume the risk involved in it (Nandrajog's 1992).

Cole's view of entrepreneurship, however, is coterminous with the general managerial activities. It is a "purposeful activity of an individual of ________ group of associated individuals, undertaken to initiate, maintain or aggrandize a profit oriented business unit for the production or distribution of economic goods and services.

Jean Baptiste Say perceived the entrepreneurial function in broader perspective. He described entrepreneur as the agent, who combines the necessary factors into production organism, thereby playing a central role both in production and distribution, whether it is agriculture or industry.

According to Schumpeter, 1947 the entrepreneurial function is one of innovation. His innovation represents the first dynamic concept of the entrepreneurial function and thus, he is the first one to put the human agent at the centre of the process of economic development.

Studies on Women Entrepreneurs

Research and experiences have indicated that women entrepreneurs in comparison with men are not different in terms of their personality, cognition, achievement motivation, dependency and other related attitudes (Vinze, 1986).

Studies on women entrepreneurs with reference to personality (Malada, 1985, Reif, et. al. 1975). Achievement motivation (Archana, T.V., Rehana, G. 1985), Cognitive Abilities (Mathur and Anamika, 1987), Potential Women (Singh and Sengupta, 1984) have been able to highlight their characteristics. It has also been stated that women differ not in terms of their characteristics but in terms of their profile. Owing to the lack of clear understanding of women entrepreneurs on the part of the promoters, developers or policy makers, one does not find a very conducive entrepreneurial climate for women in India. Thus, most of the existing programmer can be described as "Cries in despair" in the face of mass unemployment, traditional ideology and various taboos (Sarngadharan and Resia Baesam, 1995).

Robert, D. Hisrich (1985) has given a comparison of characteristics between male and female entrepreneurs in terms of their motivation, departure point, source of funds, occupational background, personality characteristics, support group and types of business.

Gaikwad, V.R. and Tripathy, R.N. in their book, *Socio-psychological Factors Influencing Industrial Entrepreneurship in Rural Areas* (1970) made a case study in the Thanku region of West Godavary district in Andhra Pradesh. The study evaluated in depth the sociological and economic factors, which helped this particular area to develop at a faster rate than the surrounding areas. The study gives valuable insights to the officials and non-officials working for industrial development and enables them to identify the strong points, for such development in particular areas.

Constantina Sofilios Rothschild, 1974 in book, *Women and Social Policy* presents the theoretical background of social policy related to women. Social policy to liberate women as well as men has been discussed. Social policy to liberate society from sexism has been clearly dealt with, along with social policy to liberate marriages, the institution of the family and family life. The main thesis of the book is that, under increasing political and social pressures, men will have to go beyond tokenism not only to relinquish marginal power positions, but also to give up some essential power posts. The transition to liberation is quite slow and painful but eventually life; society and all the relationships between women and men will be much more honest, open and rewarding than they are at present. Chances for happiness and for self-actualization are going to be much brighter both for women and men.

Sharma, K.L. in his book, *Entrepreneurial Performance in Role Perspective* (1975), explores the emerging patterns of growth of entrepreneurs, their performance and problems. Against the background of government assistance in various forms, entrepreneurs and their problems call for earnest attention for the healthy and sustained socio-economic growth of Indian society. The study was conducted to tackle some theoretical and methodological issues concerned with the analysis of the entrepreneurial role of conformity and to throw light on some applied aspects of entrepreneurial growth in the State of UP. The study brings to light the lack of response of entrepreneurs to the facilities made available by the government. One may like to explore its reasons, which may be identified as the incapacity of entrepreneurs, the inadequate terms and conditions of the facilities, the ineffectiveness of the institutions providing the facilities and the inefficiency of the personal employed therein.

Srinivas, M.N. in his paper, "The Changing Position of Indian Women" (1976), discusses a subject which is vast in nature and the bewildering complexity. He has restricted his discussions to Hindu Women only. Feminine pre-occupation with religious rituals provides Hindu Women with power over men. Since the rituals are concerned with the welfare of the household and its members, men are appreciative of the fact that women are looking after an important area of family life.

Pareek, H.S., in his book, *Financing of Small Industries in a Developing Economy* (1978), highlights the problems of small scale industries with particular reference to financial and brings home to the readers an analysis of the capital structure of 181 small scale units of different capital rises belonging to various industrial groups. The study review and the role of finance institutions and state agencies in extending credit to small scale industrial units and pin-points their attitude of indifference in catering to the needs of the tiny units. The main thesis of the author is that the financial institutions have to attune their lending policies in consonance with the needs of the small-scale sector in general and the smaller among the small scale in particular.

Vimala Mehta in her book, *Attitude of Educated Women towards Social Issues* (1979), which covers women teachers and students, makes an attempt to draw a scientific research design to attitudinal study. Her purpose was to measure conservatism-radicalism operating among women towards certain social issues such as family, social and cultural affairs, education, marriage, jobs and politics.

Maithreyi Krishna Raj, in her study, Approaches to self reliance for women (1980), gives some urban modes. She has made an attempt to assess some schemes to help low income women in Bombay from the point of view of their contribution to the development of self-reliance among women, with reference to four cases, namely Manila Arthik Vikas Maha Mandal Ltd.,

Indira Co-operative Bank, Stree Seva Shakar Sangh Siyameet and Annaporna Mandal. The first assists in employment generation, the second is a credit supply schemes; the third is an industrial cooperative federation and the fourth is an association of self employed women.

In Profiles in Female Poverty (1981), Leela Gulati tries to analyse the life situation of five working women drawn from the lowest income groups in Kerala. The range of occupations covered includes an agricultural labourer, a brick worker, a fish vendor, a construction worker and a coir worker. The author tries to focus the profiles to draw a comprehensive picture in the total day to day setting in which they work.

Lalitha Devi, in her book, *Status and Employment of Women in India* (1982), tries to show that employment per se as against age, education, family type and place of residence plays a crucial role in raising the status of women. Employed women have more power and influence in the family and outside than unemployed women. The author has made the analysis of the status of women within the family in the office and in the wider society. There is hidden potential of employment that contributes to the status of women.

Ram K. Vepa, in his book *Small Industry Development Programme* (1983) covers the growth of small-scale industries in India since the adoption of a policy to this effect in 1951. His book highlights issues relating to policy, organizational structure and international co-operation, while giving details regarding various programmes of small scale industry promotion and their linkage with other development programmes. Insight into development experience of this crucial sector of our national economy, given in the book would interest policy makers and administrators in India as well as in other developing countries.

Kalpana Shah in her book, *Women Liberation and Voluntary Action* (1984) has attempted to analyze the relationship between ideology, leadership and programmes of the women's movement by focusing on the ways in which the voluntary organization, Akhil Hind Mahila Parishad organized its activities to achieve the objectives. The book examines the central issue of development of women's consciousness in the context of the mobilization of middle class women, the author highlights the limits of the welfare programmes undertaken by middle class women's movement and shows how such movements unwillingly strengthen the traditional image of women and thus perform a very restricted role. The author stresses the relationship between ideological shifts and action programmes in the women's movement.

Sarngadharan and Resia Beegam undertook a study in his book *Women Entrepreneurship* (1995) to assess the institutional support provided to women entrepreneurship in India in general and Kerala in particular. The problems confronted by the women entrepreneurs in Kerala, engaged in various industrial/business activities. Shortage of working capital and high rates of interest charged by banks were the two major problems. Traveling a long distance for procuring raw materials is also inconvenient for the women entrepreneurs.

Manimala (1999) in her book *Entrepreneurial Policies and Strategies* suggested that policies and strategies are important variables in determining entrepreneurial performance. The success is a matter of chance and one needs some luck. This is true, but it is also possible to shape luck by building networks, by exercising parsimony of investment, by seeking competitively insulated riches by moving incrementally and by continually monitoring performance.

Functions of an Entrepreneur

The broad functions of an entrepreneur can be categorized into the following three categories:

1. Innovation
2. Risk-taking
3. Organization and management
   - (a) Planning of an enterprise
   - (b) Coordination, administration and control
   - (c) Routine type of supervision

Qualities of an Entrepreneur

In an economy an entrepreneur is expected to combine all factors of production in a manner so as to get a maximum output at minimum cost by processing following main qualities:

1. Self-confidence and capacity to assume risk.
2. Technological knowledge, alertness to new opportunities, willingness to accept change and ability to initiate.
3. Ability to marshal resources.
4. Ability to organize and administer.

Types of Entrepreneurship

The sociological, economic and industrial development scenario shows emergence of following types of entrepreneurship:

1. Agricultural oriented Entrepreneurship
2. Art and craft based Entrepreneurship
3. Profession oriented Entrepreneurship
4. Occupation Oriented Entrepreneurship
5. Business Oriented Entrepreneurship
6. Local resources based Entrepreneurship
7. Human resource based Entrepreneurship

Classification of Entrepreneurs

I. There are four categories of entrepreneurs:

1. *Innovating entrepreneurs:* They are characterized by aggressive assemblage of information and the analysis of results deriving from novel combinations of factors.
2. *Imitating entrepreneurs:* They can work only when a certain level of development is already achieved and people look forward to change and progress. They are also revolutionary entrepreneurs with the difference that they do not innovate the changes themselves: they just imitate techniques and technologies innovated by others.
3. *Fabian entrepreneurs:* They are characterized by very great caution and skepticism in practicing any change.

Their dealings are determined by customs, religion, and tradition and past practices.

4. *Drone entrepreneurs:* They are characterized by a refusal to adopt and use opportunities to make changes in production. Such entrepreneurs may even suffer losses but they do not make changes in methods of productions.

II. *New Venture Gestalts/Entrepreneurial types:*

Gostner et al. (1989) has developed categories based on four sets of variables, namely,

(a) Individual characteristics, abilities, skills and motivation of the entrepreneur.

(b) Organizational strategies and structures.

(c) Environmental features, especially its competitive nature.

(d) Entrepreneurial processes, including the entrepreneur's activities and the efforts invested in these activities.

Cluster analysis of these four sets of variables has revealed eight entrepreneurial types, described as follows.

Type 1: Escaping to Something New

It is the discontented employee who wants to change his job because of the perceived oppression of being an employee. Naturally, the venture would be in a different industry. All the same, it is an established industry, with many competitors already in the field, and the entrepreneur chooses similar products/ services as those of the competitors. The products are not technically complex, and success lies mainly in effective marketing.

Type 2: Putting the Deal Together

This entrepreneur is more or less like an agent. There are two sub-types in this group. One is the real estate agent who brings the seller and the buyer together. The other may be called a 'novelty firm', whose entrepreneur commercializes a very good product idea, not by manufacturing it himself, but by getting it made by existing manufacturers and selling it through existing wholesalers and retailers. The entrepreneur usually relies on his previous experience and personal contacts.

Type 3: Rollover Skills/Contacts

The firm revolves around the entrepreneur's technical skill or professional expertise, which has been developed or reinforced in the previous job. The provocation for starting his own business is either a block to his career, or confidence that he can do a better job than his employer. Such firms offer generic services, such as auditing, personal agencies, advertising, and so forth. Better service is the key to success in such firms.

Type 4: Purchasing a Firm

The entrepreneur has had a successful career, but quits the job because of a long-cherished desire to become an entrepreneur. He purchases a firm because that is considered to be a low risk proposition, even though the firm purchased is often assessed to be a turn-around case. The products of the firm are not unique, nor are they technically complex.

Type 5: Leveraging Expertise

The individual has never thought of becoming an entrepreneur, especially because he has had a successful career as an expert in his field. He is attracted to the entrepreneurial career by the opportunities emerging in a fast-changing environment, which his employer refuses to take advantage of. The product is technically complex, the customers are sophisticated and demanding, and therefore there is need for constant adaptation and product differentiation. Quality of product is the major factor determining success.

Type 6: Aggressive Service

The individual has always wanted to become an entrepreneur, and starts his venture in the area of his prior experience. He follows a niche-strategy, and survives by serving the neglected segments of the market through differentiated products and services.

Type 7: Pursuing the Unique Idea

A unique product or service idea is the cause of the new venture. The product or service may not be technically sophisticated or difficult to manufacture. However, its novelty and uniqueness may create feelings of uncertainty in the entrepreneur regarding its quality, feasibility, and availability of resources and market acceptability.

Type 8: Methodical Organising

Though the entrepreneur has had a successful previous corporate career, he quits that to follow his long-cherished goal of starting his own business. The product idea is chosen after long research involving potential customers. Though the idea is not a total departure from existing products, it will have innovative features calculated to exploit customers' dissatisfaction with the existing products. Hence, there is need for careful planning and testing at every stage of manufacturing, marketing and servicing the product. The initial uncertainties make the entrepreneur keep his hob till the venture is reasonable well established.

III. A further classification, on the basis of the entrepreneur's use of pioneering innovative (PI) heuristics can be made (Mathew, 1999):

Individuals travel to entrepreneurship by different routes and they adopt different policies for implementing different types of projects. This is true not only of high and low PI groups, but also of all entrepreneurs. A brief description of each subtype within groups is given below:

Subtypes of high PI entrepreneurs

1. The Inventor / Tinkerer

There are people with some ability to manipulate materials. They tinker with things, and invent a new product or improve an existing product. As a means to commercially exploiting their invention, they establish business ventures. For these people, the business venture is rather secondary. Their primary interest is in constantly improving their products, and/or experimenting with new products. Examples of entrepreneurs included in this category are a man who invented a better plough and chaff cutter specially suited for Indian conditions, a Canadian who invented the snowmobile and revolutionized human movement on snow, and another Canadian who invented a more efficient garbage compactor using a different technology. As stated above, the primary interest of these people is not in the business, but in the product they made and in its improvements. In one case, for example, when the first product became a commercial success, and the sons of the entrepreneur wanted to expand the operations, the entrepreneur left all the operations to the sons, put up an 'experimental' shed, moved into it, and went on tinkering with whatever he was interested in.

2. *The Adventurer*

These are people who venture into a field, and make a big success there under circumstances which appear to the 'common man' as the least favourable for business. There is the case here of a man who developed a business empire in a place which was a backward area, and was considered to be totally unsuitable for any business because of the lack of infrastructure facilities. During British rule, no Indian could even dream of entering shipping, shipbuilding, aircraft manufacture, etc. which were under the control of British monopolies. But one Indian ventured into these and made a success of them during his time. Later, in the 1970s when the textile industry in India was going through a decadent phase, and severe controls were imposed on large textile units by the government, there was someone who ventured into textile and built one of the largest and most successful units. Entrepreneurs belonging to this category seem, to be stimulated or challenged by obstacles. They seem to take pleasure in overcoming obstacles. They are impulsive, impatient and want to grow as fast as possible. As a consequence probably some of these, become experts at networking and resource mobilization.

3. *The Searcher / Problem-Solver*

These are people who get into business as a solution to their own personal problems, or to some problem vexing the community around. Personal problems, such as material deprivation, joblessness, problems of adjustments in the family or at the job, etc., have pushed a few people on to the business road. A second type of problem solver in this group is the man who gets interested in the community's problems and tries to solve them.

4. *The Gap-Filler*

Gap-fillers are those who are quick to spot large gaps in the economy, and devise ways of filling them through innovative business ventures. This is the case of many who ventured into the indigenous manufacture of bulk drugs.

5. *The Social Visionary*

Like the community problem solver discussed above, the social visionary also promotes a business venture as an answer to macro-level problem. However, there is difference between the two. While the former seeks a solution to an existing problems of the community, the latter seeks a solution to an anticipated problem of the community, often of the country at large.

6. *The PI Opportunity Grabber*

These are people who, in the early phase of their lives, never thought of business as a serious career option. However, when circumstances in later life offered PI opportunities in business, they were quick to grab them and build successful PI ventures.

7. *The Specialist Pioneer*

There are two subtypes within the specialist pioneer group, namely, the trained specialist and the untrained specialist. The trained specialist has got high educational accomplishments, is a specialist in a particular field (generally in engineering), and has done specialized jobs in reputed industrial organizations. For some reason, such as creative frustration, the desire to be independent, the desire to be in one's hometown, etc., he decides to set up a manufacturing venture, which would usually be in the field of his specialization or in a very closely related field. These bring rare products, will be pioneering in the local context, and the person uses his training and special talents to add innovative features to it. The untrained specialist, on the other hand, has nothing to make him specially qualified for the type of business he has entered. He is there because of certain circumstances, and once he is there he has to do better than his competitors to survive in the field. Therefore, he recruits experts in the field, encourages them to add innovative features to the product, and thus gets the better of his competitors. Since the expertise he has developed in specific to some field, he is rather unwilling to diversify into other fields, and so remains a specialist in his own field and goes on adding innovative features to his products, so that he can retain the upper hand he has already gained over his competitors.

Subtypes within the Low PI Group

1. *The Chance Entrant*

Like PI opportunity grabbers, there are people who had no intention of doing business, but are drawn into it by chance events. It may be the death of someone in the family, identification of a business opportunity while working for someone else, persuasion by friends or relatives to join their ventures as a partner, availability of the assets of a failed unit at throwaway prices, etc., that makes the person enter business.

2. *The Agent - Turned Producer*

These people generally come from the trading communities. They take up agencies of other manufacturers, foreign or Indian. For several reasons, foreign manufacturers are forced to stop their operations, when their agents start producing those goods. Most often, the quality of the agent's products would be inferior, and they are sooner or later overtaken by some PI entrepreneurs. Agents of Indian manufacturers get into production when they find that the demand is too large for the principals alone to meet.

3. *The Concession - Grabber*

These are people who set up business ventures just because there is a concession, subsidy or grant associated with it. Their main aim is to take advantage of the grant, subsidy or concession, and in the process they often fail to ensure that the project is intrinsically viable. Consequently, many such units turn sick, others are rescued by further support from outside, and a few others are fortunate enough to be viable on their own.

4. The Obsessed Producer

There are two categories within this group, one with a technical bent of mind and some qualities of the inventor/ tinkerer, and the other without any of these qualities, but with a strong view that the entrepreneur's primary task is to produce. The technical man starts with some minor invention of his own, and produces it without testing its commercial feasibility or market acceptance. When one product fails, he tries another. In the process, he accepts suggestions for new products from any one, and invests heavily to produce them.

5. The Ancillary / Imitator

The imitators may be those who are low on most types of innovation. There are two sub-types within this group. One of them is the ancillary who secures the technology from and produces according to the specifications of a large unit. The other is the producer who finds that the demand for a particular product is large enough for him also to enter, and replicate the existing units.

6. The Non-Pioneer Niche-Holder

This group has some similarities with the specialist pioneer, in the sense that both of them have carved out a niche for themselves. But the difference is that the latter goes on innovating in his special field, often to get the better of competitors, while the former is satisfied with his mediocre existence. In many case of non-pioneer niche-holders, there may not be effective competitors, or there may be enough demand to sustain several producers.

Problems of Women Enterprises

Women entrepreneurs engaged in manufacturing of readymade garments, food products, chemicals, furniture and fixtures, leather handicrafts, construction materials and service like printing, engineering job work etc. face problems related to following aspects:

1. ***Caste***
2. ***Encouragement from agencies and family members***
3. ***Location***: Influences job works and availability of materials. Transportation cost gets affected and marketing facilities, too. Due to location, sometimes, delay in securing power connection adversely affect the enterprise.
4. ***Management*** : Women entrepreneurs are able to complete the promotional procedures without seeking anybody's help rarely. They avail the help of government and professional agencies', family members' help in canvassing orders as well as for sales.
5. ***Investment***: They face problems in raising funds from long term borrowings from government agencies and banks, short term borrowings from commercial banks and other sources, if they do not get funding from their own family.
6. ***Assets***: Maximum investment of fixed assets is made for acquisition of plant and machinery followed by land and buildings. Most of the women entrepreneurs face problem of insufficiency with regard to land and building for carrying out their industrial and business operations. They also face the insufficiency of furniture and fittings.
7. ***Working Capital***: On an average, total current assets are less than total current liabilities. A large portion of the working capital comprised owned funds followed by the borrowings from commercial banks. Working capital problem is faced by many of entrepreneurs.
8. ***Return***: The lowest net profit ratio is observed in enterprises if non-operating incomes and non-operating expenses are quite negligible, whatever may be the nature of enterprise.
9. ***Financial support***: They face problems if they have to support their families without having any other source of income. This happens because they are charged with the high rates of interest, in term, shortage of funds.
10. ***Capacity utilization***: Sometimes lack of finance is major reason for under utilization of capacity. Competition and

lack of demand are other reasons for not utilizing capacity properly.

11. ***Inputs***: Scarcity and uncertaintly are major problems. In some enterprises lack of skilled labour is problems. Other problems regarding inputs are availability of power, dealing with labourers regarding high turnover and absenteeism and making use of the services of skilled labourers.

12. ***Credit facilities***: They make sales both on credit and cash basis. High prices, transport and scarcity of raw material create problem in adequate production.

13. ***Marketing***: Major portion of the products and services are marketed in district or state and no export. Debt clearance is not made by customers, increased competition inversely effects the problem.

14. ***Peculiar Problems:*** Travel for canvassing orders, purchasing raw materials and marketing the products are chief problems faced by women entrepreneurs *(Summarised by Khan, M.A. 1992).*

(i) Lack of proper space to run their enterprises.

(ii) Lack of capital and finance to purchase land, building, machinery, equipments, tools, furniture and fixtures etc.

(iii) Shortage of raw materials.

(iv) Problems of water, power, fuel and lubricant etc.

(v) Problem of industrial relations.

(vi) Problem of low capacity utilization due to lack of demand, lack of power, lack of finance, lack of raw materials and labour supply and strikes and lock out.

(vii) Lack of transportation facilities at normal rates.

(viii) Problem of marketing the products and services in India and abroad.

(ix) Cut throat competition with large scale and medium scale producers.

(x) Cumbersome procedure of import and export.

(xi) Shortage of working capital and development capital.

(xii) Lack of technical services given by small industries services institutes.

(xiii) High cost of production or the problem of cost escalation.

(xiv) Poor quality of products and services.

(xv) Poor working of incentives available to entrepreneurs in various states.

(xvi) Problem of identification, crystallization, construction and implementation of the project.

(xvii) Lack of efficient communication services or communication gap.

(xviii) The problem of growing industrial sickness.

(xix) Problem of infrastructure inadequacy.

(xx) Problem of technology, upgradation of the small-scale industries.

(xxi) Lack of proper advertisement and publicity to improve the image, prestige and goodwill.

(xxii) Problem of high taxes and duties.

(xxiii) Lack of proper legislation to protect the legitimate interests of small scale industries.

(xxiv) Poor working of various government agencies.

(xxv) Incentives have failed to achieve the aim of industrialization in backward area due to the absence of proper industrial infrastructure, shortage of potential and successful entrepreneurs and lack of skilled workers.

(xxvi) Step motherly or shabby treatment from the state government to new entrepreneurs.

(xxvii) Lack of proper facilities for research and development in entrepreneurship spheres.

(xxviii) Problem of transfer of technology.

(xxix) Problem of entrepreneurial mobility and migration from backward states to progressive states.

(xxx) Other snags faced by entrepreneurs.

Conclusion

This paper confirms the taxonomy to classify to women and men entrepreneurs, in general and problems faced by women entrepreneurs while raising and nurturing the enterprises, in particular. It is clear that women are trying their knowledge, intelligence, human and financial capital, zeal and courage to soothe the economic conditions of their-selves, thus their families. Still, there is a need to make an attempt by others to enhance the quality of enterprises drawn by them.

- Shortage of working capital and high rates of interest charged by banks needs to be made easier under Government directives.
- Time taken to have consideration for loans etc. should be reduced to minimum.
- Women entrepreneurs should be oriented to spend less on land and buildings, thus reducing initial investment.
- There is need to establish an agency with an autonomous status to supply plan and machinery to women's units on lease.
- There should be an agency structured for pooling and supplying the raw material requirements.
- Managerial and technical guidance should be extended to women entrepreneurs through orientation programmes.
- Promotion agencies should take greater interest in marketing the products of women's industrial units. Through displays and exhibitions during festival seasons can improve sales.
- The government and the entrepreneurs organizations and family determined agencies to solve the woes and teething problems should act towards solving "Growth problems of small scale units" in the country.

References

Archana, T.V. and Rehana, G., 1985. Achievement Motivation and Job Satisfaction. Productivity 24(3) 231-237, New Delhi.

Cole, A.M. 1959. Appeared in International Encyclopedia of Social Sciences. (On entreprenureship). Op.Ci.f., p.7.

Constantina Safilios Rothschild, 1974. Women and Social Policy Prentice Hall, New Jersey.

Devi, Lalitha, 1982. Status and employment of women in India. B.R. Publishing Corporation, Delhi.

Gaikwad and Tripathy, R.N. 1970. Socio-psychological factors influencing industrial entrepreneurship in rural areas. A case study in Tanuka region of West Godavari, A.P., Hyderabad.

Gulati, Leela, 1981. Profiles in females poverty. Hindustan Publishing Corporation, Delhi.

Jean Babtiste Say. In: David L. Shills. International Encyclopedia of Social Science, Ibid.

Khan, M.A. 1992. Entrepreneurial development programmes in India. Kanishka Publishing House, Delhi, p.265.

Maithreyi, Krishna Raj. 1980. Approaches to self-reliance for women: Some urban models. Research unit on women's studies. SNDT Women's University, Bombay.

Malada, M. 1985. Parent's Role in Entrepreneurship. In: Laghu Udyog Samachar. UMIFIN Courtesy.

Manimala, Mathew J. 1999. Entrepreneurial policies and strategies. The Innovator's Choice. Sage Publications, New Delhi.

Mathur, P. and Anamika, 1987. Difference of personality traits among male and female successful entrepreneurs. Presented In: 29th Annual Conference of Indian Academy. Applied Psychology, Waltaire, March.

Mehta, Vimla, 1979. Attitude of educated women towards social issues. National.

Nandrajog, S. In: Khan, M.A. 1992. Entrepreneurial development programmes in India. Kanishka Publishing House, Delhi. pp. 1-44.

Pareek, H.S. 1978. Financing of small industries in a developing economy. National.

Reif, W.E. *et al.*,1975. Exploding some myths about women managers. California Management Review (Summer). California.

Robert, D. Hisrich, 1985. The women entrepreneurs versus men entrepreneurs. Laxinagton Books, Torento.

Sarngadharan, M. and Beegam, S. Lesia, 1995. Women entrepreneurship: Institutional support and problems. Discovery Publishing House. Darya Gang, New Delhi.

Schumpeter, J.A. 1934. The theory of economic development. Cambridge, Harvard University Press.

Shah, Kalpana, 1984. Women's Liberation and voluntary action. Ajanta Publishers, New Delhi.

Sharma, K.L. 1975. Entrepreneurial performance in role perspective. Abhinav Publications, New Delhi.

Singh, N.P. and Sengupta, 1984. Potential women entrepreneurs their profile. Visions and motivations. NIESBUD, New Delhi.

Srinivas, M.N. 1976. The changing position of Indian women. Oxford University Press, Delhi.

Vepa, Ram K. 1983. Small Industry Development Programmes. IIPA, New Delhi.

Vinze, M.D. 1986. Women Entrepreneurs in India. Mittal Publications, Delhi.

17
Cultivating Entrepreneurship Education

Anjali Pahad,
Avani Maniar

Introduction

This paper attempts to highlight the importance of entrepreneurship education as 'a critical resource', for achieving sustainable economic growth of the country. Efforts should be made to promote and cultivate entrepreneurship education and higher level of education. The university system resources can be exploited for the same. The paper focuses on the factors contributing for the longevity of this education, vision for entrepreneurship education as a basic field of education.

Need for Entrepreneurship

India has reached at a crossroad where it is essential to have sustainable economic growth, but unfortunately alarming statistics of unemployed population is also on the rise. To combat this situation, the consideration of the ongoing new venture formation, continuing life long education and retraining of labour force are needed to be balanced. It is only with this balance, society can experience stable economic growth and low employment, leading to improved quality of life. Wherever the productivity increases, the new ventures need to be thought of so as to keep the labour force employed. This also demands for continuous education and training to support the system. To sustain the new venture formation society must see the births of new entrepreneurs which will sustain successfully. However to sustain the new entrepreneur much needed environmental needs should be created. Many efforts should be made at societies various levels, where a growing entrepreneur can be nurtured, trained and blossomed into a successful, profit making entrepreneur contributing to a economically sustainable society.

This calls for an additional responsibility on the shoulders of academicians of the educated class, the class which imparts education in the society. The educational institutes with their dearth of resources like planned curriculums, trained administrators, policy makers, extensive infrastructure, thoughtfully planned network with industries, growing bodies of research, grants etc. can definitely and should take up the responsibilities of promoting and cultivating entrepreneurship education.

The landscape of their stream of education varies from country to country. In some places in the west there is a rapid rise of such programmes which are fueled by unprecedented students demand for an education, which will provide them with the skills to succeed in today's dynamic and divergent business world.

At the same time there are examples of many developing countries where entrepreneurship is either not thought of an element to be included in the curricula or at the most just offered as elective course. But with the changing needs of the society, there is no doubt of its potential for longevity as an academic field. The various reasons contributory to this longevity are:

- An awareness about the entrepreneurship education.
- The academic recognition of this field.
- Establishment of the fact that "entrepreneurs are not always born, they can be taught".
- Increasing demand of entrepreneurship education courses.
- Die hard need of the young generation to be successful businessmen and churn money at the earliest and
- Growing research bodies on entrepreneurship education.

Traditional and Contemporary Approach

Entrepreneurship education is a field which lays emphasis on creativity, imagination, risk taking behaviour, qualitative approach. According to Rostadt (1985), these factors were missing in the traditional concept of this education. Traditionally, this field of education was not able to make up with the fast changing needs of the society (Chia, 1996). There are two school of thoughts. Those who are born entrepreneur and hence they can't be taught the personality traits necessary to take risk. This is the traditional approach and the other that even if one is not god gifted with skills of an entrepreneur, but can at least be taught to analyze those risks, involved in business to be analytical about their choices, if entrepreneurship cannot be taught, but the mechanics to start a business can be taught, practical knowledge regarding the business can be imparted. These are the contemporary thoughts.

In our own country, the professions are associated with caste one belongs to the Brahmins are the educators, the Kshatriyas are the warriors, the Baniyas are the businessmen and so on ...But are we still abiding by this caste system? Today the Tata's, Birla's, Ambani's are known by their success in their respective business and obviously not by their castes. Thus the traditional approach to this field of education is under great criticism due to under emphasis or the quantitative corporate technique rather than providing theoretical and quantitative skills primarily for students, who see their future with large co-operations.

However, it always takes some period of time to bring sea difference's in any system and so is the case of entrepreneurship education.

Presently our society is in great need of successful entrepreneurs. So as to enhance the economic growth of the country. In order to do so, developing research and educational programmes with an aim of improving entrepreneurship education would have a desirable effect.

Universities can and should be definitely involved in this process of graduating successful entrepreneurs.

Envisioning Entrepreneurship Education

If our society has to attain a status of sustainable economic growth then entrepreneurship education should be provided to those who have entrepreneurial talent or who are interested to develop skills in the same. Opportunities have to be developed in the form of the courses which emphasize the skills and knowledge needed to enter business world.

According to Porter, L. (1994), the courses should be planned for imparting skills and knowledge needed to be an entrepreneur. The course formats should be more informal in nature and should focus on hand on experiences to be entrepreneurs. Skills and content of entrepreneurship course should emphasize.

- Analytical thinking
- Thinking about entrepreneurship as a career that allows multiple ventures.
- Creativity skills.
- Venture strategy and evaluation skills.
- Networking deal making and harvesting skills.
- Personal ethical assessments.
- Use of experts who are experienced entrepreneurs.

A website of Babson college Arthur M. Blank emphases that among entrepreneurial courses the general format which is fairly a standard format includes:

- Concept of entrepreneurship
- Characteristic of an entrepreneur
- Value of entrepreneurship
- Building a business
- Assessing opportunities
- Developing an idea
- Finding the capital
- Starting up the business
- Managing a business

With these concepts in the course on entrepreneurship education one would be able to develop competencies required to become eligible to be an entrepreneur.

A wide variety of curricular approaches other than above are available and exist though many common elements are found across various institutions and settings.

However to envision programmes to promote and cultivate entrepreneurship education following points should be focused upon:

- Well planned curriculum providing sound knowledge and skills should be designed.
- Well co-ordinated internship programme should be planned to impart hand-on experiences to students necessary to fully absorb classroom learning.
- Comprehensive set of seminars and workshops should be held both for students and teachers to gain insight into the recent developments in the field.
- Developing a system to facilitate access to funding sources.
- Creating research facilities to serve as a link between academic and the business world for the documentation to provide basis for further research in new venture formation.
- Sponsoring the exciting business plan competition to attract the attention of prospective entrepreneurs.

Thus, the above mentioned ambitious agenda if adopted religiously can prove effective to establish the longevity of entrepreneurship education and create sustainability of the same as a basic field of education. As Kourilsky (1996) summarized: "In response to the rapidly changing national landscape, not only of employment but more generally of economic growth and job creation entrepreneurship is being increasingly emphasized as a critical resource.

Conclusion

The need of the hour is to have sustainable economic growth, for which new venture formation, continuous life long education are needed. This can be solved by seeing the birth of new entrepreneurs. Efforts should be made at university level, through proper utilization of resource like administrators, teachers, grants and infrastructures. Courses should be planned in entrepreneurship education, emphasising on the concepts of entrepreneurship skills and knowledge required to be an entrepreneur. Thus, good competency based courses should be designed and made available to promote and cultivate entrepreneurship education at higher level of education. This will ultimately help in increasing the economic growth of the country.

References

Chia 1996. Teaching paradigm shifting in Management Education: Journal of Management Studies. (C96660).

Kourilsky, M.L. 1996. Opportunity in search of a curriculum. Kansas city. Eming Marion Kauffmon Foundation.

Lord, M. 1999. Attention, aspiring capitalists B-school students are studying entrepreneurship; U.S. News Online at usnews.com (C992600).

Porter, L. (1994). The relation of entrepreneurship education to business education simulation and gaming (C96664).

18

Women Entrepreneurs: Problems and Difficulties

Shilpa Kapadia,
Shetal Barodia

Definition

The word "Entrepreneur" is derived from the French verb entrepredr which means to undertake. An Entrepreneur is an individual with knowledge, skills, initiative, drive and spirit of innovation who aims at achieving goals. An Entrepreneur is an economic agent who plays a vital role in the economic development of a country, (Kumar, Poornima, Abraham and Jayashree, 2003).

Women Entrepreneurs

Since the past two decades there has been a gradual change in the status of women in most of the developing countries.

Women are discovering themselves and trying to create a niche for themselves in all fields.

In order to improve their living conditions and increase their income there is an increase in the number of women seeking employment. Women are often the main economic agents to ensure the survival of a poor family, hence, increase in the number of women entrepreneurs assumes critical importance. There is a growing awareness among women to start their own business and to be self employed. There is a wide scope for women's economic empowerment if they are led towards entrepreneurship, thus becoming not "job seekers" but "job creators" (ICECD, 1997).

The term "women entrepreneur" deals with that section of the female population who venture out into industrial activities, i.e., manufacturing, assembling, job works, repairs/servicing and other business (Shukla, 2003). Women are venturing out in all fields and leading enterprises like electronic, multimedias, garments, catering business etc.

However, women have to face many obstacles to build in their social status. They have to work much harder than men before establishing a successful business. The problems faced by women are manifold like finance, personnel, social, psychological and others.

Financial Problems

Obtaining finance to start a business is one of the major problems faced by women. In our society males have power over women through control of property and household income (Shah & Pathak, 1994). Since female economic independence is limited this leads to lower status in relation to man and acts as a problem in approaching banks and financial institutions for loans. Banks view women applicants as high risk compared to men as they do not have faith that they will be able to repay the loan. As women lack the basic capital or any assets they have nothing to fall back on in case they are not successful in their businesses. For some reasons the banks do not have faith in women entrepreneurial abilities.

Also family members and friends hesitate to sign as guarantors for women as they are not sure about whether the woman will be successful in her business. In case the business falls apart they will have the responsibility of repaying the loan.

Lack of Education and Technical Knowledge/Skills

Women from rural and urban slum areas often lack adequate education to venture out on their own. They are unclear about the procedure for initiating a business i.e. whom to approach for finance, infrastructure needed in order to start on their own, manpower etc. They lack technical knowledge/skills and even if they do have the skills they are not aware of it, or are unable to put them to use. For example, in a project conducted by the Continuing Adult Education, the M.S. University of Baroda on "Bankable Schemes for Women", there were two women who were very good in preparing simple decorative items from beads, yet they could not think in terms of undergoing training in making jewellary from beads and starting their own business. Thus, women often lack the knowledge and initiative to undergo training to enhance or learn new skills.

Social Problems

In our society, economic independence of women may be regarded as disruption family life. Many women face problems at home i.e. either the husband, in-laws or other family members are not happy to see women venture out on their own. Women are discouraged from being involved in self employment or entrepreneurial ventures (Shah & Pathak, 1994). The family members feel that the household work will suffer and also, the women will be away for long hours from home. Interacting with other men and outsiders is always viewed suspiciously, resulting in insecurity of the family members. Starting their own business also requires the women to travel and many times saddled with small children they are not comfortable going out. Family members usually do not like the idea of women becoming independent and self reliant, and thus powerful.

Psychological Problems

Many women have low self esteem and lack in self confidence to venture out on their own. Whatever they do, is always viewed with an eagle eye by people around them. This makes them self conscious and more prone to making mistakes. They are not sure about their abilities and skills and there always lurks the fear of failure in undertaking any business.

They lack the ability and desire to take a risk which is one of the traits needed to become an entrepreneur. Women on the whole are accorded an inferior status in society and hence they lack an initiative to do something.

Lacking of High Achievement Motivation

Many women lack the achievement motivation to do something on their own. They lack the desire to do something new, be it undergoing specific training in any field or starting their own business. They do not have the experience or background and are not encouraged by family members, banks or financial institutions to grow in life. In a project conducted by the Continuing Adult Education in Gotri Community, many women were very good in stitching and stitched all the clothes of their family members. However, even though they were approached by outsiders to stitch for them, these women did not want to do so. They lacked initiative and did not want to stitch clothes for others, earn more money and generally, improve their life. They did not see themselves as major wage earners of the family.

Other Problems

Hunting for resources to start a business and approaching the correct people is another problem faced by women. At times the quality of the product is not maintained which lands the women into problems, i.e., in a business started by women on garments, the colors were not fast and were bleeding. The person who had bought the dress leaked this information to others and people were reluctant to approach the women. Many times their businesses do not take off because they lack a standard trademark. Often people do not buy products which are not branded, even though they are of good quality. Hence, marketing skills are necessary to sell the product. Women, often do not know how to market their products, advertise it and sell it to people, and are stuck with the products themselves.

Also, often government policies keep on changing which affects the business. In one such case, a woman had started fertilizer business and was doing fine until the Government started selling the same product at a subsidized rate. Thus, resulting in a loss as nobody bought fertilizers from these women.

Women go through manifold problems and attempts should be made by all to help them overcome the problems. The government and banks on their part should encourage women to obtain loans and become self employed. The government should provide the necessary environment for entrepreneurship growth. There should be less government formalities and more encouragement from them.

The rate of interest of the banks should be low, there should be more vocational training programmes for women, introducing new skills and technical knowledge and enhancing skills they already possess.

The family members should encourage women to better their lives as well as that of the family by encouraging them to start their own businesses. Rather than creating obstacles they should help the women at home as well as in business.

Once all the problems are soothed out there is no looking back at all. Women are capable of being as good, or even better than men in business. If formal training is imparted to women they could acquire skills required and can contribute in a big way to the nations prosperity. Given the right opportunities and encouragement they will be very successful and eventually overcome all the problems.

References

Shah, H. and Pathak, C.H. 1994. *Group Entrepreneurship for Rural Women. Trainers Manual.* International Centre for Entrepreneurship and Career Development. Ahmedabad: Marm Communications.

Shukla, M.B. 2003. *Entrepreneurship and small Business Management.* Allahabad: Kitab Mahal.

International Centre for Entrepreneurship and Career Development 1997. *Out of the shadows in to the line,* Ahmedabad; Mass Communications.

Kumar, S.A., Poornima, S.C., Abraham, M.K., and Jayashree, K. 2003. *Entrepreneurship Development.* New Delhi; New Age International (P) Limited Publishers.

19
Women Entrepreneurship

Varsha Parikh

Introduction

Education has to be a process which prepares the student to learn to develop a way of thinking, that is know how to seek information, know the sources for obtaining it, how to sort out the information, analyse it and make meaning out of it for conceptualisation and application (As said by Dr. A.S. Desai, Former Chair person, University Grants Commission, Excerpts).

The Indian view of education aims at an even higher ideal which seeks to equip the students for the task of not only nation building, but also world-building. This ideal is far more relevant today in the age of globalisation than it ever was in the past. At no time in history has the world been so inter-connected and inter-independent as it is today in the age of globalisation. The problems being faced by people in different parts of the world are becoming increasingly common. The convergence of the local and global is true not only for problems in the economic sphere but also visible even into culture, religion and social customs.

Universities in modern India have been by and large an intellectual, academic and administrative product of the British imperial regime and the country was subject to for about a hundred and fifty years. Universities in India represent a very vital nation building enterprise. As said by Thomas Jefferson "Every generation needs a new revolution". Change is going to be the only constant thing. In a dynamic society change is bound to be a part of life. We should learn to manage the change and lead the change.

Innovation and entrepreneurship are required in a changing society not only in the business sector but also in academic institutions, as they are flexible, and self renewing for a society. Innovation and entrepreneurship are focused on opportunity and need and therefore, have to become an integral part of our life.

Academic Entrepreneurship Refers to the Empowerment of Academicians to Design, Develop and Implement the Need Based Programs

In the contemporary society, various *reasons* like to cater to the changing needs of the industries, to reduce the lead time in the procedure, to empower the academicians, to develop innovative and non-conventional courses and many more highlight the *need for Academic entrepreneurship.* Though entrepreneurship is the lifeblood of any economy, more so in the developing economy. Not only that Entrepreneurial development and management has come to be recognised globally as the key to rapid and sustainable economic development the foundation of effective entrepreneurial development and management needs to be determined and make known from the academic institution itself.

A Paradigm Shift

Universities are primarily a power house that fires the imagination of the youth of the country to embark upon a journey of adventure into the unknown. A country of the size of India, with its enormous potential in the form of its human resource, cannot remain condemned to a 'developing' status for long. Emancipation from it lies in super-education that its universities should offer through their metamorphosis into entrepreneurial agencies of human resource development. This of course, would need a paradigm shift from abject conformity to aggressive entrepreneurship in all respects, for entrepreneurship it is the clear call of the age of the globalisation.

Most significant ingredients of entrepreneurship in higher education are viz.:

- Strategic thinking in respect of curriculum designing, methods and media development etc.

- Flexibility in course offering and in others.
- Risk taking in adopting unconventional initiatives in academics and many more.
- Networking in respect of human resource, technology etc.
- Proactive functioning in goal setting, course planning and transaction etc.
- Benchmarking with reference to methods and materials, especially of knowledge and learning.
- Focussing program, innovations, achievements.
- Debureaucratising all its dealings at all levels with people, students, their parents, teachers.
- Quality assurance with academics, research.
- Funding both autonomous and responsible ensuring cost-effective strategies that must promote self reliance to a large degree by adopting self financing projects.

Indian universities should benchmark universities with the entrepreneurial universities of other countries like Europe, U.K who have already launched this movement.

Academician and Entrepreneurship

To develop entrepreneurship among academician the universities and colleges should create a conducive environment that promotes such qualities as initiative, persistence, information seeking attitude, opportunity sensing, concern for quality work, commitment, efficiency orientation, problem solving ability, assertiveness, self-confidence, communication skill, creativity, risk bearing capacity and capacity to manage stress. Entrepreneurs are those who learn and listen, take risk and responsibility, know their own uniqueness, innovative and creative in their own way free from fear of failure or success always add value in what they do or produce and have achievement motivation. They are essentially doers and achievers, adaptable winners and dreamers. Hence the universities and colleges which are public service institutions, required to be as innovative and entrepreneurial as any business/

industrial establishment. The rapid changes occuring in the society technology and economy are both a threat and greater opportunity for them.

Academic institutions should not remain teaching shops but grow into centres of professional excellence and corporate cultured enterprise. Industry and business should support these institutions through interaction and financial help to make them academic enterprises.

Conclusion

The university must create a climate for change to happen. The human environment is the largest contributor to impacting on learning. In a fast changing competitive environment, a public service institution cannot afford to be away from promoting academic entrepreneurship. The development of academic entrepreneurship in educational institutions will play a significant role in building a strong base for our country. The preservice or induction training programs, continuing education, short-term courses on entrepreneurship and such other measures would go a long way in promoting academic entrepreneurship. The divorce between academician and business/industry has resulted discouraging academic entrepreneurship in India. In a knowledge based economy of the twenty first century, we have hardly any option other than to promote 'Academic Entrepreneurship' which also calls for developing leadership qualities that would result in excellence in education sector.

References

Desai, Vasant, Dynamics of Entrepreneurial Development and Management, Himalaya Publishing House, 2000.

Kalkundrikar, A.B., Charninath, P.M., Academic Entrepreneurship, University News, March 2001, Vol. 39, pp. 1-3.

Ghanchi, D.A., Entrepreneurial Orientation to University Management in India, University News, December 1999, Vol. 36, pp. 1-4.

20
Entrepreneurial Competencies

Bishnupriya Dasgupta

Entrepreneurial activities may be classified into two major categories:

(a) Entrepreneurial Tasks, such as setting up business, planning, team-building and marketing (including promotional activities),

(b) Custodian Tasks, such as purchasing, managing finance, supervising production, managing conflicts.

Entrepreneurial Tasks are less delegable than are custodian Tasks. In the formative stage the entrepreneur has to handle both types of Tasks. Subsequently however, it may be advisable that he starts delegating custodial tasks to the extent possible to hired professionals, without loosing control. In accordance to the 80/20 principle (achieving 80% result with 20% effort), an entrepreneur must resist the temptation of achieving perfection in executing each task all by himself, and delegate skilled Custodial tasks to managers. He/she should rather concentrate on Entrepreneurial Tasks that need vision and creativity.

Personnel Management

As the organization evolves, the entrepreneur assumes the role of key visible interface between the company and the outside world. To fulfill this role effectively, a small entrepreneur has to delegate 'Custodial tasks' to three or four senior executives (directly reporting to him). A typical organizational structure includes experienced managers, assuming independent responsibilities in well-defined portfolio such as Finance, Operations (production, purchase, etc.), Sates/Marketing,

Engineering. However there must be enough flexibility in such structure and system. While recruiting personnel in such key positions, especially in the small-scale sector it is difficult to generalize whether stress should be given to experience or to talent. In most cases it may be preferable to choose a talented (but relatively less experienced) person over senior, experienced one.

It is important to maintain an optimum climate of creativity in the organization, without over doing it. New ideas must be elicited, evolved impartially and implemented as warranted, as in brainstorming technique. Due recognition/reward must be awarded to the inventor (originator of the idea) and the innovator (one who implements it successfully). Awards may be in terms of cash or even through simple acknowledgement.

Enough attention must be given to pay-structure, financial incentives (such as bonus, commission, profit sharing, stock options) and other perquisites (such as leave, group insurance). Employees must be paid accounting to their market worth and not less. Other areas in which small new firms may compete favorably with large, established ones are in offering flexibility in working hours and hiring retired people. A formal interview strategy is always beneficial while recruiting, with precise job descriptions.

The most important resource of any company is its people. It is important to match the hiring of people to the actual job, it is fallacy to hire for future needs at the formative stage. Comprehensive programs for training and motivation should follow. The entrepreneur must pay special attention to create compensation and incentive packages, managing conflicts within the team, maintaining a creative climate and weed out people with negative contribution.

Time Management

Few people in our society work harder than entrepreneurs, many big business executives put in long hours too, but entrepreneurs seem to put in even longer hours, driven by their desire to excel.

It is very important for every entrepreneur to manage his/her time effectively through conservation of his energy and proper organization in the use of his time. Without proper planning, an entrepreneur often ends up getting exhausted and losses the vitality necessary to get customers excited and employees inspired. Several techniques may be employed to manage one's time well. There include:

1. Reserving hours best suited for creative work (according to ones own creative cycle).
2. Incorporating small attainable goals in planning of daily schedules.
3. One must not become a slave to the telephone.
4. Batching of meetings, travel, and correspondence helps in utilizing time to the optimum.
5. One must not overdo priorities.
6. Time must be set aside for thinking and planning.
7. Get regular exercise.
8. Get out of office/home for focused work, meet new people, get fresh ideas.
9. Use the principle of Enlightened Procrastination.

The entrepreneur must instill in his employees a sense of day-to-day urgency to get the allotted task done on time, to enlist their commitment and pride in making sure it happens. An employee should be judged on the output (task completed on time), and not input (working hours spent). Other methods to help people meet their goals include.

1. Written schedule and progress review.
2. Flexitime
3. Off-site meetings (in a pleasant environment).

Negotiation

Negotiating skill is the crux of enterprise management. It is vital to the success of any enterprise. In the early stages of operations in a new company, the entrepreneur has to carry out negotiations with every one he deals with.

In any business negotiation, both parties must perceive some potential benefit from the deal. It is therefore, important to strive towards a higher trade off curve in a win-win situation. It is not wise to extract an agreement under duress, nor assume a prematurely frozen position (take-it or leave-it).

Concerted effort must be made to learn in advance about the basic facts and profile of the negotiating individual and the organization. Additional advance preparation in visualizing the meeting, anticipatory objections and preparing counter arguments, and working out the detailed arrangement for the meeting helps in the long run.

Management of Fixed Assets

Unwisely capital expenditure is a major contributing factor in the failure of any new enterprise. Tying up capital in non-essential plant and machinery, frequently results in shortage of cheap working capital needed in other areas such as promotion, inventory and product development. Specialized equipment may be detrimental in switching over to other products. Apparent cost savings due to improved expensive machinery is often illusionary. Hidden costs must be cautiously identified, especially in an elaborate plant.

In order to reduce the fixed cost and maximize variable cost, following options may be considered.

1. Buying the product wholly or in components.
2. Producing through job working in other's plant.
3. Equipment/Premises to be taken on lease.

Financial Management

The entrepreneur must give greatest importance to planning cash-flow and guard it jealously. Failure to honor financial commitment is very serious and may even lead to bankruptcy. Proper method must be adopted to balance expenditure against receivables. Collection problems must be attended as soon as they occur. Major cash payments must be scheduled so that the aggregate does not hide reality. Financial planning must be done six months ahead, reviewed and updated weekly. Cash shortage must be foreseen well in advance and corrective action must be taken immediately.

Contingency planning should be ready against likely delayed payments or growth rates faster than anticipated. When one of these actually happen, investors should be kept informed. It is imperative for a new entrepreneur to be able to establish his/her credibility by keeping schedule and hitting early targets.

Budget and Control

It is important that even new ventures establish quickly some form of formal budgeting that connects tasks to the executing business plans with some organizational goals.

As a tool to implement business plan, a budget should clearly draw the limits of money and time to be spent for each conceived activity. It should also define the executing authority and limits of money/time for each specified task. Thus it becomes a tool for communication to all concerned, the quantitative statement of the enterprise's priorities and executing authorities.

By considering in advance the need to spend money for each class of expenditure, and through quantitative estimation of each need, a budget acts as an effective tool for cost control. However, the budget should have enough detail so that inefficiency in one area does not get hidden by saving in another. The assessment of the ability to meet goals on budget becomes a key tool for appraisal of an employee's performance.

Marketing and Selling

Selling is the central activity of any business enterprise. The top-line of monthly profit and loss statement consists of the value of dispatches during the period. This is the base of the entire business plan, the yardstick against which the enterprise will be measured. However when the selling is carried out through an independent sales organization (selling agent) it is often seen that the agent is actually taking the cream, i.e. higher gross margin and net profit than the manufacturer himself.

As the adage goes 'nothing happens unless you get the purchase order'. However, a lot of groundwork has to be done to make it happen. Selling is in fact a subset of marketing, other functions being market research, product specification, pricing policy, literature, advertising and publicity, technical services and support, analysis of competition and selection of sales channels. It is not wise to undermine the value of market research and other activities as 'fancy'. A little effort may yield enormous returns of information and increase credibility.

The first step in marketing program is identification, measurement and determination of the need for the product. It is vital to gather the following information:

1. Unique advantage of the product over the competitors and quantifiable benefits. How much was the customer willing to pay for it.
2. Size and rate of growth of the targeted market versus competition. If the market is large and varied which segment/class and customer/location will be concentrated upon.
3. Current selling/distribution arrangement and buying habits of customers.

Market information may be obtained from some common sources like

1. Library research, trade journals, research reports, published statistics etc.
2. Questionnaire survey, professional market survey.
3. Experts in the field, trade association, business and credit service.

In addition to the above, utmost importance must be given to gather information on technology available/employed, availability of raw materials and infrastructure etc., which is beyond the ambit of traditional market research.

References

Baty, B.G. "Entrepreneurship for the Nineties" 1990. Prentice Hall, Inc., New Jersey.

Bireley, S., Muzyka, F.D. "Mastering Enterprise" 1997, Pitman Publishing, Pearson Professional Limited, London.

Taneja, S., Gupta, S.L. "Entrepreneur Development" New Venture Creation, 2001, Galgotia Publishing Company. New Delhi.

Siropolis, N. "Entrepreneurship and Small Business Management" Sixth edition India Haoughton.

Mifflin Company Boston New York 1998 Education Publishers Chennai. All Publishers and Distributors Redg.

21
Institutional Support for Women Entrepreneurs

Sarjoo Patel,
Vrushali Datar,
Veena Gandotra,
Ms. Sonia Thakur

Institutional Support

During the last few years, a lot has been done in the country to develop new women entrepreneurs through training, and at present most of the states are involved in WED (Women Entrepreneurship Development) programming and SEP/IGP (Self Employment and Income Generation Programmes). A number of institutions/agencies are rendering assistance to women entrepreneurs by giving training, providing financial assistance and marketing assistance.

National Level Standing Committee on Women Entrepreneurs

A National Level Standing Committee on Women Entrepreneurs was constituted under the chairmanship of the Minister of State for Sports, Youth Affairs, Women and Child Welfare to look into the problems of women entrepreneurs and evolve policies for promotion of entrepreneurship among women in the country. The committee is represented by all agencies connected with the entrepreneurship development, women entrepreneurs and officials.

The committee has evolved certain policies for the promotion of entrepreneurship amongst women. The committee has also recommended a definition of women entrepreneurs, which has been subsequently adopted by small scale Industries Board. A women's cell has also been functioning in the office of the DC (SSI) to attend to the problems faced by them and to provide necessary liaison. A model syllabus has been developed for conducting exclusive programmes for women under different categories including tiny units.

Small Industries Development Organisation (SIDO)

It is an apex body which formulates, coordinates as well as monitors the policies and programmes for promotion and development of small-scale industries in the country both at central and state level. It maintains close liaison with central ministries, Planning Commission, State Governments, Financial Institutions, voluntary organisations and other agencies concerned with the development of small-scale industries. The activities of SIDO exclude those which fall within the purview of specialised Board such as all India Handloom, Handicrafts, Sericulture, Coir boards, and Khadi and Village Industries Commission.

The office of the Development Commissioner (Small Scale Industries) headed by the Development Commissioner (SSI) and ex-officio Additional Secretary, is an attached office of the Ministry of Industry. Office of the DC (SSI) is commonly called as SIDO.

Functions

It provides a comprehensive range of extension services ranging from selection of suitable line of production to marketing of the final products. These services are provided through a network of small Industries Service Institutes, Branch Institutes Extension Centres and Regional Testing Centres, Products wise Process Development Centres, Central Footwear Training Centres Production Centres and Field Testing Stations in areas of concentration of specific types of industries. In addition, there are also specialised institutions which provide training and technical services in specialized fields. They are as under:

1. Central Institute of Tool Design, Hyderabad.
2. Central Tool Room and Training Centres at Ludhiana and Calcutta.

3. Central Institute of Hand Tools, Jalandhar.
4. Institute for Design of Electrical Measuring Instruments (IDEMI), Bombay.
5. Integrated Training Centre, Nilodheri.
6. National Institute for Entrepreneurship and Small Business Development (NIESBUD), New Deihi.
7. Product-cum-Process Development Centres (Foundry and Forging at Agra and Sports Goods and Leisure Time Equipment at Meerut).
8. Electronic Service and Training Centre, Ramnagar.

National Institute for Entrepreneurship and Small Business Development (NIESBUD)

It was established in 1983 by the Ministry of Industry, Government of India, as an apex body for coordinating and overseeing the activities of various institutions / agencies in entrepreneurship development, particularly in the area of small industry and small business. The institute is also the secretariat for the National Entrepreneurship Development Board (NEDB), the apex body which determines policy for entrepreneurship development in the country. The institute, thus, performs the task of processing the recommendations made by the board. The activities of NIESBUD are as under:

The institute organises training programmes for different categories like, Trainers Training Programmes, Small Business Promoters Programme, Top Executive Orientation Programmes or General EDP's for women, Defence of SE's beneficiaries etc.

- The institute evolves model syllabi for the training of various target groups. It formulates standardized procedures of identification and selection of potential entrepreneurs.
- It prepares training aid materials like manuals, video films, learning texts, handbooks, lesson plans, cases, etc.
- Evolve standardized materials, processes and vital research publication. The institute conducts researches on topics related to entrepreneurship and widely

disseminates the findings. Status Analysis Study on Entrepreneurship in India, potential women entrepreneurship in India, successful women entrepreneurs their identity expectations and problems, etc. are some of the notable research publications of the institute. Periodical directory of experts, reports based on different studies, newsletters covering topics like new products, processes and technology, agency profile, entrepreneurial profile, etc. are also published.

Entrepreneurship Development Institute (EDI)

It is the first of its kind in Asia and was set up in May, 1983 at Ahmedabad by All India Financial Institutions, Industrial Development Bank of India, Industrial Credit and Investment Corporation of India, Industrial Finance Corporation of India, and the State Bank of India.

- The institute conducts result-oriented Entrepreneur Development Programmes in a systematic and methodical manner, which are so designed to suit the intellectual level and socio-economic background of target group.
- Special EDPs are conducted for target groups, science and technology graduates, women, for rural self-employment and existing entrepreneurs.

EDI also provides expertise for choosing prospective projects and offers achievement motivation training (AMT). Women are treated as a speentrepreneurial development.

National Institute of Small Industries Extension Training, Hyderabad (NIESIET)

The Government of India established an institution known as the small industry extention training institute (SIET) in 1960 under the Ministry of Industry for promotion and development of small industries. The institute has been raised to the level of National Institute and renamed as National Institute of Small Industry Extension Training (NISIET) from September, 1984.

The institute is conducting training programmes in the area of development, promotion and management of small, rural and artisan industries including entrepreneurship development, preparation of feasibility reports, project reports, project management, financing, self-infrastructural planning, marketing, information storage and retrieval systems, training methods etc. and state government departments/organisations, financial and other promotional institutions in their programmes for small industry development. Some studies on women entrepreneurs based on the EDP programmes for them are being done by the institute.

National Research Development Corporation of India

It is a Government of India enterprise established in December 1953 as a non-profit organisation, under Section 25 of the Companies Act. It is a repository of indigenous technologies and inventions. The corporation is engaged in the development and promotion of appropriate technologies, and in carrying the same to rural areas for improving the quality of life of the weaker sections of the population. Realising that economic independence would accelerate the improvement in the status of women. NRDC is also promoting technologies, which are appropriate for women. The corporation has brought out a publication, which serves as a ready reference for women entrepreneurs and voluntary agencies working for the uplift of women in India.

Small Industries Development Bank of India (SIDBI)

- provides training and extention services support to women entrepreneurs according to their skill and socio-economic status;
- extends financial assistance on concessional terms to enable them to set up industrial units in the small scale sector;
- the programmes for training, consultancy support and extension services for women entrepreneurs are organised through designated agency, such as Technical Consultancy Organisations, Entrepreneurship Development Institute of India, Central; State Social

Welfare boards, KVIC or other recognised training and management institutes under Mahila Udyam Nidhi scheme SIDBI provides;

- equity type assistance to women entrepreneurs who set up new industrial projects in small scale sector.
- the eligible units are all new industrial projects in the Small Scale Sector as also service activities which are eligible for finance as per SSI norms set up by women entrepreneurs, would be eligible for assistance under the Scheme provided the cost of the project does not exceed Rs.10 lakh.

National Small Industries Corporation (NSIC)

- The corporation provides industrial finance by way of supply of machines on hire purchase to small industrial units all over the country.
- The corporation envisages larger markets for the products of small-scale industries.
- Ensures availability of certain scarce raw materials, indigenous as well as imported.

State Bank of India

The State Bank of India offers several schemes suitable for women entrepreneurs. The bank has a number of schemes for financing small-scale industries. The liberalized scheme caters to all the financial needs of SSI entrepreneurs, viz. term loans, cash credit for working capital, letters of credit, bank guarantees, packing credits for exports, etc. In addition to this the Bank has special schemes for SSI units, viz. Entrepreneur scheme and equity fund scheme where loans can be given at a very low/nil margin to technically qualified and experienced persons. The *Equity Fund Scheme* provides equity support to needy small-scale units by way of interest free long-term loans repayable over a period of 5 to 7 years after a moratorium of 5 to 7 years. To make the assistance to women entrepreneurs more effective and ensure a wide coverage, the banks have consolidated the above schemes under the recent introduced *Sthree Shakti* package. This involves a financial package aimed at reinforcing the Bank's efforts in the area of developing entrepreneurship among women. Concession in respect to margin and rate of interest has been built into this package. A 5 per cent reduction in margin for all categories of advance, and concession in the rate of interest varying from 0.5 per cent to 1.5 per cent are the two distinct benefits of this package. Also envisaged in the package are Entrepreneurship Development programmes, designed exclusively for providing entrepreneurial and managerial skills to those women entrepreneurs who have no formal training on exposure to business, thereby to put them on a sound footing. These programmes are free of cost. A beginning has already been made in this direction.

Industrial Development Bank of India (IDBI)

The IDBI has floated a special scheme for women entrepreneurs with twin objectives namely, (1) to provide training and extension services support to women entrepreneurs through a comprehensive package suited to their skills and socio-economic status, and (2) to extend financial assistance on concessional terms to enable women entrepreneurs to set up industrial units in the small scale sector. These programmes (EDPs) for women are to be organised through recognised institutions such as TCO, EDI, Khadi Village Industries Commission (KVIC), voluntary agencies, etc. The IDBI provides assistance upto Rs. 10,000 per women trainee, an amount expected to take care of training, stipends, cost, of course material, market visits, consultancies, post-training follow-up and escort services. The IDBI has set up a new fund of Rs.5 crores called *Mahila Udyam Vidhi Scheme* to provide seed capital assistance to women entrepreneurs.

IFCI Scheme of Interest Subsidy for Women Entrepreneurs

The main objective of the scheme is to provide incentives to women having business acumen and entrepreneurial skills so that avenue of self-development and self-employment are created for them. The scheme covers all industrial projects, whether in rural, cottage tiny or small-scale (including ancillary) sectors (with project cost upto Rs.10 lakh), if set up by a woman entrepreneur, on her own with the minimum financial stake of 51 per cent in the unit. Eligibility conditions for availing the subsidy under the scheme are as follows:

- She should have preferably (though not necessarily) undergone a full course of an entrepreneurship development programme (EDP).
- She should be unemployed before taking up the industrial venture and after taking up the industrial venture should not have engaged herself on a part time or full time basis in any other business, trade, profession or vocation.
- The enterprise should be owned and administered by the woman entrepreneur herself with a minimum financial interest 51 percent in the share capital of the venture and must be giving at least 50 percent of the employment generated in the enterprise to women.
- The industrial venture undertaken should be her first venture and she should be devoting full time to her venture.
- She must have been sanctioned and disbursed financial assistance by and SFC or a sate level financial institution performing the role of SFC or a bank for block capital/ meeting capital cost of the project.

National Association of Women Entrepreneur and Executives

The National Association of Women Entrepreneurs and Executives (NAWEE) is an all India body, which is nonpolitical, non-profit, membership organisation. It performs the following functions.

- Acts as a clearinghouse on problems and opportunities facing women entrepreneurs and executives of all levels and to assist them in their self-development and protection.
- Acts as a Training and Development Institute so as to further equip women to be able to meet the various challenges in their respective environments.

- Works closely with industries and organisations concerned with women entrepreneurs and executives in establishing benchmarks on successful operations through research and analysis.
- Establishes hostels, dormitories and apartment facilities for women entrepreneurs and executives and provide any other facility required for such working women.
- The assistance under the schemes will be in the form of one time subsidy, determinable on a case to case basis, and will be equivalent to the amount of interest payable by the industrial unit set up by the women entrepreneur(s) to the SFC or the state level financial institutions performing the role of SFC or bank, for the loan assistance dispersed for the project for a period of one year, subject to a ceiling of Rs. 20,000 per annum, provided the unit is promoted wholly by a women entrepreneur and there is no other corporate investment, otherwise.

On review of the functions of various institutes listed above, it was observed that there exists no separate institution exclusively dedicated to the promotion of women entrepreneurs. Various institutes formulated for general entrepreneurial development and assistance were also operating separate schemes for women entrepreneurs. However women entrepreneurs receive more attention and additional concessions than general entrepreneurs in the small-scale sectors.

Suggested areas as Suitable to Indian Women Entrepreneurs

A woman should consider her family background, education, attitude and skill she has acquired. She cannot venture totally in a new area. Following are the suggested areas where uneducated women can venture:

- Aggarbatti manufacturing
- Papad making
- Embroidery

- Handicrafts
- Catering service
- Pickle manufacturing
- Milk distribution
- Small retail shops

The following are some of the entrepreneurship programmes for women graduates:

- Catering
- Confectionery, ice cream parlours and bakery
- Preservation
- Fast foods/salad bar
- Guidance centers
- For keeping fit-management of obesity
- Hobby centers
- Interior enrichment units
- Grooming centers-providing hair/skin care-to select jewellery/hair style/face make up.
- Fashion Designing
- Readymade Garments
- Dyeing and dry-cleaning units
- Computer aided designing
- Child care/crèches
- Guidance and counseling cells
- Old age homes
- Rehabilitation centers for children with special needs
- Hospital management
- Assembling of watches, radio, transistors, telephones, computer and other such modern gadgets.
- Running advertisement services.
- Stationery items – manufacturing and selling
- Xeroxing, typewriting and computer services

- Telecommunication and fax, operation services
- Maintenance of dairy, poultry and related products
- Hulling and flouring machine operation and service

Problems Faced by Women Entrepreneurs

Apart from the general problems confronting the entrepreneurs, a woman who aspires to become an entrepreneur is faced with some specific problems.

1. ***Family related:*** In India, a woman has to perform her family duties irrespective of her career as a working woman or an entrepreneur. She is in a continuous conflict between the household and business work performed by her. Biasness towards any one of them creates problems for her. If she is in a joint family she may get help of the other family members to shoulder family responsibilities. In addition she may get their moral support in difficult situations. In nuclear family she is alone to take care of the family though she has more independence. There are also families, mostly rural, where women are not allowed to work outside the home, in that case potential of the women remains enclosed within the four walls of the home.

2. ***Culture and society related:*** Our socioculture set up is such that it imposes a lot of hurdles in the path of women entrepreneurs. Being a male dominated society women are seldom treated as equals. The social norms, beliefs, attitudes are all against the independent functioning of women. Women entrepreneurship, in India is looked upon as offending the traditions, and thus the cultural values impinge on her self-confidence (D. Lalitha, 1996). It is harder for the women entrepreneur, therefore, to attempt changes for the betterment or development (Vinze, 1987). Women are looked upon as custodians of the society in matters of maintenance of cherished values, habits, accepted norms of conduct etc. It is harder for them to take even calculated risks, which is a part of entrepreneurship (UNRISD – UNESCO, 1997

and Vinze, 1987). In the Indian context, sex role stereotyping and social norms serve as a major barrier which makes the women entrepreneurs a target of discrimination by both men and other women (D. Lalitha, 1996). Our social conditioning is such that women start believing that they are not good enough to take up activities and challenges of an independent nature. This has a retarding effect on a woman's desire to take up entrepreneurial activities (Job, K.T.). Social attitudes against women taking up entrepreneurial activity has an inhibiting effect particularly on those involved in risk taking ventures. The attitude of society has culminated in developing a widespread complex among women that inhibits them from entering profitable, modern small scale business ventures. (Job, K.T.).

3. ***Finance related:*** Women have limited access over external sources of funds. Commercial banks are reluctant to lend loan to women entrepreneurs who are basically housewives with less exposure to business and risk. Banks show less confidence in proposals made by women entrepreneurs. Bankers claim that marriage, child birth or even a crises in the family can make the women close down their business (Kaza, 1996). So the financial institutions are hesitant to lend to women entrepreneurs as they may quit even a well running business in order to take care of their family (Kaza, 1996). The negative attitude of banks and other financial institutions towards women entrepreneurs is also because they don't have property rights and security.

4. ***Limited access to information and training:*** Women often face only a limited access to a variety of technical and skills training such as–technical, vocation, managerial, organisational, financial, personnel, production process, self-confidence building negotiation skills and assertiveness. They gave limited access to business related services such as business counselling, follow ups and escort services after the training or

counselling program. In addition to this, they also have limited access to information in all aspects such as marketing strategies, credit facilities, financial marketing strategies, credit facilities, financial services, technology, training and education. They also lack information and skills of how to select an activity for venturing.

5. ***Legal problems:*** Women entrepreneurs often face discriminating laws with regard to property rights and inheritance laws which deprive them of capital or collateral securities. Another threatening factor is police harassment on grounds of certain regulations such as license requirements and restriction regarding operation of units in certain areas (e.g., residential areas).

6. ***Restricted mobility:*** One's own business often demands greater mobility in meeting suppliers and customers. Women by their nature are less mobile and they are deprived of the benefits of low cost and high efficiency. Their actual physical condition, and related cultural factors and safety provisions are responsible for their low mobility. Dependence on others for mobility is deterrent in planning business tours.

7. ***Discriminating behaviour of various officials:*** Women go through discouraging experience while dealing with various officials concerned with labour, sales tax department, etc. Officials usually do not have positive attitude about projects started by women. Studies conducted abroad (James and Paul, 1979; Eric and Bary 1982; Robert and Marie, 1981) also revealed similar findings.

Conclusion

Economic development is essentially a process of upward change whereby the real per capita income of an economy increases over a period of time. Entrepreneurship plays a premium role in promoting the economic development of the country. Men have been the part of the entrepreneurial culture for long. But it's only recently that Indian woman joined their counterparts. They have steadily moved from the status of housewives to educated women, employed women and now women entrepreneurs. They are now contributing their share of potential towards economic development of the country though not equally but to some extent. Initially they confined themselves to the traditional business of pickle and papad making. But now they can also be seen in the technical fields such as engineering, electronics, and energy. Government support and social changes have been largely responsible for the development of women entrepreneurs. But still the growth is not satisfactory. Women entrepreneurs constitute a negligible proportion of the total number of entrepreneurs. An array of factors could be ascribed as hindering the growth of the women entrepreneurs. The most dominant ones are the lack of proper training, inadequate financial assistance, inherent weaknesses in Indian women namely poor self image, inadequate encouragement and motivation, lack of courage and confidence, fear of failure and criticism, and last but not the least societal attitudes. To rectify the situation a lot is needed to be done on the part of the government women herself and society at large.

It can be said that women entrepreneurship has crossed the stage of transition and it is finally in flight, but still there is a long way to go till they actually can compete on par with men, and emerge as successful business giants. Thus the need of the hour is the creation of congenial social, political and economic environment where the entrepreneurial skill of the women can be nurtured and developed which, in turn results in the economic development of the country.

Suggestions

The planning commission, the central government and various state governments in India are becoming greatly aware of the fact that women should be brought into the mainstream of economic development and that women should be assisted in their entrepreneurial development in rural and urban areas. Still the present condition is deplorable. Some suggestions have been made which can be worked out in the direction of development of women entrepreneurs. Better results can be obtained by generating greater awareness, better mobilisation of resources and having more scientific approach towards women's entrepreneurial development programmes.

- To make women entrepreneurship movement a success, cohesive efforts of all the concerned institutions viz., training, financial and marketing are greatly required. They are needed to work in collaboration with each other. A single co-ordinating agency, which facilitates the flow of adequate working capital, technology power, and marketing of finished products, is desirable. Training programmes must be organised through concerted efforts of NGO's and governmental organisations.
- Information centres should be set up at appropriate places, in both rural and urban areas so that the information related to entrepreneurship (whether it is regarding training, finance, marketing or any other) is easily accessible to the aspiring women entrepreneurs, and to those who are already in the field. Information should also be disseminated using other media of communication.
- More finance should be given for the small units started by women at lower interest rate without stress on collateral security. There should be improvement in the method of accessing credit. There should not be any delay in sanctioning and receiving of funds. It is also very necessary to identify the poorest women in rural and urban areas to provide financial assistance by banks. These women should be encouraged to take up retail business, household consumer goods producing activities etc.
- The provision of bank finance for women entrepreneurs shall be made under the existing bank lending schemes like DIR priority sector lending etc. and also by devising new schemes exclusively. Therefore, banks should be given more freedom in this regard.
- Training component should include skill formation knowledge on different technologies, handling of better

equipments, legal aspects of running a business, reparation of feasibility reports, better marketing and communications. The content of the training programme should be planned keeping in mind the intelligence level and interest of the target group. The venue of the programme should be such that more and more women come to participate in it.

- Crash literacy programme can be undertaken for those who are resourceful but illiterate.
- Depending upon the resources available, entrepreneurial activity should be decided upon. The type of enterprise feasible at one place might prove out to be completely unsuccessful at another. The easy availability of the raw materials should be considered.
- If the individual lacks enough motivation and confidence, the efforts made by the concerned organisations are of no significance. Counselling centres must be established where women can be helped to overcome their weaknesses and encouraged to take up entrepreneurial programmes.
- Since family members do have influence on the decision making of the entrepreneurs, family counselling must also form part of the entrepreneurial programme for women.

References

Soundarapandian, M. 1999. Women entrepreneurship issues and strategies. Kanishka Publishers Distributors, New Delhi.

Padmanabhan, A. 2000. Search for an identity, Zest for entrepreneurship. India Abroad.

Rani, I. 1996. Women entrepreneurs. A.P.H. Publishing Corporation, New Delhi.

Ramana, A.V. 1999. Entrepreneurship and economic Development. Kurukshetra, pp. 8-10.

Govinda, G.T. 1999. Rural women entrepreneurship. Constraints strategies. Kurukshetra, pp. 11-14.

Job, K.T. 2000. Women entrepreneurship development – an alternative for gender empowerment pp.81-90 in women entrepreneurship, Sasikumar, M. (ed.). Vikas Publishing House Pvt. Ltd., Delhi.

Raju, G. 2000. Women entrepreneurship development through DWACRA pp. 131-139 in women entrepreneurship, Sasikumar, M.(ed.) Vikas Publishing House Pvt. Ltd., Delhi.

Begum, R. 2000. Problems encountered in promoting women enterprises, pp. 109-129 in Women Entrepreneurship, Sasikumar, M, (ed.) Vikas Publishing House Pvt. Ltd., Delhi.

Das, J. 2000. Problems faced by women entrepreneurs pp. 141-148 in women entrepreneurship, Sasikumar, M. (ed.) Vikas Publishing House Pvt. Ltd., Delhi.

Abraham, V.L. 2000. Factors influencing and shaping women entrepreneurship in Kerela. pp. 181-189 in women entrepreneurship, Sasikumar, M. (ed.) Vikas Publishing House Pvt. Ltd., Delhi.

Vinze, M.D. 1986. The women entrepreneurs versus men entrepreneurs, Laxinagton Books, Toronto.

Archana, T.V. and Rehana, G. 1985. Achievement motivation and job satisfaction productivity 24(3).

Mathur, P. and Anamika, 1987. Difference of personality traits among male and female successful entrepreneurs. Paper presented at the 29th annual conference of Indian Academy of Applied Psychology, Waltaine, March.

Singh, N.P. and Sengupta, 1984. Potential women entrepreneurs their profile, visions and motivations, NIESBUD, New Delhi.

Symons, G.L. 1990. Women occupational carriers in business, managers, entrepreneurs in France and Canada (ed.). Nancy, J. Alder Dufia N. Izraeli, Women in Management, Annie, Phizacklea.

Aiyadurai, K. 1999. Women entrepreneurship in India: A Review in Women.

Entrepreneurship Issues and Strategies. Soundarapandian (ed.) Kanishka Publishers, New Delhi.

Kohli, S.C. 1999. Development of women entrepreneurship, Mittal Publications, New Delhi.

Singh, N.P., Shegal, P., Tithani, M. and Sengupta, R. 1986. Successful women entrepreneurs their identity, expectation and problems. National Institute for Entrepreneurship and Small Business Development, New Delhi.

Pillai, R.R. 1998. Promote entrepreneurship among women. The Indian Express.

Sasikumar, 2000. Women entrepreneurship. Vikas Publishing House Private Limited, Mumbai.

Dhameja, S.K. and Saini, J.S. (ed.) Entrepreneurship and small business, Rawat Publications, Jaipur.

Sarngadharan, M. and Beegam, S. 1995. Institutional support and problems. Discovery Publishing House, New Delhi.

Ghosh, B. 2000. Entrepreneurship development in India, National Publishing House, Jaipur and New Delhi.

Bhatia, B.S. and Batra, G.S., Entrepreneurship and Small Business Management. Deep and Deep Publications Private Limited, New Delhi.

22
Women Entrepreneurship Training: A Need of an Hour

Asha Patil,
Dimple Kshatriya

Introduction

Entrepreneurship has become popular and respectable area today. Entrepreneurship is the key to rapid growth of a country. A country with able entrepreneurs will always go faster on the path of Industrialization as compared to a country, which has no able entrepreneurs.

Entrepreneurship is an activity that aims at starting establishing and increasing the size of an enterprise that produces and sells goods or services in market. Doing new things and doing things that are already done in a new way is therefore a simple definition of entrepreneurship.

Entrepreneurship has two distinct aspects

The Entrepreneurs themselves and other is Enterprise

Entrepreneurship thus refers to general trends of setting up of new enterprise in a society. It is a process of actual working. Thus, Entrepreneurship concept does not have any gender bias.

Entrepreneur

The entrepreneurship is the real backbone of economic development. Mr. Cantillon, an Irishman living in France during the early part of eighteenth century was the first to coin the word "entrepreneur". The entrepreneur has been derived from the French word "Entrependra" which connotes "undertaker".

Is a person involved in business activity, he produces as well as sells a product or service and makes profit, this may include manufacturing, trading or services oriented business.

Entrepreneur can be characterized as a person with a high drive and high activity level, constantly struggling to achieve the goals. An entrepreneur is considered to be energetic, resourceful, alert to new opportunities, able to adjust to changing conditions and willing to assume risk involved in change.

Realization for Development of Women Entrepreneur

It is pointed out that, over the years while adopting industrial policy resolution Government of India has not taken special note of women entrepreneurs as a separate and potent factor in economic growth. Earlier negligence towards women entrepreneurs was due to prevailing male dominant thought in the society. However, training programme is also designed to motivate and help to develop certain qualities essential for prospective women entrepreneur to run small-scale industries of their own.

A separate programme for training of women entrepreneurs was started in 1978-1979. The number of Entrepreneurial Development course organized exclusively for women increased from the nine in the year 1978-79, the year of inception of such training programme, to twenty seven in 1982-83. It shows three fold rise in number of training programme for women entrepreneur in four years. Similarly the number of women trained in the Entrepreneurial Development training also increased from seven hundred nine in 1978-79 to nine hundred ninety-three 1982-83.

Entrepreneur attributes can be improved to a certain extent through training. Training further stimulates the development of the competencies in individuals. The entrepreneurship training thus help the women to identify the weaknesses and ways of improving them. Entrepreneurship training will enrich women with latest information.

Entrepreneurship Development Programmes

The International Management Development Network (INTERMAN), in cooperation with United Nations Development

Programme (UNDP) and International Labour Organization (ILO), brought out a publication titled, "Profiles of Entrepreneurship Development Programme" in 1991. It is a study based on the status of entrepreneurship development programme conducted in seventy-one countries.

As defined by INTERMAN, entrepreneurship development programmes are to:

- Create awareness about entrepreneurship.
- Provide career oriented interprises.
- Lead to the creation of new enterprises through training of potential entrepreneur.
- Promote self-employment.
- Train existing entrepreneurs for business survival and growth.
- Stimulate entrepreneurial values in the community.

Entrepreneurship Programme Contents

The trainees are exposed to inspirational lectures highlighting the benefits of entrepreneurship to consolidate their motivational levels.

This followed by lectures of faculty members and experts drawn from various organizations, financial institutions and by successful entrepreneurs dwelling on topics such as entrepreneurial competencies, preparation of a project report, personnel management, sources of financial assistance, market survey, taxation, publicity and advertisement, account keeping, general management, marketing strategy, etc. apart from all above inputs, field visits are arranged for practical exposure.

Need for Developing Women Entrepreneurship

Women entrepreneurship is a new phenomenon, which is recently being recognized as a full-fledged profession among women. Women are increasingly seeking entrepreneurship as an avenue for economic growth of their families as well as of nation.

Some researches have been done on entrepreneurship but very little has been done on women entrepreneurs. Data are available on entrepreneurial characteristics and motivation of men but very negligible data are available regarding women entrepreneurs. We know about women's socialization pattern, behaviour, how their role and responsibility do not allow them to think and behave in an entrepreneurial way. This is because women have primary responsibility for child care and household work. Hence, they are not encouraged to set their personal goals. They make decisions only after seeking the approval of their families and do not show much imitative for personal career development. This has resulted in women acquiring attitudes and behaviour not conducive for entrepreneurship. Assessing and developing behaviour and attitudes of women for becoming successful is the most important component of women entrepreneurship development. Thus project worker thought of helping women to become entrepreneurs by motivating and providing training on entrepreneurship. This training would help women to get equipped with latest information for becoming entrepreneurs and also help in availing loans from the banks through District Industries Centre. The project worker was more concerned with development of women and specially women's economic independence. This training helped them to develop the entrepreneurial competencies among them. Due to all these reasons, the thought of undertaking this action project was further provoked.

Title: An Action Project to Promote Entrepreneurship Among the Women of Baroda City in the Year 1999-2000, was undertaken

Broad Objective

- To impart entrepreneurship training amongst the women of Baroda city.
- To help women in developing their own enterprises.

The project to promote entrepreneurship among the women of Baroda city was planned in order to make the entire programme attainable and successful.

The steps followed, to implement the project were as below–

1. *Identification of centers providing training in entrepreneurship and training of project workers*

In order to identify centers for entrepreneurship, the project worker visited District Industry Centre at Baroda for collecting information regarding the center offering entrepreneurship training. Thus, the project worker contacted the center for Entrepreneurship Development at Baroda and Institute of Technology at Baroda. The purpose of visiting these centers was to gather information regarding duration, content, experts to be called, and related procedure for organizing entrepreneurship training programme.

Thus, the project worker had selected the center for Entrepreneurship Development for undergoing the entrepreneurship training. The project worker had selected this institute because it is a government institution and reputed institution among the Entrepreneurship Development Centres. The project worker discussed the project with Regional Officer of Centre for Entrepreneurship Development for coordinating one for the training programme. Thus project worker participated in organizing, co-coordinating and executing training programme at Wahgodiya. To gain more knowledge of entrepreneurship training, the project worker enrolled herself in the same training programme. Thus, training helped the project worker to get updated with latest information about entrepreneurship.

2. *Organizing training programme for women of Baroda city.*

After collecting the list of women, the project worker approached different institutions, friends, relatives. Publicity through newspaper was made so that more number of women could get enrolled in this training programme.

The project worker contacted Karelibaug Bhagini Samaj for availing help in organizing training programme on entrepreneurship in their premises. Based on the training received at Wahgodiya and considering the women who were going to attend the programme, the inputs were decided. The project worker thus finalized the time; date, hours, experts and subjects to be covered during the programme. The project worker was successful in collecting twenty-three women for the training.

3. Plan of Entrepreneurship training programme

The entrepreneurship training programme was planned from 10th June, 1999 to 24th June, 1999 for two weeks from 3.00 p.m. to 5.00 p.m. the following experts were invited to give lectures on different subjects.

No.	*Date*	*Day*	*Topic*	*Name of the Expert*
1.	10/6/99	Thursday	Entrepreneurial Competencies	Dr. Asha Patil
2.	11/6/99	Friday	Information on computer	Ms. Sapna (computer expert)
3.	12/6/99	Saturday	Govt. Schemes for loans	Mr. Ajit Jadava (Field Investigator)
4.	14/6/99	Monday	Market Survey	Ms. Deepa Kumari (M.B.A.)
5.	15/6/99	Tuesday	General Management	Ms. Deepa Kumari
6.	16/6/99	Wednesday	Marketing Management	Mr. Shailesh Shah (Marketing Officer)
7.	17/6/99	Thursday	Account Keeping	Mr. Shachin Mehta (C.A.)
8.	18/6/99	Friday	Preparation of project proposal	Mr. Diplip Parikh
9.	19/6/99	Saturday	Communication	Ms. Dimple Kshatriya
10.	21/6/99	Monday	Publicity and advertisement	Ms. Deepa Kumari (M.B.A.)
11.	22/6/99	Tuesday	Taxation	Mr. Sachin Mehta
12.	23/6/99	Wednesday	Visit to Karelibaug Bhagini Samaj	Mr. Navneet Thakar
13.	24/6/99	Thursday	Visit to Narmada Bhavan	Mr. Dimple Kshatriya

4. Implementation of training programme

The project worker started the programme with welcoming the experts. The session was given to expert to deliver necessary information regarding the subject. The project worker had given full freedom to the participants to ask question and clarify their doubts, if they had any regarding the subjects. The project worker found difficult to interact individually with the large group. But as the training programme proceeded ahead, the project worker was able to build good rapport with all the women participants individually. The project worker helped them individually to develop their respective project proposals. In total there were twenty-three who attended entrepreneurship training programme, but only fifteen continued to consult the project worker to start their enterprises.

5. *Preparation of loan application*

The project worker guided the women in collecting the loan application forms and other documents like light bill, experience certificates, quotations of requirements, guarantors, pay slip and project proposal. The project worker went along with the women to submit the loan application form at the District Industry Centre. Out of fifteen, ten women had submitted their loan forms related to different Business in the month of June and remaining five women submitted forms later in the month of July due to the problem in collecting documents.

The project worker and women contacted the field investigator to check the progress of the loan application at District Industry Centre and revealed that it takes minimum of

Table 2
Showing the Amount and Month of Receiving Loans by Women Entrepreneurs from Bank

Month of receiving loan and year	*Type of enterprise*	*Amount in Rupees*	*No. of Women*
August '99	Paper tubes, Pouch making, Fall beading	60,000 10,000 6,000	1 1 1
October '99	Day care centre Computer Job work	40,000 80,000	1 1
November '99	Wood Carving	57,000	1
January 2000	Jewellery manufacturing	95,000	1

fifteen days for processing it to the head office at Gandhinagar after submission of papers. In case of seven women out of fifteen it took longer time, about three months in sanctioning the loans.

Table 2 shows month of receiving loans by women entrepreneurs. Out of fifteen, eight women entrepreneurs had received the loans from bank. Out of eight, three women entrepreneurs had received the loans in the month of August, 1999 and January 2000 respectively.

6. *Marketing strategy adopted by women entrepreneurs*

Sale is the major aspect of entrepreneurship training programme. This needs to be thought of much in advance before starting manufacturing. Exhibition is one of the marketing strategies adopted by the present project worker. The main purpose of organizing exhibition was to provide the place to the women for selling their products.

Exhibition-cum-sale will encourage women and increase self-confidence among them. The project worker helped the women in organizing exhibitions at four different places.

- First exhibition at Karelibaug Bhagini Samaj Trust, Baroda.
- Second exhibition at Karelibaug Bhagini Samaj Trust, Baroda.
- Third exhibition at Oil and Natural Gas Corporation Limited, Officer's club, Baroda.
- Fourth exhibition at Department of Home Science Extension and Communication, Faculty of Home Science, The M.S.U., Baroda.

Different products were displayed such as ceramic pot, nib painting, pillow covers, bed sheets, handkerchiefs, bags, imitation Jewelry bags, blouse covers, sari covers, key chains, and so on.

Other women entrepreneurs engaged in paper tubes, pouch making and yellow duster making contacted wholesale dealers, in computer job work service, contacted different company's as well as department of Home Science Extension and Communication. In activities like beauty parlour, fall beading and for selling of coconut oil, women contacted different people in the society. Women engaged in day care center and video shooting had made use of different publicity material to inform people regarding the services. Women engaged in woodcarving and zero received their orders through their contacts.

7. *Account in their enterprise*

Accounts are the eyes of enterprise and it shows financial conditions of enterprise very clearly. Whatever may be the size of the records? Absence of account of such system is one of the important reason of failures of enterprise.

Table 4
The Total Income Earned by Women Entrepreneurs till March 2000

Type of Enterprise	*Loan Received (Rs.)*	*Raw Material Used (Rs.)*	*Total Sale (Rs.)*	*Income Earned (Rs.)*	*Installment Paid (Rs.)*	*Net Profit (Rs.)*	*Amount Invested on their Enterprise (Rs.)*
Jewellery	95,000	9,720	19,720	10,000	2,000	8,000	-
Paper Tubes	60,000	16,000	31,000	15,000	7,000	8,000	-
Wood carving	57,000	11,300	18,400	7,100	2,800	4,300	-
Day Care Centre	40,000	9,000	25,500	16,500	5,000	11,500	-
Fall Beading	6,000	740	1,688	928	3,500	-	2,572
Computer	80,000	1,000	4,000	3,000	5,000	-	2,000
Zero	1,00,000	300	1,200	900	4,500	-	3,600
Pouch making	10,000	4,850	7,760	2,910	3,500	-	590
Painting	N.R.	1,020	2,800	1,780	N.A.	1,780	-
Yellow duster	N.R.	1,590	5,890	4,300	N.A.	4,300	-
Blouse and Sari Cover	N.R.	7,300	14,300	7,000	N.A	7,000	-
Beauty Parlour	N.R.	6,000	10,500	4,500	N.A.	4,500	-
Bed Sheet	N.R.	5,200	7,000	1,800	N.A.	1,800	-
Coconut Oil	N.R.	16,000	20,450	4,450	N.A.	4,450	-

NR – Not Receive the Loan
N.A. – Not Applicable

Table 4 indicated that the amount of loan received by women entrepreneurs from the banks, raw material used and other expenses. It also shows total sale made by the women entrepreneurs and by earned income, installment repaid to the bank by women entrepreneurs. With reference to the women who have not received the loans from the bank they have started their enterprise with their own investment and made the profit.

Out of fifteen eleven women entrepreneurs had made profit whereas four women entrepreneur purchased the machinery from the loan received from the bank, had paid the installment from their resources. Four women, entrepreneurs who had received the loan, earned money after selling the product from which they had paid installment to the bank and still had profit at the hand.

8. *Repayment of loan installment*

Women's access to credit is seen as one of the most important and difficult aspects. The amount of repayment depends upon the loan received from the bank.

Table 5
Shows the Amount and Number of Installment Paid by Women Entrepreneurs

No.	*Type of Enterprise*	*Amount of Installment Rs.*	*Number of Installment*
	Manufacturing		
1.	Jewellery	Rs. 1,000	2
2.	Wood Carving	Rs. 700	4
3.	Pouch making	Rs. 500	7
4.	Paper tubes making	Rs. 1,000	7
	Services		
5.	Day Care Centre	Rs. 1,000	5
6.	Fall beading	Rs, 500	7
7.	Computer Job Work	Rs. 1,000	5
8.	Xerox	Rs. 1,500	3

Thus, the above table shows that almost all women had started repaying their installment. The amount of installment varied from Rs. 500/- to Rs. 1500/-.

9. *Reference material on entrepreneurship*

Reference material on entrepreneurship will always help the women entrepreneur to refer to the content whenever needed in future. The following topics were covered in the reference material for women entrepreneur, which were:

- Entrepreneur: Meaning and qualities
- Women Economic Development Schemes
- General Management
- Market Survey
- Marketing Management
- Account keeping
- Communication
- Advertising important part of sale
- Taxation
- Computer information
- Project proposals

The reference material was prepared on the basis of lectures given by the experts during the training programme. Different books were refered to make complete and sound reference material. The notes provided by lectures were used for developing reference material. The reference material was distributed among the women entrepreneurs.

10. Evaluation of the accomplishment

Evaluation is the process of determining the extent to which objectives have been attained. Evaluation of any programme identifies a well-planned process to measure the entire programme in terms of the objectives, which examines the success or failure of the programme.

Evaluation is an essential step in the extension process. It is a systematic process, which determines the value effectiveness or significance of a programme or of a particular situation.

A reaction scale was prepared by the project worker to identify their reaction regarding the project. The experts from the department validated the reaction scale, which was later filled by the target group trainees for the programme. The reaction scale had four sections.

- Section 1 — Background Information
- Section 2 — Entrepreneurship training programme
- Section 3 — About their own enterprise
- Section 4 — Opinions and suggestions

Analysis of the result revealed the following information–

All the respondents opined that

- Entrepreneurship training programme was useful to them.
- They understand the language used by the experts in the training programme.
- They were satisfied with training programme.
- In future they would like to attend the related programme on entrepreneurship.
- They would advise their friends, relatives who want to become entrepreneurs to join entrepreneurship training programme.

All the respondent opined regarding their own enterprise that

- They would able to expand their enterprise in future.
- Their family members were satisfied with enterprise.
- They were satisfied with their enterprise.
- Majority of the respondents (46.67%) were engaged in manufacturing of products.
- Majority of respondents (53.33%) had received the financial loans.
- Majority of respondents (93.33%) opined that entrepreneurship training programme was useful as it oriented to the problems that may arise in running an enterprise.
- Majority of the respondents (60%) had a financial problem of limited working capital.

11. *Problems faced during the project work*

Various problems were faced during the planning, execution and evaluation stages of the action project. They were as follows:

- It took lot of time to locate who were interested in starting their enterprises from Baroda city.
- Though women were keen and interested in starting their enterprises, but due to family problems they were not in a position to start their enterprises.
- Based on previous experience banks were not ready to provide the loans to these women entrepreneurs. The project worker had to spend time in persuading the bank people to offer loans to these women entrepreneurs under the project. This took longer time, which demotivated some women.

12. *Conclusion*

The following conclusions can be made after the completion of the project.

- The project helped women to start their own enterprises.
- The project helped women to deal with their enterprise effectively.
- Out of twenty-three women, fifteen women (little over half) started their own enterprises. Out of these women eight women received financial loans from bank through District Industry Centre, Baroda.
- The project helped them to generate income from their own enterprise and thus making them self-confident and self-sufficient.

Bibliography

- Ali Arshid, Entrepreneurship Growth and Development, Charegh Publication. Allahabad, India, 1980, pp. 36-42.
- Mutsuddi Nalinksha, "You too can become an entrepreneur", Wheeler Publishing, New Delhi, 1996, pp. 194-196.
- Pandya Raina, An Action project to promote awareness

regarding HIV/AIDS through jatha of women from village Dakar of Padra taluka, district Baroda.

- Dissertation (M.Sc.) Department of Home Science Extention and Communication, Faculty of Home Science, M.S. University of Baroda.

23
What Motivated Women to Adopt an Entrepreneurial Career? A Study

Dr. Neerja Jaiswal

Abstract

An attempt has been made in the present descriptive study to identify the motives responsible for their entrepreneurial career and line of enterprise selection of 113 women entrepreneurs, of Baroda city. The pre-tested interview schedules were utilized as a tool to collect the data by personally interviewing them. The major findings indicated that "economic independence" emerged as dominant motive among the respondents for taking up entrepreneurship as their career "achievement in life" was reported to be the strongest motive for running their enterprise. An idea generated from "within themselves" was the main source of their enterprise initiation, and "opportunity to exercise creativity" was the prime motivator among the respondents to select their present line of enterprise.

Introduction

> *"What accounts for the rise in civilization is not the external resources such as markets, minerals or factories but the entrepreneurial spirit which exploits the resources - a spirit found most often among business people".*
>
> – D.C. McClleland

Undoubtedly the entrepreneurs both in developed and developing countries have been in the forefront in economic growth, employment generation, innovation and capital formation. The entrepreneurs are leading the world into the 21st Century - a bright future. The entrepreneurs, both men and women, are in many ways unsung heroes.

Entrepreneurs are not born. Entrepreneurship is a highly personal process, when a "determining event" decides the starting of a business - a set of practices or skills developed out of dissatisfaction with the existing job, need for recognition, to gain independence or job security with economic gain. Desai, 1996 found that men were drawn more by money and independence, while women appear to be drawn more by recognition. A great many of the latter also had chosen the entrepreneurs' world because of compelling urge of "wanting" to do something positive" in their lives.

The stage is set for social take-off for women from a low development path to an accelerated pace in achieving higher level of self-sustaining economic growth. Women entrepreneurs have been making a significant impact in all segments of the economy in Canada, Great Britain, Germany, Australia and the United States. Their mark in business is accountable for the reasons that; (a) they want new challenges and opportunities for self-fulfillment, (b) they want to prove their mettle in innovative and competitive jobs and (c) they want the change to control the balance between their family responsibilities and their business.

Women entrepreneurs in India represent a group of women who have broken away from the beaten track and are exploring new vistas of economic participation. Today we find women in different types of industries, traditional as well as non-traditional.

According to McClelland and Winter (Year not mentioned), motivation is a critical factor that leads one towards entrepreneurship. This apart, challenge and adventure to do something new, liking for business, and wanting to have an independent occupation are some of the pulls of women. These are the factors that indicate a relatively deeper commitment to entrepreneurial profession on the part of entrepreneur.

To what extent is this true for the women entrepreneurs of Baroda city, was yet to be explored. Thus the present research was conceptualized. The findings of the study would answer the queries viz, What motivated the women of Baroda to take up an entrepreneurial career? What were the motives behind running their enterprise? Who was the motivating source for idea generation for setting-up their enterprise? And what motivated them to select their present line of trade? The findings of the study would be an eye opener for the new aspiring women entrepreneurs. At the same time the findings would also enrich the existing data base in the related field. It would also assist in understanding the behavioural aspect of women entrepreneurs, of a certain locale. The findings would also present a platform for the training institutes to mould their training packages accordingly.

Objectives of the Study

1. To identify the motives responsible for entrepreneurial career of women entrepreneurs of Baroda city.
2. To determine the motives of women entrepreneurs for running their enterprise.
3. To find out the sources of idea generation to set-up their enterprise.
4. To explore the reasons for the choice of their present line of enterprise.

Methodology

The present study is descriptive in nature. The locate of the study was Baroda city. 113 women entrepreneurs having a controlling stake in their venture, (be it proprietorship, partnership or a limited company), and who were managing one or more than one of the functional departments of their enterprise independently; and having enterprise of minimum three years or more than 3 years of age were selected as respondents for the present study. The selection of the respondents was done through snowball sampling technique.

Interview method was utilized to collect the data on a pretested interview schedule, personally by the investigator. The data was further subjected to coding, tabulation and statistical analysis by employing descriptive statistics.

Major Findings of the Study

The findings of the study are categorized under four parts as:

1. Motives responsible for the respondent's entrepreneurial career,
2. Motives for running the enterprise,
3. Sources of idea generation to setup their enterprise, and
4. Reasons for the choice of the present line of enterprise.

Motives Responsible for the Respondent's Entrepreneurial Career

Among the various financial, social, personal, and familial motivations of the respondents for adopting their entrepreneurial career, personal factors outshined as the dominant one over others (Table 1). Analysis of each motivating force separately, however, highlighted certain facts.

Financial

Among these motives, which dealt with finance related matters, "to achieve a sense of economic security" was the important force among 40.71 per cent of the respondents for adopting their entrepreneurial career. The second strongest force was the "financial crisis in the family" which forced 12.39 per cent to become entrepreneurs. The third force emerged to be "the productive investment of their funds". Very few respondents

Table 1
Motives Responsible for the Respondents' Entrepreneurial Career

Motives	*N = 113*	
Financial	F	%
Economic security	40	40.71
Utilization of funds	9	7.96
Financial crisis at home	14	12.39

Contd...

Table 1 Contd...

Motives	*N = 113*	
More return on investment	13	11.50
Quick profit earning	10	8.85
Unemployment	10	8.85
Enough money to take risk	5	4.42
Social		
Social service	11	9.73
Providing employment	26	23.01
Gaining social prestige	19	16.81
No other alternative	1	0.88
Personal		
Utilization of time	44	38.94
Disinterest in service	8	7.08
Pursuing one's interest	36	31.86
It is challenging	48	42.48
To exercise creativity	49	43.36
Utilization of skill	52	46.02
Fulfillment of one's ambition	43	38.05
To become independent	54	47.79
It gives power to command	12	10.62
No qualification required	4	3.54
Achievement in life	43	38.05
Any other	3	2.65
Familial		
Family welfare	1	0.88
Continuity of family business	26	23.01

Note: Total exceeds due to multiple respones,

who gave the reason for choosing entrepreneurship, only, "to take risk of their funds" can undoubtedly be generalized as real entrepreneurs because of their risk taking characteristic.

Social

"Providing employment" and consequently "gaining social prestige" emerged as the first and second social motivator among the respondents.

Personal

A strong urge for "independence" received top priority as personal motivator among nearly one-half of the respondents. Other personal motives accounted for the respondent's entrepreneurial career in the ranking order were "utilization of skill", "to exercise creativity", "to meet a challenge", "to utilize their time", and "achievement of life".

Familial

"Continuity of the family business" was the prime motivator among 23.01 per cent of the respondents for their entrepreneurial career. On the whole "economic independence" ranked as the reason of greatest importance followed by "utilization of skill". "To exercise creativity" and "to meet challenges" ranked third and fourth consequently in their order of importance followed by "economic security".

Motives for Running the Enterprise

When inquired about the motivating forces for running their enterprise, majority of the respondents reasoned "achievement in life" as the most important force while running their business ventures (Table 2). The succeeding strongest motive stated by 71.68 per cent of the respondents was "gaining independence". Running of enterprise seems to be incomplete and useless if the profit oriented motive lacks among the entrepreneurs. "Earning profit" ranked third among nearly two-third of the respondents, followed by motives of "progress in life" and "meeting a challenge". The prime motive "economic independence" as detected earlier must have exerted great influence on the respondents to be the self-initiator of their enterprise.

Table 2
Motives of the Respondents for Running their Enterprise

Motives	*N = 113*	
	F	%
Achievement in life	83	73.45
Independence	81	71.68
Earning profits	74	65.49
Progress in life	72	63.72
Meeting a challenge	69	61.06
Earning social prestige	63	55.75
Welfare of the family	60	53.10
Accomplishing by one's own efforts	59	52.21
Achievement of the goal	57	50.44
Satisfaction of the soul	56	49.56
Providing employment	42	37.17
Getting tasks done by others	24	21.21
Continuity of family business	21	18.58
Any other	4	3.54

Note: Total exceeds due to Multiple Responses.

Source of Idea Generation

An idea generated from within themselves was the main source for setting-up their enterprise (Table 3). The next

Table 3
Sources of Idea Generation to Set-up the Enterprise

Sources of Idea Generation	*N = 113*	
	F	%
Husband	31	27.43

Contd...

Table 3 Contd...

Sources of Idea Generation	*N = 113*	
Parents	6	5.31
Relatives/friends	13	11.5
Self	44	38.94
Successful entrepreneur	2	1.77
Family business	11	9.73
Training institute	3	2.65
Any other	5	4.42

Note: Total exceeds due to Multiple Responses.

successive outstanding source of idea generation was their husbands, followed by their relatives/friends.

Reasons for the Choice of the Present Line of Enterprise

Analysis of the data in Table 4 made it evident that the reason "opportunity to exercise creativity" which is stated by 35.40 per cent of the respondents was one of the prime motivators for selecting the present line of their enterprise. Reasons ranking fourth "opportunity to exercise possessed skill" and fifth "utilization of professional qualification" made it very clear that respondents were quite self-confident about their potentials and wished to exercise them in a constructive manner. Slightly more than one-fourth of the respondents who reasoned "better prospects" for choosing the present line of their enterprise reflect

Table 4
Reasons for the Choice of the Present Line of Enterprise

Reasons	***N = 113***	
	F	%
Great demand	24	21.24
Better prospects	35	30.97

Contd...

Table 4 Contd...

Reasons	***N = 113***	
Family business	28	24.78
Availability of ready market	22	19.47
Low capital requirement	17	15.04
Utilization of professional qualification	26	23.01
Past experience	8	7.08
Short gestation period	6	5.31
Opportunity to exercise creativity	40	35.40
High rate of return	7	6.19
Typically feminine	5	4.42
Opportunity to exercise possessed skills	27	23.89
Socially acceptable	13	11.50
Low mobility	12	10.62
Low break even	2	1.77
Easy availability of raw material	6	10.62
High profitability	12	10.61
Self interest	7	6.19
Any other	14	12.39

Note: Total exceeds due to Multiple Responses.

their foresight and good knowledge of their business. Others gave varied reasons.

Conclusion

Reasons stated by the respondents to pursue entrepreneurial career and the motives behind running their enterprise clearly indicated that they were confident, wanted to be independent, achieve something in life, and wished to utilize their skills, creativity, and their educational qualifications productively. "Self-motivation" as a source of idea generation to set-up their enterprise showed their inclination and their firm determination for entrepreneurship. Their vision in selecting their present line of enterprise proved their foresightedness and an indication of their aptitude for an entrepreneurship.

References

Desai, V. 1996. Entrepreneurial Development, Vol. 1, Bombay, Himalaya Publishing House.

Desai, V. 1996. Entrepreneurial Development, Vol. 3, Bombay, Himalaya Publishing House.

Hisrich, R.D. and Brush, C.G. 1986. The Woman Entrepreneur: Starting, Financing and Managing a Successful New Business, Canada, Lexington Mass.

Hisrich, R.D. and Peter, M.P. 2002. Entrepreneurship, New Delhi, Tata McGraw Hill Publishing Company Ltd.

Jaiswal, N. 1998. "Determinants of Entrepreneurial Growth Process Among Women Entrepreneurs". Unpublished Doctorate Dissertation. Dept. of Home Management. Faculty of Home Science, The Maharaja Sayajirao University of Baroda, Vadodara.

Kale, J.D. 1990. "Women Entrepreneurship in Gujarat, Indian Management, Nov.-Dec.

Kulshrestha, A. 1985. "Attitudes, Motivation and Experience Profile of Women Entrepreneurs". News-Corp 2(2) : 28-29.

Kumar, R. 1993. Women Executives Attitudes. Motivation, Leadership and Communication Skills. New Delhi: Deep & Deep Publications.

Shah, H. (Year not mentioned). "Fostering Women Entrepreneurship - A study of Distinctive Features". Research Report Serial 3. New Delhi: NIESBUD.

Sharma, J. 1992. "Study of Women Entrepreneurs : A Follow-up of 55 Trainees from CED, Baroda". Unpublished M.Sc. Dissertation, M.S.U., Vadodara.

Singh, K. 1992. Women Entrepreneurs. New Delhi: Ashish Publishing House.

Singh, N.P. and Gupta, R.S. 1990. "Potential Women entrepreneurs - Their Profile, Vision and Motivation". Research Report Serial 1. New Delhi: NIESBUD.

Varghese, M.A. 1990. Women Administrators in Education, New Delhi, Vikas Publishing House.

Verma, S.K. and Valulla, S. 1991. "Self-Employed Women in Gujarat". Social Welfare 38(2).

Vinz, M.D. 1987. Women Entrepreneurs in India - A Socio-Economic Study of Delhi - 1975-1985, Delhi, Mittal Publications.

24
The Role of Banking to Encourage the Entrepreneurship in Women

Bharti V. Oza

Abstract

The economic and industrial development of a country largely depend upon how efficiently the funds are managed by its banks and financial institutions. Efficient management of banks and financial institutions will not improve their profitability but also enhance their contribution to the industrial and economic development.

Small entrepreneur is regarded as one of the important contributors to the economic growth of a nation. The commercial banks after the nationalization and expansion of branch network are playing key role in the development and growth of small industries in the country. Bank take as much interest so as to give strong financial support and are playing their entrepreneurial role efficiently and effectively.

The survey carried by estimated method. Comprised of 40 women entrepreneurs from Jamnagar - Rajkot Gramin Bank. General information about finance, loan, management of unit, why they want to become entrepreneurs, training and problems were considered.

Results revealed that women entrepreneurs had taken loans from Gramin Bank to establish new units.

Fifty per cent women manage their unit without the help of family members. Fifty-seven per cent women reported it was for, to improve their economic condition thirteen per cent desired to achieve something, thirty per cent said they got social prestige on becoming an entrepreneur. Ninety per cent, women took training for setting up their units.

Experience of borrowing loan from the bank, 85% women entrepreneurs were satisfied with bank procedure like the repayment period, rate of interest, legal formalities, recovery procedure and total service of bank. Branch manager's opinion was that, women borrowers are very accurate and serious about repayment of loan. He was satisfied with the recovery performance and faced no difficulties in recovery of the overdues from women entrepreneurs.

Today, most of the women have strong desire to progress and they even get sufficient support from family. The social circumstances are changing. Now women entrepreneurs have become ambitious, acquired experience and basic-skills of competency and self assurance, required for becoming successful entrepreneurs.

Introduction

The entrepreneur is one of the most important inputs in the economic development of country or a region within the country. 'Entrepreneur' has been defined in various ways, an innovator, a risk taker, an organization builder and so on. The concept of entrepreneurship will certainly, undergo a change with the advancement of technology and information boon. There is a phenomenal increase in the number of self employed women after the world war.

Majority of woman entrepreneurs are from the middle class families. Today there is great awakening among women, that if given an opportunity, they will deliver the results like-wise in officers and industries, many have shown better performance.

The government and the non-governmental organization have a bigger role in stimulating and nurturing the spirit of entrepreneurship amongst woman.

Finance is one of the basic requirements for entrepreneurs. At every stage of the project, finance is now made available to entrepreneurs by commercial banks for purchase of plants, machinery and equipment and for working. Even after nationalization of the banks central government decided to set up Regional Rural Banks (R.R.B.) through the country for giving facilities to the small entrepreneurs. The head office of the R.R.B. is located in district. R.R.B. also periodically publish booklets detailing the various schemes for the entrepreneurs, which help them to become aware and update with information.

Banks should stimulate people to take up entrepreneurship through imparting entrepreneurial environment. Banks have their various financing schemes, workshops, awareness camps, motivations camps, external support to the entrepreneurs, the security and margin requirements. The banks role in nursing the sick and rehabilitating the sick units is also noteworthing.

If there is an enterprising entrepreneurs, the doors of the bank and financial institutions are always open for her, for her bright future and countries prosperous economy. The economic and industrial development of a country largely depends upon how efficiently the funds are managed by its banks and financial institutions.

Materials and Methods

A questionnaire was prepared to collect the information which comprised of 40 women entrepreneurs from Jamnagar-Rajkot Gramin Bank, Jamnagar Branch.

Questionnaire for Entrepreneurs

1. Personal profile - name, age, address, education, sex.
2. Background information on which name of unit, sources of finance, name of bank, address of unit, purpose for borrowing the forms of loans, rate of interest, relationship with bank, market, how they manage the unit, why she wants to become an entrepreneur? From where she had taken Training? How many times this information was taken.
3. Miscellaneous : subsidy, time lag for sanctioning the loan, repayment period, security, rate of interest, legal formalities, recovery procedure, services of bank.

Result and Discussions

On the basis of information obtained by the questionnaire method, result are presented in Table I, II.

Table 1 - general information

Table 2 - experience of borrowing loan from bank

Table 3 - types of women enterprises

Opinions of women entrepreneurs and details of discussion with the branch manager are given below. Women entrepreneurs are from Jamnagar-Rajkot Gramin Bank, Jamnagar Branch.

Table I
General Information

1.	Age, education	Women between 25 to 35 age group (Graduate)
2.	Source of finance	100% have taken a loan from the Jamnagar-Rajkot Gramin Bank, Jamnagar branch.
3.	Purpose of borrowed the loan	100% women have taken a loan to establish new unit.
4.	Management of unit	50% manage without the help of family members. 50% manage with the help of family members.
5.	Factors influenced her to become an entrepreneur	57% said to improve their economic condition. 13% desired to achieve something. 30% said to get social prestige.
6.	Training	90% women take training for 1 to 2 years. 10% women have no training.
7.	Indicate the general problem faced by her unit	70% said, we have no problem. 20% said, problem of space for unit, 10% said, our area is not suitable for our enterprise.

Table II

1.	The time lag for sanctioning the loan was Normal 80% Moderately lengthy 20%
2.	The repayment period was Sufficient 85% Insufficient 15%

Contd...

Table II Contd...

3.	Rate of interest is Normal 90% Moderately high 10%
4.	Legal formalities followed is Rigid and complicated 5% Fairly simple 95%
5.	Recovery procedure is Strict 20% Liberal 80%
6.	Total service of bank are Very good 70% Good 20% Average 10%

Types of Women Enterprises

45%	Sewing machine
15%	Computer
20%	Readymade garment
20%	Novelty store

Opinion of the Women Entrepreneurs

- Fifty-seven per cent said, there is a big improvement in standard of living of Entrepreneurs.
- Twenty per cent Ready made sellers get an advantage of meeting so many people as they have to go far, place to place sell their materials, but it is a very time consuming process.
- Fifteen per cent Computer Entrepreneurs get large amount of job works and at the same time they can also learn new techniques.
- Twenty per cent ready made garment sellers often traveling to Surat, Baroda etc. for goods variety, cheap raw materials, to get better marketing. Get Experience by undergoing such travels.
- Eighty-five per cent women entrepreneurs have very positive experience from bank they satisfied with bank.

Branch Manager's Opinion

Jamnagar - Rajkot Gramin Bank

- Head office in Jamnagar.
- Jamnagar city 2 branches.
- In Jamnagar district 44 branches.
- Rajkot district 4 branches.
- He is satisfied with the recovery performance and faced no difficulties in recovery of the overdues from women Entrepreneurs.
- Women come for loan directly to bank or some times with their husbands or brothers.
- Women borrowers are particularly very accurate and serious for repayment of loan.
- In rural areas, women have very little education.

So it is very difficult to advise them. They always come with their family members, which is the rural culture. They want to come forward for entrepreneurship but have family responsibilities.

Conclusion

The survey of 40 women entrepreneurs from R.R. Bank was carried for the purpose of the present study to know the Women's interest in doing work and role of bank for encouraging women entrepreneurship.

The Survey and data revealed that banks take much interest to give strong financial background and are playing their entrepreneurial role efficiently and effectively.

Further, regarding the legal formalities, rate of interest, repayment periods and total service of bank for entrepreneurs all women are satisfied.

The present results reveal that most of the women have strong will to work to get success in their enterprise. Desire to achieve something and even to get sufficient support from family for setting up successful enterprises.

25
Farm Oriented Microenterprises for Women

Shobha Nagnur,
Channamma N.,
Geeta Channal

Women in agriculture work from dawn to dusk by combining homemaking and nurturing roles in agriculture. However, their work and their contributions do not receive the due attention. Many a times they exhibit their powerful position by combining their multiple roles is agriculture with farm oriented income generation activities. The upcoming phenomenon in the present rural society shows a trend of combining micro entrepreneurship with home and family. It is contended that these women who undertake micro entrepreneurship and are able to contribute to families cash income through economically productive work tend to elevate the social status of their family.

Meaning of Microenterprise

The term microenterprise must be understood with reference to economically productive work based on farm oriented work that tender income. All those activities that employ less than 10 persons including the owner and family workers fall within the purview of microenterprise. In the context of regular and remunerative wage employment, microenterprises represent opportunities for self-employment which poor women can take up with appropriate support.

From a gender perspective microenterprises represent an opportunity for women to gain direct access to income when they may have limited avenues for alternative employment. From the economic empowerment point of view microenterprises provide scope for developing and exercising competence in managing an activity, handling funds, taking responsibility for business transactions and taking decisions.

Why to Promote Microenterprises?

By promoting microenterprises the work-production relationships open up and women can justifiably select the sector for generating income. The added advantages of promoting microenterprises are as follows:

- To generate additional income that will lead to savings and improve investment capacity.
- To empower women as decision-makers.
- To build scope for women as information seekers, overcome the fear of failure and provide access to peer support.

Planning for Women's Micro-enterprises Promotion

- Start with exposure visit to the market or sharing of experiences of other entrepreneurs to provide a platform for awareness generation and decision making.
- Make women feel confident regarding their contribution to the activity both in terms of time and skill output and economic gain by planning out appropriate training strategies for confidence building.
- Provide simulation games for awareness generation on transaction of and making money, assessment of day-to-day market conditions, decision-making and acting quickly on these decisions.
- Provide education on quality parameters and need for maintaining certain quality parameters for end use or sale of product/produce.

The present study highlights on microentreprises for women in agriculture and examines the fruitful and enlightening enterprises that women can take up as economic activity and provides valuable information on experiences of women entrepreneurs in goat farming, bee keeping, vermicomposting and silk cocoon rearing.

Goat Farming

Goat often referred to, as the poor man's cow is a small sized mammal that is capable of integrating itself into dissimilar socio-economic situations prevailing in our country. The main products of goat farming are milk, mutton, wool and hide. The greatest value of the contribution of milk and meat is towards the health and nutrition of the family by way of availability of cheap and good quality mutton and milk. The importance of goat as a microenterprise in the rural economy is evidenced by its unparallel advantages such as:

A Case of Woman Goat Farmer

Lingavva Rudrappa Poojar aged 32 years is a successful goat rearing farm women from Bogar village of Dharwad district in Karnataka state. She belongs to a farming family which owns three acres of land jointly among three married brothers.

In addition to working on her own farm she is engaged in rearing goats. Four years back Lingavva started with one goat and now owns 40 goats and 10 kids. She first purchased a buck for Rs.500 as there was already a she goat at home. She got a small shed built in front of the house with just four poles and a roof of coconut fronds for the increasing herd size. She manages all activities such as feeding, milking, sanitation and postnatal management by herself. Her husband and other male members take care of grazing and consultation with veterinarian.

Male goats are sold only when money is required to buy grains for the goats or during financial emergencies. Milk is not sold as about one liter of milk is used for home consumption and the rest is towards purchase of grains (Rs. 500/- bag) for feeding. She buys one bag of grains every two months, which comes out to be six bags of grains per year.

Bee Keeping

People from ancient times have been practicing bee keeping as a subsidiary enterprise. Bee keeping these days has become a

Production Economics	
Expenditure Purchase of 6 bags of grains @ Rs. 500/bag/year	Rs. 3000/-
Expenses for prevention or cure of diseases or ailments	Rs. 500/-
Total Expenses	**Rs. 3500/-**
Income **Sale of three bucks @ Rs. 1000 to Rs. 1500 per goat**	**Rs. 4500/ -**

Note:
1. Profit is by way of increase in the herd size.
2. Better nutrition is provided to the family by using milk.

very useful agricultural enterprise because bees not only provide honey and wax which are useful to man, but also help in pollination of different crops.

A Case of Woman Bee Keeper

Sudha Venkatesh of Alnavar village of Dharwad district aged 33 years. The farm on which the apiary is maintained is a training institute where Sudha's husband is an instructor. Many flowering plants and trees for foraging are maintained and as a successful beekeeper she is managing her own apiary on the same land. Eight years back she started off with five colonies and now she is maintaining 10 colonies. She also multiplies colonies for sale.

Income generation	
Expenditure	**Rs.**
For the box	600/-
For the colony	300/-
For the stand	250/-
Total	**1050/-**
Income	
Income from 15 kgs. Honey/year @ Rs. 120 kg.	1810/-
10 colonies @ Rs. 300/- colony	3000/-
2 kgs. of wax @ Rs. 150/- kg.	300/-
Total Income	**5110/-**

Sudha is involved in most of the activities like watering, cleaning the comb and box (once in 15 days) and honey extraction (once in 15 days), fixing of honey chamber and foundation sheet. The colonies maintained by are of log, pot and basket types, which do not require much investment. In addition to selling honey, she also colonies to prospective beekeepers.

Vermicompost

Vermicompost is the compost/manure produced by the earthworms. In recent times vermicompost has gained popularity and is in great demand because of its ecofriendly nature and low cost. Earthworms produce good organic manure by degrading various organic wastes. Earthworms consume waste material, digest it and defecate. This fecal matter is termed as vermicompost. Vericompost is a rich source of plant nutrients and is a good manure especially for crop gardening and vegetable cultivation. Vermicomposting as an enterprise not only provides good manure for one's own farm but will also supplement the income when sold in tones to other farmers or sold in packets of 1-2 kgs. for use in urban home gardens.

A Case of Vermicomposting by Woman Farmer

Kalavva Malleshappa Hakkalad 45 years of Kamplikoppa village of Dharwad Taluka is producing vermicompost since 1998. She belongs to a farming family owing six acres of land.

She was introduced to this enterprise by Bharathiya Agro Industries Foundation (BAIF) and NGO working in Kamplikoppa and surrounding villages. Kalavva first started vermicomposting with 18 worms which were reared and multiplied in a bamboo basket. These worms were then let in to the waste pit. Later she got brick columns constructed and is carrying out

Income generation	*In Rupees*
Expenditure	Nil
Income	
1 Quintal worms @ Rs. 200/- kg.	20,000/-
70 bags of compost @ Rs. 130/- bag	9,100/-
Total Profit	29,000/-

vermicompost in this brick column. Since Kalavva's family maintains a small dairy, she uses the cowdung for composting. Animal feed wastes, as well as mango leaf litter from her garden is also used for composting. Kalavva waters the pit once in two days. After compost is ready she also does the sorting, drying and bagging.

Since past four years she has earned about 29,100/- rupees with no investment at all.

Silk Cocoon Production

Seri culture is an agro industry, the end product of which is silk. India has the unique distinction of being the only country in the world bestowed by nature with all four varieties of silk viz Mulberry, Tasar, Eri and Muga. Mulberry silk is the best known of all silks. Silk cocoon production is an enterprise, which does not require strenuous labour or specialized skills. It being an indoor activity women and children during their spare time can be actively involved.

Case study

Shashikala Yadal of Myakalmaradi village of Bailhongal taluka, Belgaum district of Karnataka state comes from a large land holding nuclear family. The family owns good fertile lands which are irrigated by wells. Cauliflower and beetroot were grown in abundance, which were sold in Belgaum market to be sent to Goa and Mumbai. However, poor market price due to middle men and the prevalence of drought from the past three years and the consequent drastic reduction of water in the wells prompted the family to look for alternative source of income. The success of some neighbouring farmers in silk worm rearing encouraged. Shashikala to persuade her husband to take up silk worm rearing with the help of the sericulture department.

Shashikala who is educated up to 10th standard decided to take up silkworm rearing while her husband concentrated on farming including mulberry cultivation. She took up this enterprise in the year 2001 with little initial investment. A room for storing grains was converted to the rearing room, the racks were got made with the wood of the trees grown in their own fields and there was land and water for growing mulberry. V_1 variety of mulberry is grown and bivoltine silk worms are reared. With the supervision and inputs like bleaching agents and formalin from the sericulture department, Shashikala was able to earn good profit in the first year, which was about Rs.45,000 for each harvest of 45 days.

Production economics for 1 harvest of 45 days for 200 dfls

Cost	In Rupees
Non – recurring Carpenter charges and plastic wires for racks of 150	 5,000/-
Cost chandrikes (for coco)	10,000/-
Recurring Cost of 200 DFLs @ Rs.1.50 dfl. Cost of mulberry cultivation for two acres / year	 300/- 1500/-
Labour charges 2 labour for 30 days i.e. 60 Mondays @Rs.30/- day **Total**	 2,000/- **18,000/-**
Income per harvest	
1700 kg. Cocoons	34,000/-
Sold at Rs. 200/- kg. Profit for 1st harvest	15,200/-
Profit for subsequent harvest will be Approximate	30,000/-

Shashikala is now confident that she can rear at least 300 dfls because her husband has already planted mulberry on one more acre of land. She is now taking four harvests per year and plans to take at least six harvests per year, which would work out to Rs.1,80,000 profit per year. This enterprise has abled her to maintain that standard of living of the family which existed before the drought years.

Conclusion

The ability to generate income is a key element of socio-economic upliftment of families and thereby, the communities. In the context of lack of regular and remunerative wage employment, microenterprises represent opportunities for self-employment that the women can undertake with support of other family members. Thus the women can have direct access to income and by managing the economic returns in a logical manner she further expands her work. Her positive approach, dedication and farsightness will make her economically empowered woman. The real life experiences of the entrepreneurs will be a source of information and incentive for other women.

26
Constraints in Utilization of Drip Irrigation Technology in Agricultural Entrepreneurship

B.N. Kalsariya,
M.N. Popat,
N.D. Bharad & K.M. Karetha

Abstract

The present study was conducted in Vanthali village of Vanthali Taluka of Junagadh district of Gujarat to identify the constraints in utilization of drip irrigation system and seek the suggestion to overcome these problems. Out of 180 drip irrigation adopters, 64 respondents were selected by using proportionate random sampling technique. The result of the study revealed that the high initial cost of installing drip irrigation system, uneven distribution of water due to insufficient pressure, this system is not suitable for all important crops and regular maintenance and inter culturing became difficult were the other main constraints of utilization of drip irrigation system. To increase the rate of subsidy and provide cent percent loan facility to purchase the set/s and to develop multi use bilateral pipes for various field crops were the major suggestion offered by drip irrigation adopters.

Introduction

Drip irrigation is acclaimed as one of the most modern methods of irrigation. It has been adopted now in many countries and it is not new to India. It has established its universal versatile of being advantageous under many situations. This system saves 40 to 70 per cent of irrigation water which is used judiciously for irrigating more crops. In order to popularize the drip irrigation system many efforts are being made by government, university and other private organizations in Gujarat state. In spite of this, the farmers are not adopting the drip irrigation system as they are facing many constraints. Hence, it is worthwhile to identify the constraints faced by the farmers and to seek their suggestions to overcome the constraints, this study was undertaken.

Methodology

The study was conducted in Vanthali village of Vanthali taluka of Junagadh district of Gujarat as more number of farmers of this area are having drip irrigation system. Total 180 farmers had drip irrigation system, out of which 64 farmers were selected by using proportionate random sampling technique. The data were collected through personal interview method with the help of interview schedule especially structured for the purpose.

In order to measure the constraints pertaining to adoption of the drip irrigation system, a four point rating scale, i.e., very important, important, less important and not at all important with scale value 3, 2, 1 and 0 respectively were used. The total score of each constraint was summed up and then mean score was worked out. The ranks were assigned on the basis of mean score to each constraint. The suggestions were invited openly from the respondents. The frequencies were calculated for each suggestion and converted into percentage.

Result and Discussion

Table - 1 shows that high initial cost of installing drip irrigation system (Rank-I) and extra tank is needed for high pressure (Rank-II) were the main financial constraints faced by the farmers.

The high initial cost and extra tank need more investment which may not be afforded by average farmers, might be the probable reason for these constraints.

With regards to technical constraints, uneven distribution of water due to insufficient pressure (Rank-I), problem of blocking the drippers due to salts and other impurities (Rank-II) and unavailability of spare parts at village level (Rank-III) were experienced by the farmers.

In case of administration and extension activities, the major constraints like system is not suitable for all important crops (Rank-I), lack of sufficient knowledge (Rank-II) and lack of proper training (Rank-III) were perceived by the farmers as major constraints.

The probable reason for this might be that the farmers are having insufficient technical knowledge to operate the drip irrigation system.

In relation to difficulties regarding cultural operation problems of inter culturing and weeding within the rows were faced by the respondents.

The other constraints like difficulty in maintenance of drip irrigation system (Rank-I), problems of rats and other rodents cut the rubber pipe (Rank-II) and spacing varies from crop to crop, so it becomes difficult to change the place of lateral pipes frequently (Rank-III) were faced by the farmers.

This finding is supported by the findings of Naik (1990), Parikh (1991) and Thorat & Bhoite (1992).

The data presented in Table - 2 shows that the major suggestions offered by the farmers were to increase the rate of subsidy and provide cent percent loan facility to purchase the set/s (87.50 per cent), prepare a muiti use bilateral pipe, which may be use in various field corps (81.25 per cent) and provide regular information and free service for maintenance of drip irrigation sets (78.12 per cent).

Conclusions

It can aptly be concluded from above that the high initial cost of installing the drip irrigation set, uneven distribution of water due to insufficient pressure, drip irrigation system is not suitable for all important crops and difficulties in inter culturing and maintenance of drip irrigation sets were the major constraints faced by the farmers. To increase the rate of subsidy and provide cent percent loan facility to compensate the other expenses were the major suggestions offered by the farmers.

Table 1
Practice-wise Constraints faced by the Drip Irrigation Adopters in Adoption/utilization of Improved Irrigation System

Sr. No.	Practice-wise constraints	Mean	Rank
I.	**Financial**		
1.	High Initial cost of installing drip irrigation system.	1.72	I
2.	Extra tank is needed for high pressure.	1.06	II
3.	Spare parts of drip irrigation system are costly.	0.75	III
4.	Lack of timely availability of financial help from government.	0.03	IV
II.	**Technical**		
1.	Uneven distribution of water due to insufficient pressure.	2.78	I
2.	Problem of blocking the drippers due to salts or other impurities.	2.34	II
3.	Unavailability of spare parts at village level.	0.93	III
4.	Problem of leakage of pipe.	0.34	IV
5.	Lacks of technical know - how.	0.31	V
6.	Technically complicated.	0.03	VI
III.	**Administration and extension activities**		
1.	System is not suitable for all-important corps.	2.96	I
2.	Lack of sufficient knowledge.	1.93	II

Contd...

Table 1 Contd...

Sr. No.	*Practice-wise constraints*	*Mean*	*Rank*
3.	Lack of proper training.	1.72	III
4.	Unavailability of technical manpower for installing the system on farmers' field.	0.50	IV
5.	Information regarding drip irrigation system is not available from extension workers.	0.28	V
6.	Financial procedure is complicated.	0.21	VI
7.	Lack of sufficient literature on drip irrigation system.	0.03	VII
IV.	**Cultural operation**		
1.	Inter culturing becomes difficult.	1.09	I
2.	Weeding within the rows become difficult.	0.25	II
V.	**Others**		
1.	Regular maintenance is difficult.	2.93	I
2.	Rats and other rodents cut the rubber pipe.	2.78	II
3.	Spacing varies from crop to crop, so it becomes difficult to change the place of lateral pipes frequently.	2.12	III
4.	Accumulation of extra salts in the soil due to insufficient quantity of water.	1.91	IV
5.	Problems of low voltage and irregularity of electricity power.	1.37	V
6.	Difficulty to carry from one place to other.	1.03	VI
7.	Companies/dealers are not provided proper service regarding the drip irrigation set/s.	0.72	VII
8.	Problem of uprooting due to shallow root system	0.59	VIII
9.	Lack of repairing facility at village level.	0.18	IX

Table 2
Suggestions offered by the Drip Irrigation Adopters in Utilization of Improved Irrigation System

Sr. No.	*Suggestions*	*Frequency*	*Percent*
1.	Increase the rate of subsidy and provide cent percent loan facility to purchase the set/s.	28	87.50
2.	Multi use bilateral pipes, which may be used in various field crops, should be developed.	26	81.25
3.	Provide regular information and free service for maintenance of drip irrigation set/s.	25	78.12
4.	To arrange training on drip irrigation system.	23	71.87
5.	Extension workers should arrange regular visits.	19	59.37
6.	Demonstrations should be arranged through companies/dealers.	15	46.87
7.	Use of mass media like radio, T.V., newspapers, and magazines to solve the problems regarding drip irrigation system.	07	21.87

References

Naik, M.N. 1990. Constraints in Popularizing Drip Irrigation System in Gujarat. The Gujarat Association for Agricultural Sciences. September-1990, G.A.U. Anand.

Parikh, M.M. 1991. Economics of Drip Irrigation Water Management Project. 8th February-1 991 , G.A.U. Navsary.

Thorat, D.R. and Bhoite, H.S. (1992). The Socio-Economic Constraints in the Use of Drip Irrigation. *Maharashtra Journal of Extension Education*, XI: 324 - 326.

27

Farm Women's Behaviour to Agricultural Entrepreneurship on Improved Mango Cultivation

B.R. Karkar,
M.C. Dhaduk,
B.N. Kalsariya and N.D. Bharad

Abstract

The present study was undertaken with the objective to find out the personal and socio-economic characteristics and suggestion to make training more effective by the farm women. The study was conducted at three villages, i.e. Akolvadi, Prempara and Thoradi of Talala, Visavadar and Una talukas of Junagadh district, respectively. The total number of 25 trained and 25 untrained farm women were selected proportionately by using random sampling technique. The result of the study depicted that majority of the trained and untrained farm women belonged to young age group up to 30 years. Nearly one-third of the trained farm women possessed college level of education and untrained farm women had secondary level of education.

Majority of the trained and untrained farm women belonged to large size of family. More than three-fourth of the trained farm women had medium social participation. Whereas, more than two-third of trained and untrained farm women had medium extension participation.

In case of suggestion for making training more effective, venue should be the Farmer Training Centre, time should be during-slack season, training methods should be lecture with practical followed by lecture with discussion and demonstration and field visit and preferred female teacher for training.

Introduction

Training is a powerful means to catalyses human resource development. Significance of training has been well established in the field of agriculture. From ancient days, women have played a pivotal role in agricultural production. It is felt necessary to improve their technology. This is only possible by organizing the need based intensive training programme.

Therefore, mango grower should be trained in specific operational and technical know-how and skills embracing all phases of production for maximizing their economic returns. Keeping this fact in mind, the present investigation with the following specific objectives has been taken.

1. To study the personal and socio-economic characteristics of trained and untrained farm women.
2. To seek suggestion for making the training more effective.

Methodology

The present study was conducted in the three villages, i.e., Akolvadi, Prempara and Thoradi of Talala, Visavadar and Una talukas of Junagadh district, respectively during the month of June, 2003. The total numbers of 50 trained and untrained farm women were selected from all the three villages by using random sampling technique. A schedule was developed to include questions on some of the personal and socio-economic characteristics of the farm women on improved mango cultivation. The personal interview technique was used for collecting the information from 25 trained and 25 untrained farm women.

Findings and Discussion

(A) Characteristics of trained and untrained farm women on improved mango cultivation:

The data in Table-1 revealed that a great majority of trained (92.00 per cent) and untrained (84.00 per cent) farm women were in young age group. Near about one-third of trained farm women (32.00 per cent) had college level of education followed by higher education (24.00 per cent), secondary education (24.00 per cent), primary education (4.00 per cent) and illiterate (4.00 per cent). Whereas forty per cent of untrained farm women had secondary level of education followed by primary level of education (36.00 per cent), higher education (12.00 per cent), college level of education (8.00 per cent) and illiterate (4.00 per cent) respectively.

In case of family size, majority (56.00 per cent trained and 60.00 per cent untrained) of respondent belonged to large family size. Whereas, majority of the respondents (44.00 per cent trained and 48.00 per cents untrained) belonged to small size of land holding. Thirty-six per cent trained and thirty-two per cent untrained farm women belong to medium size of land holding.

More than three-fourth (80.00 per cent) of the trained farm women belong to medium social participation followed by high social participation (12.00 per cent) and low social participation (8.00 per cent) respectively. Whereas, 68.00 per cent untrained farm women belong to medium social participation followed by low (28.00 per cent) and high (4.00 per cent) social participation group respectively.

(B) Suggestions for making training more effective:

(1) *Venue of Training*

The majority of the respondents (64.00 per cent) had suggested the Farmer Training Centre (FTC) as a suitable venue for training followed by 24.00 per cent respondent suggesting village.

(2) *Time of Training*

More than half of respondents (56.00 per cent) suggested to organize the training programme in slack season followed by 28.00 per cent prior to monsoon. The sixteen per cent respondents suggested organizing training after harvesting crop.

(3) Training Methods

The most important methods of training suggested by respondents were lecture with practical (92.00 per cent), lecture with discussion and demonstration (88.00 per cent), field visit (80.00 per cent).

(4) Any Other Aspect

The response received in this regard was that 88.00 per cent of the respondents suggested that they like to have female teacher trainer. The probable reason for the choice of female teacher trainer may be that the rural women can talk and discuss freely with female teacher.

The second suggestion received was for farm demonstration by 72.00 per cent respondents.

Another suggestion made by 44.00 per cent respondents was that the center must have audio video aids laboratory.

Conclusion

It can concluded that majority of the trained and untrained farm women belonged to young age group up to 30 years. Nearly one third of the trained farm women possessed college level of education, and untrained farm women had secondary level of education.

Majority of the trained and untrained farm women belonged to large size of family.

More than three-fourth of the trained farm women had medium social participation. Whereas, more than two-third of trained and untrained farm women had medium extension participation.

In case of suggestion for making training more effective, venue should be the Farmer Training Centre, time should be during slack season, training methods should be lecture with practical followed by lecture with discussion and demonstration and field visit and they preferred female teacher for training.

Table 1
Characteristics of the Trained and Untrained Farm Women

Sr. No.	Variable	Level of variable	Category of farm women			
			Trained		Untrained	
			Number	Percent	Number	Percent
1	Age	Young (upto 30 years)	23	92.00	21	94.00
		Middle (31 to 45 years)	02	08.00	03	12.00
		Old (above 45 years)	00	00	01	04.00
2	Education	Illiterate	01	04.00	01	04.00
		Primary	04	16.00	09	36.00
		Secondary	06	24.00	10	40.00
		Higher education	06	24.00	03	12.00
		College	08	32.00	02	08.00
3	Family size	Small	11	44.00	10	40.00
		Large	14	56.00	15	60.00
4	Size of land holding	Marginal	02	08.00	04	16.00
		Small	11	44.00	12	48.00
		Medium	09	36.00	08	32.00
		Big (large)	03	12.00	01	04.00
5	Social participation	Low	02	08.00	07	28.00
		Medium	20	80.00	17	68.00
		High	03	12.00	01	04.00
6	Extension participation	Low	01	04.00	06	24.00
		Medium	18	72.00	17	68.00
		High	06	24.00	02	08.00

Table 2
Distribution of Respondents Expressing their Suggestion for Making Training More Effective

Suggestions	*Frequency*	*Percentage*
(A) Venue of Training		
1. Farmers Training Centre	16	64.00
2. At the farm site	03	12.00
3. In the village	06	24.00
(B) Time of Training		
1. During slack season	14	56.00
2. After harvesting crop	04	16.00
3. Prior to monsoon	07	28.00
(C) Training Method		
1. Lecture	09	36.00
2. Lecture with discussion	15	60.00
3. Lecture with practical	23	92.00
4. Field visit	20	80.00
5. Lecture with discussion and demonstration	22	88.00
6. Education tour	16	64.00
(D) Any other aspect		
1. Farm for demonstration	18	72.00
2. Female trainer	22	88.00
3. Audio video aids laboratory	11	44.00

References

Chothani, S.G. 1999. Training Needs of Mango Orchard Growers of Junagadh districts of Gujarat State. Unpublished M.Sc. (Agri.) Thesis, G.A.U., Sardarkrushinagar.

Gorfad, P.S. 1993. Mango Grower's knowledge and Adoption of Improved Mango Cultivation Practices. Unpublished M.Sc. (Agri.) Thesis, G.A.U., Sardarkrushinagar.

Mehta, P.O., Sawant, P.S. and Nirban, A.J. 1989. Knowledge of Farmers in Respect of Selected Agricultural Practices of Rice and Mango Crops. *Maharashtra Journal of Extension Education*, Vol. 8: 167-170.

Patil, M.B. and Waghmare, S.K. 1989. Some Personal Socio-Psychological and Extension Variables Facilitating Adoption of Banana Cultivation Technology. *Maharashtra Journal of Extension Education*, Vol. 8: 131-134.

Siddaramaiah, B.S. and Jalihal, K.A. 1983. A Scale to Measure Extension Participation of Farmers. *Indian Journal of Extension Education*, Vol. 19 (3 and 4): 74-78.

28

Self Help Group: An Accelerate of Sustainable Production in Agricultural Entrepreneurship

N.D. Bharad,
B.N. Kalsariya,
B.R. Karkar and M.N. Popat

Abstract

Training is an integral part of any development activity. Training plays vital role in making the farmers and farm women more receptive and to equip them with new technology. But training can become effective only when it is in consonance with the needs of the clients. In the present study, an attempt has been made to assess the training needs of farm women about sustainable production of agricultural entrepreneurship.

The present study was conducted at Sardar Smruti Kendra (SSK), Gujarat Agricultural University, Junagadh with collaboration of Forest Department (Gir east and west zone). Total 112 farm women (i.e. three training classes) were included in the sample. The result of this study depicted that the demonstration on preparation of different kinds of pickles, nursery raising of flower plants, grain storage management and its different methods were the major area of training needs covered by farm women.

More than half of farm women were convened into arranging three days training programme and also agree to lecture with discussion and demonstration of same per cent of respondents. Three-fourth of respondents suggested that training should be reorganized after one year and at Sardar Smruti Kendra / institution is best venue for training.

The major suggestions offered by the respondents were lecture with practical demonstration followed by all the teacher should be speaking in local language.

Introduction

Women can significantly contribute to rural economy and assist in rejuvenating agricultural resources, if they are actively involved in agriculture, animal husbandry works and be given priority over men folk. Women should be made to improve their own capacity and overcome their own problems by building self-confidence, developing leadership and management skills through training.

Training to all is a critical input for ascertaining agricultural production as well as increasing employment and income of the farming community. Training to farm women become very meaningful aspects for rural people and prior need based training for creating awareness, improving knowledge and developing skill for generating job opportunity. It is one of the most commonly used devices that impart knowledge and skill to the farmers and farm women. Before conducting training programme, it is important to know the existing situation, i.e., what is their training? Keeping this in view, the present study was conducted with following specific objectives.

1. To identify the training needs of the farm women about home science, horticulture and general in agricultural technology.
2. To know the appropriate duration, venue, time, interval and method of training programme.
3. To identify their problem to make the training more effective.

Methodology

The present study was conducted at Sardar Smruti Kendra (SSK), Gujarat Agricultural University, Junagadh. The SSK has organized three days institutional training programme in collaboration with Forest department. In this context, SSK has organized three training courses for farm women members of Self Help Group working under Eco Development Project of Forest department during the period of October to December, 2003. All participates who belonged to Una, Talala, Visavadar, Maliya hatina, and Manavadar talukas of Junagadh districts and Dhari taluka of Amreli district. Thus, in all 1112 farm women (i.e. three training classes) were included in the sample. The data were collected with the help of structured interview schedule. Thereafter, data were analyzed, tabulated and inferences were drawn in the light of above objectives of the study.

Results and Discussion

The training centre plays a vital role in transfer of farm technology to the farmers and farm women for adoption of new innovations. Training can become effective only when it is in consonance with the needs of the farm women. The results of the training needs are as under.

(A) Area of training needs perceived by the farm women

Table-1 revealed that in case of home science, demonstration on preparation of different kinds of pickles was Rank-I followed by demonstration on preparation of masala powder (Rank-II), demonstration on making of different items from milk (Rank-III) and demonstration on fruits and vegetables preservation.

Whereas, nursery raising of flower plants was Rank-I followed by marketing facilities of flowers and nursery plants (Rank-II) and nursery raising of mango, chiku, coconut, ambla, ber etc. (Rank-III) in nursery and marketing.

In general view of agriculture, grain storage management and its different method was Rank-I followed by proper care of animal (Rank-II) and making a compost pit (Rank-III).

(B) Respondents expressed their suggestion for making training more effective

More than half (54.46 per cent) of farm women suggested

three days of duration of training followed by thirty three per cent respondents suggested five days of training duration.

Nearly eighty per cent of the respondents indicated that at Sardar Smruti Kendra / institution is best venue for training. Majority of the farm women were free from their work during slack season (78.58 per cent). In case of interval of training, 73.22 per cent of farm women suggested that the training should be after one year. Whereas, more than half of respondents agreed to lecture with discussion and demonstration (51.78 per cent) followed by lecture with discussion (17.85 per cent).

(C) Suggestion offered from the respondents to improve the training programme

The farm women were asked to offer their suggestion to make the training programme more effective in future. Their responses were presented in Table-3.

The most important suggestions were lecture with practical demonstration should be shown to the farm women if possible (66.07 per cent) followed by all the teachers were lecture with practical demonstration should be shown to the farm women if possible (66.07 per cent) followed by all the teachers should speak in local language (Gujarati) (65.17 per cent); interval between two lectures (4 to 5 minutes recess) should be given; time of one lecture should be arranged one or less than one hour.

Conclusion

It can be concluded that demonstration on preparation of different kinds of pickles, nursery raising of flower plants grain storage management and its different method were the major area of training needs covered by farm women.

More than half of farm women were convened in arranging three days training programme and also agreed to lecture with discussion and demonstration of same per cent of respondents. Three-fourth of respondents suggested that training should be reorganized after one year and at Sardar Smruti Kendra / institution is best venue for training.

The major suggestions offered by the respondents were

lecture with practical demonstration followed by all the teacher should be speaking in local language.

Table 1
Area of Training Covered by the Rural Farm Women during Training

Area of training	*Number*	*Per cent*	*Rank*
[A] Home Science			
1. Demonstration on preparation of masala powder	82	73.21	II
2. Demonstration on preparation of papad	12	10.71	X
3. Demonstration on fruits and vegetables preservation	71	63.39	IV
4. Demonstration on preparation of different kinds of pickles	103	91.96	I
5. Demonstration on making of different items from milk	78	69.61	III
6. Demonstration on the best from waste.	21	18.75	VIII
7. Demonstration on making various bakery items	39	34.82	VII
8. Demonstration on preparation of sarbat, jam, jelly, tomato ketchup/ syrup	42	37.50	VI
9. Demonstration on how to making packing of bottle and others.	16	14.28	IX
10. Demonstration on making banana and potato wafer.	67	59.82	V
[B] Nursery and marketing or horticulture			
1. Nursery raising of flower plants.	19	16.96	I
2. Nursery raising of mango, chicku, coconut, ber etc.	12	1071	III
3. Marketing facility of flowers and nursery plants	17	15.17	II

Contd ...

Table 1 Contd ...

Area of training	*Number*	*Per cent*	*Rank*
[C] General agricultural			
1. Making a compost pit	52	46.42	III
2. Making a fertilizer from waste materials by use of vermicultuer	47	41.96	V
3. Grain storage management and its different method	89	79.46	I
4. Use of medicinal plant and their introduction	48	42.85	IV
5. Teaching on use of different yojana and self employment education and training	06	05.35	VIII
6. Proper method of milking the animal	27	24.10	VII
7. Duration/timing of milking animal	39	34.82	VI
8. Proper care of animal	63	56.25	II

Table 2
Distribution of Repondents Expressing their Suggestions for Making Training More Effective

Area of training	*Number*	*Per cent*
[A] Duration of training		
1. One days	07	06.25
2. Three days	61	54.46
3. Five days	37	33.03
4. Seven days	04	03.58
5. Ten days	03	02.68
[B] Venue of training		
1. At Sardar Smruti Kendra	89	79.47
2. At the farm site	09	08.03
3. In the village	14	12.50

Contd ...

Table 2 Contd ...

Area of training	*Number*	*Per cent*
[C] Time of training		
1. During the stack season/convenience of the farm women	88	78.58
2. Kharif season	01	00.89
3. Winter season	03	02.67
4. Summer season	04	03.57
5. After harvesting crop	09	08.03
6. Before crop/s sowing	07	06.26
[D] Interval of training		
1. After one year	82	73.22
2. After two years	22	19.64
3. After three years	08	07.14
[E] Training method		
1. Lecture	31	00.89
2. Lecture with discussion	20	17.85
3. Only discussion of problem	04	03.58
4. Lecture with practical	16	14.28
5. Lecture with discussion and demonstration	58	51.78
6. Field/farm experiment visit	03	02.68
7. Educational tour	06	05.36
8. Use of A.V. aids	04	03.58

Table 3
Suggestion Offered from the Respondents to Improving the Training Programme

Suggestion	*Number*	*Per cent*
1. Time of one lecture should be one or less than one hour.	58	51.78

Contd ...

Table Contd ...

2.	Interval between two lectures, 4 to 5 minutes recess should be given/ arranged.	62	53.35
3.	All the teachers should speak in local language Gujarati	73	65.17
4.	Lecture with practical demonstration should be shown to the farm women if possible.	74	66.07
5.	Every teacher should be provided a Lecture note.	43	38.39
6.	Every teacher should use audio visual aids during delivering his Lecture.	37	33.03
7.	After two or three years, reoriented training should be organized.	22	19.42
8.	Test should be arrange after completion of training and rewarded first three for increasing/sustaining enthusiasm of trainees.	15	13.39
9.	During the training period, the subjects which are not involved in training course, provide free agricultural literature to be helpful to trainees.	08	07.14
10.	Training should be provided to young generation, who are quick to adopt new agricultural technology.	31	27.67
11.	Especially for the pest and disease, the pictures of these should be exhibited show during Lectures of plant protection.	45	40.17

References

Thakor, R.F. and Patel, K.F. (1997 and 98). Training Needs of Rural Women. *Gujarat journal of Extension Education.* VIII and IX: 134-137.

Meena, R.K. and Chauhan, M.S. (2002). Training Needs of Farmers about Improved Production Practices of Groundnut, *Rajasthan Journal of Extension Education,* 10: 117-121.

29
Correlates of Knowledge of Farm Women on Improved Mango Cultivation

M.C. Dhaduk,
B.R. Karkar,
B.N. Kalsariya and N.D. Bharad

Abstract

The study was conducted in three villages i.e. Akolvadi, Prempara and Thoradi of Talala, Visavadar and Una talukas of Junagadh district, respectively to know the knowledge level of farm women and their relationship with the independent variable. The total number of 25 trained and 25 untrained farm women selected proportionately by random sampling technique. The result of the study depicted that more than three-fourth (76.00 per cent) of trained and more than half (56.00 per cent) of untrained farm women were in medium knowledge level group.

Age and education had negative and positive significant correlation with knowledge level of trained farm women respectively. Whereas, untrained farm women, age and social participation had negative and positive correlation with the knowledge level of respondents on improved mango cultivation, respectively.

Introduction

Mango is one of the ancient fruit of India. It is most thrived age old major crop as well as the cash crop of Junagadh district. The cultivation technology of mango orchard is complex and sophisticated. Wide gap exists between its innovations and applications on the farmer's field. From ancient day women have played a pivotal role in agricultural production in India, it is felt necessary to improve their technology. This is only possible by organizing the need based intensity training programme. Therefore, mango growers should be trained in specific operational technical know-how and skills embracing all phases of production for maximizing their economic returns. Keeping this fact in mind, the present study was undertaken with the following objectives.

1. To know the knowledge level of respondents regarding the improved mango cultivation.
2. To study the relationship between the characteristics of the respondents and their knowledge regarding the improved mango cultivation.

Methodology

Three villages, i.e., Akolvadi, Prempara and Thoradi of Talala, Visavadar and Una talukas of Junagadh district were selected purposely for the study during the month of June, 2003. The total number of 25 trained and 25 untrained farm women, i.e., sum of total 50 respondents were selected from the entire three villages by using random sampling technique.

For measuring the level of knowledge of improved mango cultivation by the farm women, the teacher made scale was developed and used. The scale of 25 items concerning improved mango cultivation. The respondents were asked to answer correct or incorrect, right or wrong, yes or no against each item. One score was given to correct response, while zero score was given to incorrect answer. The knowledge score was calculated as sum of the scores of correct responses converted into percentage and simple correlation co-efficient was calculated.

Findings and Discussion

The data indicated that a great majority of trained (76.00 per cent) and untrained (56.00 per cent) farm women fall in the category of medium knowledge level group. The 16.00 per cent and 8.00 per cent trained farm women possessed high and low level of knowledge about improved mango cultivation, respectively. While in the case of untrained farm women, 36.00 per cent and 8.00 per cent of respondents had low and high level of knowledge, respectively.

This finding is in conformity with the finding of Darbh et.al. (1999) and Sakariya (1991).

The Table-2 revealed that in case of trained farm women, only two variables i.e. age and education were found negative and positive correlation with the knowledge level of farm women about improved mango cultivation, respectively. Whereas, family size, size of land holding, social participation and extension participation had non significant correlation with the level of knowledge of respondents.

The probable reason may be that the young farm women were generally more educated and with greater receptive power, more exposed and wider mental horizons.

In case of untrained farm women, age and social participation had negative and positive correlation with the knowledge level of respondents on improved mango cultivation, respectively.

Whereas education, size of land holding, family size and extension participation were found non significant with the level of knowledge of respondents.

These findings are similar with the findings of Charu Lata (1995) and Chothani (1999).

Conclusion

It can be concluded that more than three-fourth (76.00 per cent) of trained and more than half (56.00 per cent) of untrained farm women were medium knowledge level group.

Age and education had negative and positive significant correlation with knowledge level of trained farm women, respectively. Whereas, in untrained farm women, age and social participation had negative and positive correlation with the knowledge level of respondents on improved mango cultivation, respectively.

Implication

1. To raise the level of knowledge, the extension workers should strive to bring up the characteristics such as reading habit, education, training received, extension participation.
2. Efforts should be made for extensive use of audio video aids in the training programme.

Table 1
Level of Knowledge about Improved Mango Cultivation by the Respondents

Knowledge level category	*Category of farm women*			
	Trained		*Untrained*	
	Frequency	*Per cent*	*Frequency*	*Per cent*
Low	02	08.00	09	36.00
Medium	19	76.00	14	56.00
High	04	16.00	02	08.00

Table 2
Relationship between Selected Characteristics of Trained and Untrained Farm Women and their Level of Knowledge of Improved Mango Cultivation

Characteristics	*"r" value*	
	Trained	*Untrained*
X_1 Age	-0.4848*	-0.2932*
X_2 Education	0.3810*	0.2568 NS
X_3 Family size	-0.2869 NS	-0.1884 NS
X_4 Size of land holding	0.2670 NS	0.5646 NS
X_5 Social participation	0.1628 NS	0.5392*
X_6 Extension participation	0.1947 NS	0.3122 NS

* = Significant at 0.05 level
NS = Non significant

References

Chandel, R.S. 1978. A Handbook of Agricultural Statistics. Achal Prakashan Mandir, Kanpur: 297 - 304.

Charu Lata, Verma, S.K. and Vinita Jain (1993). Cognitive Access of Men and Women Regarding Paddy Cultivation on rural Haryana. *Indian Journal of Social Research*. 34(3): 241-247.

Chothani, S.G. 1999. Training Needs of Mango Orchard Growers of Junagadh district of Gujarat State. Unpublished M.Sc. (Agri.) Thesis, G.A.U., Sardarkrushinagar.

Darbh, S., Bhople, R.S. and Shinde, R.S. 1999. Determinants of Knowledge and Adoption of Recommended Cultivation Practices of Custard Apple. *Maharashtra Journal of Extension Education*, 17: 279-284.

Sakariya, K.M. 1991. Level of Knowledge and Training Needs at Groundnut Growing Farm Women in Respect to Groundnut Production Technology. M.Sc. (Agri.) Thesis, GAU, Sardarkrushinagar.

30

Scope of Women Entrepreneurship through Home Science Curriculum in Traditional University

Kamble Rajkumar and Shinde Ulka

Introduction

The process of human evaluation goes parallel with the education of the human beings as is evident from the history of civilization. Home science education has become an important integral part of our education system and has tenets in the community all over the country. Home Science is a dynamic profession with a richly diverse range of practice, theories, research and skills, which the qualified practitioners can adopt in so many problem solving situations. There is great need that Home Science education should be focused on the knowledge objectives, attitude objectives and skill objectives. However, this implementation is rarely possible in the home science education under social science in traditional university. Hence, there is an emerging need to establish the training center of women entrepreneurship for the professional approach and wide identity of Home Science students.

Comparison of Home Science Education Between Science Oriented and Social Sciences Stream

By comparison of these 10 characters social science stream has less opportunities in economically self reliant and professional

Sr. No.	*Science Oriented*	*Social Sciences oriented*	
1.	Knowledge coverage areas	More	Less
2.	Examination system	Semester	Annual
3.	Duration of degree course	Four years	Three years
4.	Research areas	As per specialization	General
5.	Extension work	As per Specialization	General
6.	Motivation for the subject	As per specialization	General
7.	Acquiring knowledge	More, each semester offers different courses	Less, students are having option to choose the other subject papers also
8.	Percentage for higher studies (i.e. PG, M.Phil, Ph.D.)	More	Less
9.	Percentage of passing NET, SET qualifying examination for lectureship and research scholarship	More	Less
10.	Professional exposure and job settlement	More	Less

identity in wide range. Hence, these students do not get, viable and reliable exposure after graduation. Therefore, the training centre of women entrepreneurship will provide a platform to these students for the development of self confidence, self expression, motivation to run small scale business, able to earning at early age while learning, and independent professional identity.

Entrepreneurship through Home Science Curriculum

In the three year degree course students covered at least one paper from five specialization areas of Home Science. Hence, they get basic knowledge or idea about each specialization. By using this knowledge students will be able to boost themselves as a entrepreneur through training centre. There is wide scope of entrepreneurship training areas like traditional and novelty areas such as:

Sr.	*Traditional Areas*	*Sr.*	*Novelty Areas*
1.	Ideal planning of crèche and preschool management.	1.	Landscaping and gardening, flower preservation and bouque center, windows treatment
2.	Dietetic counseling center-to start independently or in consultation with other medical hospitals.	2.	Bakery Unit – with emphasize on high fibre bread, biscuits, etc.
3.	Traditional textile and dress designing including embroideries, paithani, narayan pethi, batik, tie-die, etc.	3.	Formulation of weaning mixes and supplementary foods and their marketing.
4.	Interior decorator – Independently or in collaboration with the architecture in home, hotels, hospital, executive offices.	4.	Cultivation of vegetables and fruits with soil fortification of minerals or consultation with farmers or cultivators.
5.	Cultivation and preservation of mushroom and its marketing	5.	Project management, organizational structure, leadership development and use of advanced technology.
		6	Communication, marketing, profit margin and linkages with agro based industries, village industry, food processing textile designers, national-international organizations and NGO's dealing and co-operation techniques.

On the whole it can be concluded that, Home Science graduate students acquire basic knowledge during their course work but they are unable to implement their gained knowledge into professional and in practical utility. There is a wide scope to the Home Science student to develop as a good entrepreneur training centers and modification of curriculum according to the new trends, technology and need base.

31
Entrepreneurship: A Key to Empowerment

Sangeeta Patel

Introduction

Woman is often described as the better half of man. But the actual condition of women in the world does not match with this description. By and large across the world, women have not achieved even equality with men. Nearly 70% of the world's 1.4 billion poor people are women. Of the world's 30 million refugees 80% are women and children, of the world's one billion illiterate adults two-third are women and of the 150 million children world wide who are not in schools, two-third are girls.

In India, women constitute about 48 percent of the population but their participation in economic activity is only 34 percent. There is a continuing concentration of women in low paid and low status occupations which indicates that women are marginalized in the labour force. There is a common assumption that men are the bread winners and that most of the female work is either done in the leisure time or serves as the procurer of supporting income for the family.

The major reason for this is social prejudice is that women's world is required to be focused around family and household. In addition to this, in India's rural areas there is lack of education, lack of health care facilities and lack of effective opportunities of employment for women. Such constraints and social traditions largely inhibit the emergence of this vast potential of women power which remains the nation's greatest untapped resource.

Empowerment of Women

It is believed that economic strength is the basis of social, political and psychological power in the society. Thus the lower status of women mostly stems from their low economic status and subsequent dependence and lack of decision making power. Therefore, if women gain economic strength, they gain visibility and voice.

Among the various approaches, the empowerment approach in development programmes is considered the best. This approach is modeled to 'power' itself and gain control over the self, the resources and freedom to decide. This process of gaining control over the self, the resources and the decision making power may be termed as empowerment. Ideally, the empowerment process should aim at "women finding time and space of their own" and should provide mechanisms for their active participation in the development process.

Further it should ensure their role in decision making and should foster self reliance both socially and economically. Significant contributions towards women empowerment can be made by facilitating their direct participation in income generation activities and decision making capacity. This will enable to take initiatives for their development into their own hands. Through a well directed package of skill enhancement, credit facilities and educational inputs, women can discover their economic role and gain recognition in the society.

Entrepreneurship can help women's economic independence and improve their social status. Automatically the women get empowered once they attain economic independence. The development of women entrepreneurship enables society to understand and appreciate their abilities. It enhances their status and leads to integration of women in nation building and economic development. It provides the needed psychological satisfaction and imbibes a deep sense of achievement to create their enhanced identify in society.

Status of Women Entrepreneurs

Since the turn of the century, the status of women in India has been changing due to growing industrialization and urbanization, spatial mobility and social legislation. Over the years, more number of women are going in for higher education, technical and professional education and their proportion in the labour force has also increased.

With the spread of education and awareness, women have shifted from the extent of kitchen, handicrafts and traditional cottage industries to non-traditional higher levels of activities. During the 1970s the decade of the International Women's Year, efforts to promote self-employment among women received greater attention from the government and private agencies. The new industrial policy of the Government of India has laid special emphasis on the need for conducting special entrepreneurial training programmes for women to enable them to start their own ventures.

Financial institutions and banks have also set up special cells to assist women entrepreneurs. The result has been the emergence of women entrepreneurs on the economic scene in recent years, though the number of enterprises initiated by women is still quite low. Women's entrepreneurship has remained a much neglected field.

Almost half the population of our country comprises of women while businesses owned and operated by them constitute less than 5 percent. This is a reflection on social, cultural as well as economic distortions in the decades of development.

In fact, women's contribution and participation in economic activity and production of goods and services is much greater than statistics reveal, since much of it takes place in the informal sector and also in the households.

As education has spread and compulsions for earning have grown, more and more women have started to go out of the homes and opt for employment - wage, self or entrepreneurial career.

However, for women there are several handicaps to enter into and manage business ownership due to conservative and orthodox Indian society.

1. Problems faced by women entrepreneurs

The problems and constraints experienced by women entrepreneurs have resulted in restricting the expansion of women entrepreneurship. The major barriers encountered by women entrepreneurs are:

1.1 Lack of confidence

Women have lack of confidence in their own capabilities. Since long women are accepting a subordinate status. Even at home, members of family do not have confidence on their abilities and their decision making.

Society in general also lacks confidence in women's strength, traits and competence. This is quite apparent as the family is reluctant to finance women's venture, banker is reluctant to take risks on projects set up by women and individual is unwilling to stand guarantor for loan to a women.

1.2 Problems of finance and working capital

Another problem faced by women entrepreneurs is lack of access to funds as they do not possess any tangible security and credit in the market. Since the women do not enjoy right over property of any form, they have limited access over external sources of funds. Even the family members have no confidence in the capability of women in running the business.

The serious problem encountered by women entrepreneurs is obtaining working capital for financing day-to-day operations of the enterprises, including purchase of raw materials and meeting pay rolls. The chronic shortage of working capital leaves women entrepreneurs extremely vulnerable to competition and other emergencies.

The complex and complicated procedure of bank loans, the delay in obtaining the loans and running about involved, deter many women from establishing enterprises.

1.3 Socio-Cultural barriers

Women has to perform her family duties irrespective of her career as working woman or an entrepreneur. In our society, more importance is given to educating male child as compared to female child. This results in lack of schooling and vocational training of women, their lack of attaining technical skills and thereby lack of awareness of opportunities available.

This adds to constraints for establishing enterprise by women. Even the male labour do not prefer working under lady boss. Woman entrepreneurs are not taken seriously by labour force. This all hinders the women entrepreneurship.

2. *Production problems*

Production in manufacturing enterprise involves coordination of a number of activities. While some of these activities are in the control of entrepreneur, there are others over which she has little control. Improper coordination and delay in execution of any activity cause production problems in industry. Inability of women entrepreneurs to keep pace with latest advances in technology and lack of technical know how results in high cost of technology acquisition and machinery utilization. These problems result in increasing the cost of production and adversely affect the profitability of the unit.

2.1 Inefficient marketing arrangements

Heavy competition in the market, lack of mobility of woman makes the dependence of women entrepreneurs on middlemen indispensable. For marketing the products, women entrepreneurs are at the mercy of middleman who pocket major chunk of profit. Further, women entrepreneurs also find it difficult to capture the market and make their products popular. There is lack of information on changing market. In addition, for women entrepreneur, there is difficulty of collection of payments.

Recommendations

In small and medium enterprises majority of functions have to be performed by owners themselves due to limitation of resources. In case of women entrepreneurs the problems get compounded because certain problems have gender dimensions attached to it.

The domestic commitments and child-care support are the two main responsibilities of women. This along with narrow outlook of the society in still accepting woman as a separate entity as an entrepreneur makes the life of a woman entrepreneur more difficult. To meet all these challenges and to encourage woman entrepreneurship some recommendations are suggested. These are:

- To overcome the initial resistance from husband and family members at the time of setting up of a venture, the prospective women entrepreneurs are suggested to maintain their cool and persistently convince them, without confronting them regarding benefits of setting up of an enterprise. Strong inherent will power of woman is required in such difficult times. The inflow of money in the home will eventually solve this problem.
- The responsibilities of shouldering dual duties of an entrepreneur and home management by a woman entrepreneur can be effectively undertaken by adopting better time management. The family members or other business partners can also be involved in the business which will help in sharing the burden of entrepreneurial work. Moreover, woman entrepreneur must try to make her husband and children self-sufficient at home. Using little tact and diplomacy, she should solicit cooperation from family members.
- A woman can set up home based business. By operating her business from home a woman can coordinate household and business responsibilities in a smoother way.
- A woman can start her business when her children have reasonably grown up to take care of their own small needs. This gives enough time to woman for managing her enterprise.
- Confidence building training should be given to women to do away with traditional feeling that women are interior to men and are dependent on men. Women must acquire education which makes them mentally strong.
- For marketing of products, women entrepreneurs must establish their credibility first in terms of quality and

competitiveness of product or service. She should acquire relevant techniques and skills on winning customer's loyalty. E-commerce business will also help greatly in this regard. For publicity and advertisement, the women entrepreneur can work on alternatives like cable TV, pamphlets, leaflets, slides in cinema halls, displaying banners at strategic locations etc.

- Effective and efficient use of information technology like internet can help in assimilating information about variety, range and quality of products, publicity and marketing of products and services.
- Workshop and seminars should be organised frequently for the officials of financial and support agencies and the women entrepreneurs to make their relations more cordial.
- Simplification of procedures for providing financial assistance by banks and government organizations is another area required to be taken up. Women inspectors if available, should be asked to inspect women enterprises.
- It has been observed, that there is tendency to project higher value of sales, production and profits in project reports to impress the bankers. Such project profile is not appropriate from a good financial management point of view. So, women entrepreneur need to undertake training in various aspects of financial management to understand its finer implications.
- Most of the times it is difficult to acquire loans from government financial agencies and banks due to complicated lengthy procedural difficulties.It is suggested that women entrepreneur can search for non-formal sources of finance like private financiers, relatives, friends and committees etc.
- In banks and financial institutions, minimum target of loan to be disbursed to women entrepreneurs should be followed. Collateral security should be dispensed away in the case of women entrepreneurs because women have

hardly any property or other assets in their name to be guaranteed as collateral. Marginal money for projects to be undertaken by women entrepreneurs should not exceed ten percent. Subsidy under the schemes should also be given to the women entrepreneurs at the initial stage itself.

- Women entrepreneurs should acquire relevant training in technology and in details of their plant and machinery. They should have knowledge about the functioning of machines and processes so that labour cannot befool them. They need to be more assertive towards their employees. She should prefer employing more number of women workers in her enterprise. They must undergo training in management skills to help them in handling of human resources, training in effective communication skills and practices and legal aspects of running a business.
- Group entrepreneurship is a viable option for weaker sections of the society and it is an instrument which helps the poor women to overcome their poverty. It empowers women and provides necessary mental confidence for entrepreneurship. Women's organizations, women's cooperatives and NGOs should be promoted to assist self-employment for poor women.

Conclusion

"When women move forward, the family moves, the village moves and the nation moves". These words of Pandit Jawahar Lal Nehru are an accepted fact. Employment gives economic status to women. Economic status gives way to social status and thereby empowerment to women.

In present scenario due to modernization, urbanization, globalization and development of education, with increasing awareness women are now seeking gainful employment in several fields.

Women are entering into entrepreneurship even while facing socio-cultural, economic, technical, financial and managerial difficulties. Women entrepreneurship movement can gain momentum by providing encouragement, appropriate awareness, training, environment and support. This would definitely enhance their socio-economic status, a pre-requisite of women's empowerment.

32

Women Entrepreneurs in Lower Middle Class Families and Their Problems

Kamalamani Rao

Introduction

The dream of becoming the owner of her own business is no more a vision in the lower middle - class women entrepreneurs in this changing society, even though this field is no bed of roses to her and that the society is still not ready to accept woman in a separate entity as an entrepreneur, which makes her life more difficult.

This has not barred the young and older women to start some or the other small scale or home industry in the field of education, health and home industries like tailoring, pappad, pickle making etc. with very less finance in their hands but with self-confidence and self-respect.

In carrying on her enterprise, the woman has not forgotten to keep up her cool and maintain cordial relationship among the family members. Time management also becomes one of the main responsibilities of a woman entrepreneur of any field along with income earning, then only she can discharge her dual role of an entrepreneur, wife and mother.

By working hard they have proved that they are par with men folks and have raised their standard in the eyes of the society and wiped out the dependency syndrome, at the same time to tide over the problem of "male ego", an atmosphere of cooperativeness and humility need to be established in the home so that there are no ego-battles.

This has encouraged me to do the survey of women entrepreneurs in lower middle class families in Rajkot and problems faced by them.

Material and Method

A survey was carried on Women Entrepreneurs in lower - middle class families by questionnaire method in Rajkot and the sample size being 25 women entrepreneurs and grouped in three categories according to their nature of work. The questionnaire includes following format.

Questionnaire

Women Entrepreneurs in Lower-Middle Class Families and their Problems

(A) 1. Name

2. Age

3. Education

4. Family Income

5. Family Size

(B) *Nature of Period of Business:*

Education	*Period*	*Health & Physique*	*Period*	*Miscellaneous*	*Period*
Tuition		Beauty Parlour		Household Industries	
				Papad	
Play house				Masala	
				Pickle	

Contd ...

Table Contd ...

Education	*Period*	*Health & Physique*	*Period*	*Miscellaneous*	*Period*
				Tailoring and Embroidery	
				Artificial and Fancy Jewellery Making	

(C) Reason for Starting the business:

1. Big Family Size:
2. Death of husband:
3. Disability of income earner:
4. Divorce:

(D) Marketing and Sales Income:

Market Income - Below Rs.1500/- Rs.1500-3000/-

1. Local
2. Outside

(E) Problems faced during the work:

1. Arrangement of finance:
2. Arrangement of material:
3. Availability of market:
4. Limited work space:
5. Inadequate publicity:
6. Collection of payment:

(F) Attitude and Co-operation of:

1. Husband:
2. Family members:
3. Relatives:
4. Neighbours:

(G) Contribution to the Society / Family by you:

1. Work satisfaction

2. To bring out hidden skills and potentials of women
3. Supporting family members and employment generation
4. To upgrade self respect of women in the society
5. Maintaining dual responsibility of an entrepreneur and housewife and mother.

On the basis of data collected the three groups include number of women entrepreneurs according to their nature of work.

GROUP I	*GROUP II*	*GROUP III*
Education (Tuition and Playhouse)	Health and Physique (Beauty Parlour)	Miscellaneous Household industries, Tailoring and Embroidery, Artificial and Fancy Jewellery making.

Results and Discussion

The data obtained is presented in Table I and Graph I and II.

Table I
Findings of the Survey of 25 Women Entrepreneurs in Lower Middle Class Families and their Problems

General Information	*Group I*	*Group II*	*Group III*
	Education	Health and Physique	Miscellaneous Industries
	Tuition, Playhouse	Beauty Parlour	Household Inds. Tailoring and embroidery Artificial fancy Jewellery
Women entrepreneurs in %	28	24	48
(A) Background			
Age (years)	32-40	31-44	18-40
Education	Graduate	Graduate	Under Graduate
Family size	2-6	3-4	5-6

Contd ...

Table 1 Contd ...

General Information	*Group I*	*Group II*	*Group III*
(B) Period of Business (years)	2-10	2-10	2-7
(C) Reasons for Starting the Business			
1. Big family size	As a Hobby Some as to meet family needs	For livelihood As a hobby and for mental peace To avoid loneliness	Due to single male earner Disability of male earner
2. Death of husband			
3. Disability of income earner			
4. Others			
(D) Marketing and Sales			
1 Income Rs. month	2000 - 2900	1300-3000	900 - 2250
Local	Nearby	Customers	To shops
Outside	Children, of friends and working women	from nearby area, friends	friends, Relatives and nearby people
	Education	Health and Physique	Miscellaneous Industries
	Tuition, Playhouse	Beauty Parlour	Household Inds. Tailoring and embroidery Artificial fancy Jewellery
(E)Problems faced during the work			
1. Arrangement of finance	Self finance, Relatives, friends, advance payment	Self finance	Self finance Part Advance payment

Contd ...

Table 1 Contd ...

General Information	*Group I*	*Group II*	*Group III*
2. Arrangement of material	From local market	From local market	From local market
3. Availability of market	Friends, Relatives and Neighbour	Nearby area, friends and Relatives	Shops, friends and Relatives local people
4. Work space	Sufficient with equipped facilities	Well equipped rooms	Limited space
5. Publicity	Mouth to Mouth Pamphlets	Mouth to mouth pamphlets	Unawareness cannot afford advertising
6. Collecting payment	Advance Cash	Advance Cash	Advance against order balance cash payment
(F) Attitude and Cooperation of			
1. Husband 2. Family members Relatives and Neighbours	Full Cooperation From everybody Few husbands do not cooperate	Full Cooperation From everybody Few are teased by in-laws and relatives	Full Cooperation From everybody
(G) Contribution to society/family by you			
1. Work satisfaction	Satisfied, feel they are training children	Satisfied, get mental peace	Satisfied, want to expand business
2. To bring out hidden skills and potentials of women	Want to teach others and develop qualities in unemployed women	Want to train others and develop qualities in unemployed women	Want to train others and to save old traditional art and do training class for unemployed women for employment

Contd ...

Table 1 Contd ...

General Information	*Group I*	*Group II*	*Group III*
3. Supporting family members and employment generation	Financial support	Financial support	Financial support
4. To upgrade self respect of women in society	Women must come forward for any challenging job to do	Women must come forward for any challenging job to do	Women must come forward for any challenging job to do in any circumstance
5. Maintaining dual responsibility of entrepreneur and housewife	Carry out dual responsibility	Carry out dual responsibility	Carry out dual responsibility

Discussion

Regarding the socio-economic profile of these women, the data indicates that women entrepreneur is graduate in Group-I 28% and Group-II 24%. The data therefore proves that a good educational background helps to be a successful entrepreneur. In Group-III 48% women entrepreneur were undergraduate but had good skill in their work and practical experience.

Age-wise Group-I was in the age of 32-40 years, Group-II 31-44 years and Group-III between 18-40 years when they started their enterprise. This shows that there is no age bar to start own enterprise.

Some women entrepreneurs of Group-I started business as hobby while others to meet family needs whereas Group-II started to avoid loneliness, for mental peace and as a livelihood Group-III started business to meet family needs due to large family size, and disability of male earner.

Group-I shows earning of Rs. 2000-2900 month, Group-II 1200-3000 month and Group-III 900-2250 month. Women entrepreneurs of all groups had self-finance arrangement or borrowed from friends or relatives to start and continue their enterprise.

The survey also shows that most women entrepreneurs received better cooperation from all members. Few women entrepreneurs in Group-I and II were humiliated by in-laws.

Graph 1 : Percentage Women Entrepreneurs having Different Enterprises

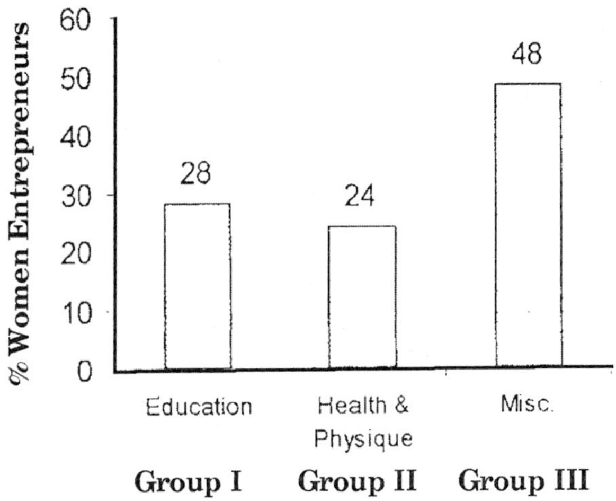

Graph 2 : Women Entrepreneurs monthly income in different Enterprise

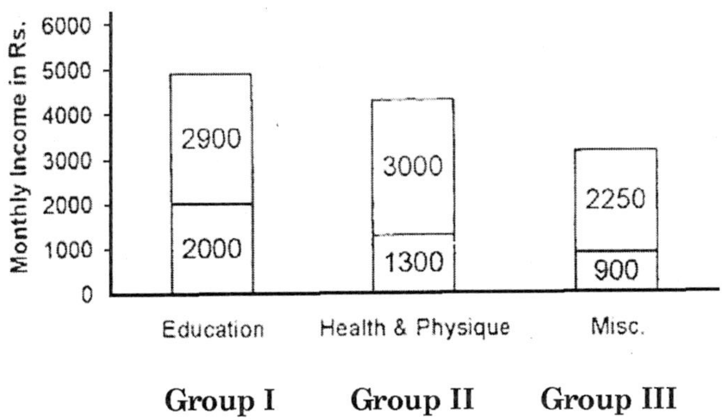

Conclusion

It is clear from the survey that women entrepreneurs are efficient, hardworking, follow a disciplined routine and effectively discharge the dual role of a family responsibility and entrepreneur. They should solicit love and cooperation from family members by using, if required, a little diplomacy.

Acknowledgement

I than all women entrepreneurs for their kind response and cooperation during the survey.

Reference

Sharma, D.D. and Dhameja, S.K., Women and Rural Entrepreneurship in India, pp. 9, 11, 31, 32.

33
Constraints of Women Entrepreneurs

Neerja Jaiswal

Abstract

The present descriptive research was undertaken with the objective of identifying the constraints encountered by the women entrepreneurs' while establishing and running their enterprise and to determine the nature of problem solving adopted by them. A sample of 113 women entrepreneurs of Vadodara city, selected through snowball method, based on a set criterion, were interviewed personally on a pre-tested interview schedule by the investigator for data collection. The major findings of the study high-lighted that women entrepreneurs experienced all sorts of problems related to finance, technical, labour, marketing, legal and general ones. Solving the problem jointly with husband pre-dominantly existed among the women entrepreneurs.

Introduction

New industrial policy of Government of India has highlighted the need for special entrepreneurship programs for women entrepreneurs, with an objective of enabling them to initiate entrepreneurship. Due to the growth of industrialization, urbanization, education and democratic system in the country, the tradition bound Indian society has seen a major technological change and the women are now seeking gainful employment in several fields in increasing numbers. The women entrepreneurship movement has taken off the ground and it is felt that the moment has crossed the stage of transition. It is during the last 15 years, women have started becoming entrepreneurs and started enterprises and business. They are yet to go a long way to be at par with men. The fact however cannot be denied that constraints always exist in an enterprise irrespective of their size and nature. Though magnitude of problems or constraints may vary from enterprise to enterprise, whether it be owned by a women or men.

Women entrepreneurs experience multidimensional constraints. The problems follow like a shadow. If she can overcome a problem, few more will crop up. The entrepreneur faces problems in the beginning, i.e., starting problems. She is confronted with problems when the enterprise is running. She therefore, has to look after the entire spectrum of problems despite the great limitations under which she functions.

Women as a group faces additional hurdles when compared to their male counterparts (Rao, 1995). Bhadwar, et.al. (1988) points :

> *"One must remember that the very concept of entrepreneurship will cease to exist unless there is the element of struggle. So women will have to brave the odds and succeed".*

In the post independence period, the Government at the centre and in the states have established a number of specialized institutions to cater to the need of women enterprises. These promotional institutions assist all and sundry in setting-up units with a view either to fulfill their objectives or over-reach their targets; but they do not ensure the provisions of adequate working capital, raw material, power supply, nor do they assist them in developing marketing outlets for the sale of their products. This situation has arised because of the absence of a meaningful co-ordination among the concerned agencies.

The schemes and programs intended for the women entrepreneurs had good intentions and despite the growth and the overall contribution in the Indian economy, the women entrepreneurs have suffered many problems. The plethora of institutions without any effective co-ordination and subsequent snags/lacunae at the implementation level has resulted in much gap between the plans and their implementation.

Review of literature have made it evident that few studies have been conducted on women entrepreneurs studying different entrepreneurial aspect at different geographical areas. The nature of problems experienced by women entrepreneurs of Baroda city was thought to be an area yet less explored which motivated the investigator to conceptualize the present research. The problems faced by the respondents would serve as an informative experiences guiding the existing and the new emerging women entrepreneurs. It would also assist the policy makers at government and non-governmental level to understand the problems of women entrepreneurs more precisely and pragmatically and thus modify and plan their programs based on the actual desired needs. Thus, the present research was undertaken with the following objectives:

Objectives of the Study

1. To identify the constraints encountered by the women entrepreneurs while establishing and running their enterprise.
2. To determine the nature of the problem solving adopted by the women entrepreneur.

Methods and Procedures

The present study was carried in Baroda city of Gujarat. It is descriptive in nature as it elaborates at the existing facts regarding the various problems faced by the women entrepreneurs. Simultaneously it also describes the nature of the problem solving adopted by them. The unit of enquiry of the present study constituted 113 women entrepreneurs, selected out of 245, based on a set of criterion. Only those women entrepreneurs were selected who had been in the business for at least 3 years at the time of data collection.

The snowball sampling technique was adopted to collect the data on a pre-tested interview schedule. The data was collected by personally interviewing the respondents, with prior appointments. The data was then coded, tabulated and subjected to descriptive statistical analysis.

Findings of the Study

The constraints encountered by the respondents while initiating or at different stages of operating their enterprises have been discussed underneath. These constraints have been categorized into financial, technical, personnel, marketing, legal and miscellaneous heads.

Finacial

Table 1
Financial Problems Encountered by the Respondents while Initiating and Running the Enterprise

	Financial Problems	*N=113*	
		F	*%*
1.	Apprehensions of financial institutions for recovery of the loans	20	17.70
2.	Unawareness about the sources of borrowing	5	4.42
3.	Lack of collateral security to secure the money borrowed	10	8.85
4.	Limited working capital	60	53.10
5.	Economic incredibility regarding women	13	11.50
6.	Supply/sales on credit	42	37.17
7.	Delays in sales/cash realization	47	41.59
8.	Complicated/lengthy procedures of loan sanctioning	28	24.78
9.	Non co-operative attitude of bank personnel	23	20.35
10.	Cost price squeeze	20	17.70
11.	High rates of taxation	27	23.89
12.	Miscellaneous	8	7.08

Note: Total exceeds due to Multiple Responses.

Nearly one-half of the respondents expressed the problem of limited funds hindering the growth of their enterprise (Table 1). 41.59 per cent and 37.17 per cent of the respondents respectively were troubled by delays in sales/cash realisations and supply/sales on credits. About one-fifth of them complained about the high rates of taxation specially sales tax and octroi and three times high royalty in the state as compared to other states. Harassment caused by tax personnel and octroi department dissatisfied one of the respondents. One-fifth of them had difficulty with the non co-operative attitude of the bank personnel. 24.78 per cent complained about the complicated and lengthy procedures of loan sanctioning. High rate of interest for working capital, push required for availing loans through somebody, non-availability of government subsidy, non-availability of loans even after making lot of efforts and demand of husband's guarantee as security by the financial institutions were some of the other problems faced by 7.08 per cent of the respondents.

Technical

One-fifth of the respondents encountered difficulty in repairs and maintenance of the machineries and another one-fifth lacked specialized skills to undertake specific projects (Table 2). Other problem faced were availing of unmatched machinery due to unawareness about it and lack of technical inputs for innovations, overall development and modernization of the unit.

Table 2
Technical Problems Encountered by the Respondents while Initiating and Running the Enterprise

Technical Problems		*N=113*	
		F	*%*
1.	Lack of technical know-how involved	15	13.27
2.	Non-availability of modern technology	13	11.50
3.	Difficulty in repairs and maintenance of machinery involved	23	20.35
4.	Lack of specialized skills to work to specific projects	23	20.35
5.	Miscellaneous	3	2.65

Note: Multiple Responses

41.59 per cent of the respondents were found to be quite anxious about the non-availability of skilled and experienced personnel (Table 3). Slightly higher than one-fourth of them reported absenteeism as a very major and frequent problem with no abatement, directly affecting the productivity of the enterprise. Insufficient quality of personnel was stated by nearly one-fifth of the respondents. Miscellaneous problems highlighted among 7.96 per cent of the respondents included pro-labour policy of the government, delayed deliveries due to dependence on the labourers specially during festive seasons like Holi and Deepawali when they visit their native place irrespective of the workload at hand, without intimating any specific date of their return. Problems related to lending of money to the labourers, who later quits the job suddenly, against no security and untrustworthy lower level workers indulging in stealing of the materials were reported to be very serious in nature. Problem of quitting the job even when paid high salary or/when offered more by somebody else were also experienced by the respondents.

Table 3
Labour/Personnel Problems Encountered by the Respondents while Initiating and Running the Enterprise

Labour / Personnel Problems		*N=113*	
		F	*%*
1.	High turnover of the staff/workers	16	14.16
2.	Non-availability of skilled and experienced personnel	47	41.59
3.	General insufficiency of the personnel	25	22.12
4.	Absenteeism	31	27.43
5.	High salary/wages/bonus demands	18	15.93
6.	Unrealistic demands of service terms and conditions	9	7.96
7.	Frequent strike/go slow movements	7	6.19
8.	Strained labour relations	6	5.31
9.	Miscellaneous	9	7.96

Note: Total exceeds due to Multiple Responses

Marketing/sales problems

Stiff competition was the dominant problem faced by slightly less than one-half of the respondents (Table 4). High cost of advertising ranked second (28.32 per cent). One-fourth of the respondents were encountered by the fluctuating demand of their

Table 4
Marketing and Sales Problems Encountered by the Respondents while Initiating and Running the Enterpreise

Marketing and Sales Problems		*N=113*	
		F	*%*
1.	Lack of required marketing infrastructure	20	17.70
2.	High cost of advertising/sales promotion	32	28.32
3.	Stiff competition	51	45.13
4.	Lack of adequate market orientation	4	3.54
5.	Inability to approach clients/customers directly due to limited mobility	20	17.70
6.	Fluctuations in the demand of product/service	29	25.66
7.	Fluctuations in the prices of products	27	23.89
8.	Miscellaneous	4	3.54

Note: Total exceeds due to Multiple Responses

product/service. Other problems dealt with the search for dealers, industry recession affecting the sales, unscrupulous brokers and poor location of the unit, thus reducing the business.

Legal Problems

17.70 per cent of the respondents complained about the applicability of too many legislation and equally the same percentage were unhappy with the requirement of compulsory

Table 5

Legal Problems Encountered by the Respondents while Initiating and Running the Enterprise

Legal Problems		*N=113*	
		F	*%*
1.	Too many legislations applicable	20	17.70
2.	Complexity of applicable law/procedures	18	15.93
3.	Costly legal assistance	14	12.39
4.	Multiplicity of compulsory licensing/registration required	20	17.70
5.	Cumbersome import/export policy and procedures	17	15.04
6.	Miscellaneous	7	6.19

Note: Total exceeds due to Multiple Responses

Table 6

Other Problems Encountered by the Respondents while Initiating and Running the Enterprise

Other Problems		*N=113*	
		F	*%*
1.	Lack of regular and timely availability of raw material	29	25.66
2.	Lack of infrastructural facilities	15	13.27
3.	Inadequate quality control measures	7	6.19
4.	Lack of personal/political influences for getting the things done	7	6.19
5.	Corruption/bureaucracy/red tapism to the extent of frustration	38	33.63
6.	Non-availability of communication facilities	12	10.62
7.	Power cuts	32	28.32
8.	Lack of adequate transportation facilities	10	8.85
9.	General incredibility regarding women	2	1.77
10.	Miscellaneous	13	11.50

Note: Total exceeds due to Multiple Responses

licensing and registrations (Table 5). Miscellaneous problems that came to light were cumbersome procedures regarding the establishment of the unit, licensing and labour laws, complexity of existing taxation and other laws which change constantly and necessitates costly expert help.

Other Problems

One-fourth of the respondents experienced difficulty due to irregular supply of the raw material (Table 6). One-third of them complained about the corruption/bureaucracy/red tapism which led to frustration. 28.32 per cent experienced excessive power cuts affecting the unit operations. 11.50 per cent experienced problems of varied nature viz., change in import and export policy of the government, copying of designs, non-availability of government subsidy and loan (due to complex formalities). Though SSI units are entitled to receive payments within 30 days as per government orders, they were troubled by delayed payments. Accumulation of dead stock, resulting into loss of money and lack of professionalism were also stated by the respondents. Some were very much dissatisfied for giving 'haftas' regularly to police people in order to avoid unnecessary problems created by them. Some faced problem as they did not give bribes. Contrary to this some complained that their work was not accomplished smoothly even after bribing the concerned authority. Some were very much dissatisfied with the government staffs who were non-conversant with the procedures and the related subject matter which delayed their work.

Nature of Problem Solving

Solving the problem jointly with husband predominantly existed among 41.59 per cent of the respondents (Table 7). Only 36.28 per cent enjoyed a high status in problem solving as they handled the problems independently on their own. Singh (1986) found that there existed a direct correlation between higher age and the ability of women entrepreneurs to overcome problems.

Table 7
Nature of Problem Solving by the Respondents

Nature of Problem Solving		*N=113*	
		F	*%*
1.	Independently	41	36.28
2.	Jointly with the husband	47	41.59
3.	Jointly with the partner	12	10.62
4.	Jointly with family members	13	11.50
5.	Jointly with employees	12	10.62
6.	Jointly with experts	6	5.31
7.	Others alone	4	3.54

Note: Total exceeds due to Multiple Responses.

Conclusion

Problems always exist in enterprises irrespective of their size and nature. Viewing these problems as challenges or constraints depends a lot on the attitude of the women entrepreneurs. Some who take it as a challenge directs their path to advancement. In absence of hurdles, problems or challenges, women entrepreneurs tend to feel complacent, which is the beginning of her degeneration. An optimistic and problem solving attitudes always benefit them. Thus, any expected or unexpected constraint or challenge be treated in this spirit.

An overview of the constraints encountered by the respondents while initiating or running their enterprises highlighted that respondents experienced all sorts of problems related to finance, technical, labour, marketing, legal and of general nature. However, limited working capital under financial problems, non-availability of skilled and experienced personnel under labour/personnel problems and stiff competition under marketing problems and corruption/bureaucracy/red tapism to the extent of frustration were found to be the most pressing ones among others. Solving the problem jointly with husband pre-dominantly existed among the women entrepreneurs.

References

Bhadwar, I., Pratap, A., Madhukar, U. and Tripathi, S. (1988). Women Entrepreneurs : Blazing New Traits. *India Today*, July, p. 8.

Desai, V. (2003). *Dynamics of Entrepreneurial Development and Management*. Mumbai. Himalaya Publishing House.

Hisrich, P. (1998). *Entrepreneurship*. Boston. McGraw Hill.

Hisrich, R.D. and Michael, P.P. (2003). *Entrepreneurship*. New Delhi. Tata McGraw Hill Publishing Company Ltd.

Jaiswal, N. (1998). Determinants of Entrepreneurial Growth process among Women Entrepreneurs. Unpublished Doctoral dissertation. Department of Home Management, Faculty of Home Science, The M.S. University of Baroda, Vadodara. pp. 164-171.

Singh, N.P. (1986). Successful Women Entrepreneurs : Their Identity, Expectations and Problems. *Research Report Serial 2*. New Delhi. NIESBUD.

34

Women Entrepreneurship and Micro Enterprises - Some Potential for Economic Development

Anuradha Mathu

Challenges of Women Entrepreneurship

Women have been regarded as the nuclei of nation and the builder and moulder of its destiny. It is an accepted fact that "when women move forward, the family moves, the city moves and the nation moves." Days are gone when women in India remained confined to four walls of their homes and their immense strength and potential remained unrecognized and unaccounted, now women entrepreneurs are important an input of economics development. A woman is a catalyst of development and with her we prosper, but without her we are poor.

Entrepreneurship happens to be one of the best ways towards self sufficiency and poverty alleviation for women in a country where employment is not guaranteed. The women entrepreneurs need not be highly educated. It is enough if they possess basic knowledge of a language, entrepreneurial skills and the knowledge of the system. And also entrepreneurship is a more suitable profession than regular employment in public and private sectors, since they have to fulfill dual roles. In emergence of nuclear families and diversification of labour activities has resulted in the non-availability of servants, limited baby care facilities at home and work is pushing women towards entrepreneurial activities. Women entrepreneurship is the process where women take lead and organize a business or industry and provide employment opportunities to others. Though women entrepreneurship is a recent phenomenon in India which came into prominence in late 1970's now more and more are venturing as entrepreneurs in all kinds of business and service sector. There are successful women entrepreneurs today heading enterprises like electronics, multimedia, garment, industry and so on.

The problems follow the women entrepreneurs like shadow.

Women entrepreneurs have to struggle much more and face the following problems.

- In a traditional society women have been trained to listen, obey and leave decision to men in the family.
- Family environment is not generally helpful. Women entrepreneurs have to take time off from their household duties.
- It is also difficult to find men prepared to work under women.
- The women entrepreneurs suffer from a number of problems at the pre-investment stage, investment stage and post-investment stage. The problems mainly relate to finance, raw material and marketing. Getting finance is a big problem because women generally do not have property in their name. They cannot offer property as collateral security. Banks too consider women less creditworthy.
- The rural women entrepreneurs particularly do not know how to synhronise their skills with the market requirements.
- Inefficient management for marketing and sale.
- Stiff competition
- Low mobility
- Social attitudes
- Low ability to bear risk
- Lack of education
- Low need for achievement

- Inadequate infrastructure

The risk are even more for the women entrepreneurs as she has to work in a male dominated area. The main drawbacks to women's success are lack of experience, and inaccessibility of resources to develop the entrepreneurial skills like independence, self confidence, assertiveness, drive. Development as entrepreneurs is a recently discovered phenomenon for women for which they need of motivation, training and family members support. Facilities are provided by governmental and non-governmental agencies to motivate and to impart training to develop entrepreneurial skills in women. But most of the women are kept away from such developmental programmes due to social norms, values and attitudes towards women.

If the women decide to go in for a small business the basic ability cannot really be in question. The issues relating to self-confidence, lack of knowledge and information and absence of role models can partly be solved by education and experience. Business risks can be minimized by careful planning and expert guidance. There are several specialized agencies, financial organizations and voluntary organizations offering guidance and financial help. Increasing number of entrepreneurial development programme (EDP) is offered by these agencies which help develop project profiles, feasibility reports, personal counseling about one's unit, marketing skills etc. The EDPs range from general to industry–specific programmes which are product or process oriented. Some additional concessions are required. Bank and other financial institution should come forward to give loans to women entrepreneurs without obtaining security from them and at low interest rate. Maximum possible assistance should be provided to women for completing documentation and other formalities. Lastly to ensure women entrepreneurship development integrated efforts by various institutions and corporations are needed so that required assistance may be provided to potential women entrepreneurs.

Entrepreneurship would to a great extent solve two major problems – mass poverty and widespread unemployment. India will have to pay a lot of attention and search for encouraging entrepreneurship especially in small sector, which involves low capital and high labour intensity.

It is rightly observed that small scale sector not only provides larger employment but also mobilizes local resources, skills, savings, and take up industries for wider distribution of wealth.

It is also seen that in the past two decades, many attempts have been made to develop a network of small scale and cottage industries or micro enterprises. Many government efforts to design special programmes to promote entrepreneurship on scientific basis were also made. We have also witnessed many indicators and paramenters to prove the worth of such efforts and programmes for achieving national goal. We all know that this problem of unemployment is enormous and is taking 'Gigantic Form'.

The effort of academicians, policy and programme planners should be develop and train hundreds and thousands of women entrepreneurs to meet this ever growing challenge.

Entrepreneurs play a pivotal role in the economic development of any country. Entrepreneurs are considered to be the most important economic agents for the economic augmentation and growth of any country. They act as the owners, producers, coordinators, market makers, decision-makers, risk takers and innovators. They provide an improved allocation of resources for the best interest of their enterprises as well as the country. They are considered the economic pioneers initiating changes in the economy. They strive to increase productivity and improve the quality of output though the application of more efficient production technique, better plant layout and effective marketing policies. They ensure production of better quality of goods and services at lowest cost. They generate employment opportunities and arrange for the betterment of the standard of living.

Entrepreneurship is also considered a life moving force behind any economy. It is also believed that without entrepreneurial activities the process of industrialization is not possible.

Leibenstein (1968) defines an entrepreneur as an individual or a group of individuals with the following four characteristics

- A person who connects different markets;
- A person capable of making for market deficiencies (gap filling);
- An input – completer;
- Creates or expands time–binding input transforming entities for firms.

Gupta (1987) states that entrepreneurship involves a whole-range of aptitudes and capabilities of an enterprising person like the capability to bear risk to forecast prospects of an enterprise, to organize various factors of production, to manage various offices of the business, to innovate or initiate new things, confidence and competence to meet the unforeseen adverse conditions.

Further, the entrepreneurs are the dynamic persons for innovation and 'gap-filling' for economic development. The role of the entrepreneur is that of an innovator who not only combine factors of production but also introduces a change over the existing one. The entrepreneur performs an important role in producing goods at lowest cost, providing the growth of the firm and maximizing profit.

In short, a successful entrepreneur should have perseverance and hard working habits, risk-taking ability, high aspiration, willingness to learn, dynamic and creative nature, adaptability, innovativeness, good salesmanship, ability to win friends, overcome crisis, initiative, self-confidence, will power, determination to succeed, pleasing personality and tactfulness, high integrity, responsibility, excellence in work and perception of time.

Also the success of entrepreneurship depends on some personality factors, which are

- Self-knowledge
- Imagination

- Practical knowledge/Experience
- Analytical ability
- Search Skill
- Foresight
- Computation skill
- Delegational skill
- Organisational skill

Successful entrepreneurs would have the following qualities:

- Sociable
- Adaptable
- Truthful
- Co-operative
- Logical
- Aggressive
- Perserving
- Practical
- Patient
- Independent
- Tough-minded
- Emotionally mature
- Free from anxiety
- Patience
- Sagacity
- Power of observation
- Discrimination
- Leadership

Bibliography

- Berna, J.J. 1960, Industrial Entrepreneurship in Madras State, Asia Publishing, Bombay.
- Bhattacharya, S. N. 1986. Development of Small Scale and Cottage Industries, Metropolitan Book Co., New Delhi.

- Coher, William, A. 1990. The Entrepreneur and Small Business Problem Solver, John Wisley and Sons, New York.
- Desai, V, 1997. Dynamics of Entrepreneurship Development and Management, Himalaya Publishing House, Mumbai.
- Greene, C.I., 2000. Entrepreneurship Ideas in Action, Washington: South Western Educational Publishing Company.
- Gupta, M.C. 1987. Entrepreneurship in Small Scale Industries, Anmol Publications, New Delhi.
- Indian Association for Women's Studies (1993). The New Economic Policy and Women, A Collection of Background Papers to Sixth National Conference, 1993, edited, printed and published by Sheilu Sreenivasan, Managing Editor.
- Khanka, S.S. 2001. Entrepreneurial Development, New Delhi, S. Chand and Company Ltd.
- Kulshreshta Kalyani, 1999. Successful Entrepreneurship, Kanishka Publishers, Distributors, New Delhi.
- Mutsuddi Nalirakshah (1996). You can become an Entrepreneur, Wheeler Publishing, New Delhi.
- Patrik Martin, 1999. Self Employment and Successful Entrepreneurship, Kanishka Publishers, New Delhi.
- Rao, R.Y. 1979. Small Industries and the Developing Economy in India, Concept Publishing, New Delhi.
- Sharma, R.K. 1983. Industrial Entrepreneurship in Developing Economies, Kalyan Publishers.
- Singh, P.N. 1986. Development Theory of Entrepreneurship: Developing Entrepreneurship for Economic Growth, Vikas Publishing, New Delhi.
- Soundarapandiar M., 1999. Women Entrepreneurship – Issues and Strategies, Kanishka Publishers, New Delhi.
- Vepa, R.K. 1983. Small Industry–The Challenges of the Eighties, Vikas Publishing, New Delhi.

Appendix

Material and Method

The information was collected using a questionnaires. The sample was 40 women who were running small scale industry in Limbadi town. After collecting questionnaires was discuss were held with working women.

The Encouragement Provided to the Women Entrepreneurship

Questionnaire

Name ____________________ Monthly Income ____________

Education _______________ Family Members ______________

1. Have you started the business because of increasing prices?
2. Had you been provided with the guidance for your business?
3. Have you an idea about the facilities provided for your business by the nation?
4. Have you gained the training for this business?
5. What must be a reason for starting business?
   - Uneducated education   Yes   No
   - High price   Yes   No
   - Unemployment   Yes   No
   - For the development of financial growth of the family.
6. Are you getting encouragement for this business from your husband?   Yes   No
7. From where have you raised the capital for starting this business?   Yes   No

8. What type of help do you get from the members of your family (other than husband/children)?
Yes No

9. People of society are helpful to you? Do your children help in your work? Yes No

10. Do you know about the loans provided from Government, Semi Government, Gramin Banks, Co-operative Banks?
Yes No

11. Why have you installed your industry in your house?
Yes No

12. Are you also able to satisfy the needs of children, husband, and family members together with business?
Yes No

13. Are you able to provide financial support to your family?
Yes No

14. Do family members appreciate that you have chosen not to go outside but do work at home? Yes No

15. Have you to face the difficulty with the responsibilities of family life? What type of difficulty do you face?
Yes No

16. Had you been even victim of envy of other women?
Yes No

17. Do you get mental satisfaction from both the responsibility of house and small scale industries that you are running?
Yes No

18. Do the family members realize the trouble which you have in doing the two works? Yes No

19. Do you get as much sympathy as the woman gets who does outdoor work? Yes No

20. Do the family members grumble when you are trying to give perfect satisfaction to the customers?
Yes No

21. What type of obstruction do you get in your work from the neighbours and guests? Yes No

22. What feeling do you experience when you have no vacation

or other leaves in your work which you are doing at your home? Yes No

23. Can you care for your physical-mental health while doing business? Yes No

Questionnaire

Women Entrepreneurs in Lower – Middle Class Families and their Problems

(A)

1. Name
2. Age
3. Education
4. Family Income
5. Family Size

(B) Nature and Period of Business

Education	Period	Health & Physique	Period	Miscellaneous	Period
Tuition		Beauty Parlour		Household Industries	
				Papad	
Play house				Masala	
				Pickle	
				Tailoring and Embroidery	
				Artificial and Fancy Jewellery Making	

(C) Reason for Starting the business

1. Big family size
2. Death of husband
3. Disability of Income
4. Divorce

(D) Marketing and Sales Income

Market Income – Below Rs. 1500/- Rs. 1500-3000

1. Local
2. Outside

(E) Problems faced during the work

1. Arrangement of finance
2. Arrangement of material
3. Availability of market
4. Limited work space
5. Inadequate publicity
6. Collection of payment

(F) Attitude and Co-operation of

1. Husband :
2. Family members :
3. Relatives :
4. Neighbours :

(G) Contribution of the Society / Family by you

1. Work satisfaction.
2. To bring out hidden skills and potentials of women.
3. Supporting family members and employment generations.
4. To upgrade self respect of women in the society.
5. Maintaining dual responsibility of an entrepreneur and housewife and mother.

Appendix – Questionnaire

Questionary Form

Bhavan's Shri A.K. Doshi Mahila College, Jamnagar

A STUDY OF SMALL SCALE INDUSTRIES TRAINING CENTRE BY N.G.O. FOR WOMEN ENTREPRENEURS

Name

Address

Type of enterprise

Methods of training

Strength of trainees

Time limit of training course

Part time

Full time

Education of trainees

Education of instructors

Time of the training

Information for the training place, equipments, training batch etc.

Questionnaire

1. How do you do the adult of the time for the training?
2. Are your skills developed by the training?
3. Are you experienced?
4. Do the modern technology and equipment useful in acquiring knowledge?
5. Do you have full knowledge of theory before doing the practical?
6. Do you take the help of books, magazines, internet and experts after training?
7. What is your plan to start your enterprise in future?
8. What is the aim of the business?
9. Do you get co-operation of your family members?
10. Do you have any problem in the training centre during the training?
11. How will you manage the money for the business after training? Do you have any knowledge of bank loan?

12. Will you employ skilled workers in your business?
13. How will you do the marketing of your product?
14. What will you do for the development of your business?
15. Your future dream about your business?

Appendix – Questionnaire

Place: ________ Date: __________

Name: ____

Address: ____

____

Education: _____________ (current) Age: _______________

1. What kind of enterprise would you prefer to do?

   ____

   Make following with (   ) sign matters concerning you:

2. Why do you want to start this enterprise?
   - 2.1 Because of my interest.
   - 2.2 Because I have taken training.
   - 2.3 For self-development.
   - 2.4 To keep pace with the society.
   - 2.5 To acquire an economic-social position in the society.
   - 2.6 For upbringing of family's economic condition.
   - 2.7 Because it is difficult to get job now-a-days.
   - 2.8 Because the limits of job is unacceptable.
3. Which member of family will assist you in this enterprise?
4. How will you cope up with both, enterprise and family?
5. Enlist the basic amenities required to start an enterprise?
6. How much money is required for your enterprise?
7. From where will you procure this money?

8. Do you have any information regarding government plans for this?
9. How much monthly profit do you expect in the beginning?
10. How will you take care of raw material, management, marketing?
11. What kind of difficulties will you face?
12. Do you need to take training to make this enterprise a success?
13. Enlist various useful enterprises.

Appendix – Questionnaire

Questionnaire

Name :

Address :

Type of Enterprise :

Education :

Monthly Income :

Q. 1. Which type of problems you face in your enterprise:

(a) Shortage of material
(b) Deficiency in capital
(c) Lack of your education
(d) Lack of training centre related to your enterprise
(e) Lack of knowledge from where we get loans
(f) Delay in loan sanction
(g) Difficulties to manage marketing due to multinational attack.
(h) Lack of skill and experienced worker.
(i) You feel corruption is a major problem?
(j) You see internet marketing?
(k) Whatever time you spent in your enterprise will you get adequate profit.

(l) Do your family members co-operate with you.

(m) You feel difficulty in marketing.

(n) You feel any difficulty as you are women entrepreneur?

(o) You have to do time to time modification in your enterprise to compete in market.

(p) How does advertisement effect in your enterprise?

(q) Any other problem.

Q. 2. Write in sequence which major 6 problems do you feel in your enterprise.

Q. 3. Which steps were taken by government to solve above problems?

Q. 4. How much effect does your enterprise have in your social life?

Q. 5. How much effect does your enterprise have in your family life?

Q. 6. Is your standard of living lifted up due to your enterprise?

Q. 7. Do you feel your personality is developed due to your enterprise?

Q. 8. Give your opinions about how you plan to expand your enterprise in future?

Q. 9. How many trained workers work in your enterprise?

Q. 10. Are you flexible with changing trends?

Q. 11. Do you wish that government should run the training centre to develop skill of entrepreneurs and training is for which type of industry?

Q. 12. Do you feel training should be made compulsory?

Index